D1550159

*W*ildlife
Travelling Companion

FRANCE

*W*ildlife
Travelling Companion
FRANCE

Bob Gibbons
and Paul Davies

The Crowood Press

First published in 1992 by
The Crowood Press Ltd.
Ramsbury, Marlborough
Wiltshire SN8 2HR

Field Guide plates 1–7 by **Michael Benington**,
plates 8–12 by **Chris D Orr** and plates 13-20 by
Amanda Yektaparast.
Maps by **Kathy Merrick.**

Title page photograph: Chamois (*Rupicapra
rupicapra*) on look-out duty in the Maritime
Alps.
Photograph this page: Little Egret (*Egretta
garzetta*).

British Library Cataloguing in Publication Data

A catalogue record for this book is available from
the Brirish Library.

ISBN 1 85223 579 9

**Edited and designed by
D & N Publishing**
DTP & Editorial Services
5 The Green
Baydon
Wiltshire SN8 2JW

Phototypeset by FIDO Imagesetting, Witney,
Oxon

Printed and bound by Times Publishing Group,
Singapore

CONTENTS

SECTION I
COUNTRY GUIDE

INTRODUCTION

Our intention in this book is to allow the visitor to France, with some interest in natural history, to find and visit a range of natural sites that collectively possess the best features that France has to offer. France is a huge and varied country, with immense potential for the naturalist, and inevitably we have been able to detail only a small proportion of what is there. However, it is our hope that this selection of a range of the best sites will help the visitor to find quickly the types of places that they are interested in, and to visit them during the best season.

Before detailing the sites, let us look at France as a whole, its geography, people, climate and of course its wildlife.

THE COUNTRY

With an area of approximately 547,000km^2, France is the largest country lying wholly within Europe. It not only has the largest surface area, but is also, almost certainly, the most varied country in Europe. It straddles several climatic zones, has coastlines on two quite different seas, and a vast range of habitat types, from warm dry coastal habitats in the extreme south-west to the highest mountains in Europe in the Alps. To the naturalist, France occupies a strategic position, sharing species with a range of the countries and areas surrounding it. Thus, it has an

Opposite: a field of colourful Dandelions in the Maritime Alps.

exceptionally rich and varied natural history, though conversely, there are relatively few endemic species that occur only in France.

The coast of France is one of its great glories. It is about 3,200km long, bordering the English Channel, and the Atlantic and Mediterranean Seas. Apart from being the basis of a huge tourist industry, it is also a mecca for the naturalist with its rich bird-life in winter, and superb range of species-rich semi-natural habitats. Despite the pressures of millions of holidaymakers, much of interest remains, though the Mediterranean coast has lost a great deal of its richness through over-development and pollution.

The north of France, (the area roughly north of a line from Tours to Mulhouse), is predominantly low-lying, with the notable exceptions of the Vosges and the Ardennes in the north and east. Apart from the area west of Cherbourg, the rocks of this area are largely of recent sedimentary origin, frequently giving rise to fertile soils that are easily cultivated. There is a vast ring of chalk around Paris, occupying much of central and north France, bounded by a ring of Upper Cretaceous and Jurassic rocks that are frequently somewhat hillier than the chalk, with a less intensive agriculture. Beyond this ring, the geology becomes more complex. For example, the Ardennes is formed from Devonian rocks. The centre of the chalk ring, the Paris basin, is formed of more recent rocks such as those from the Eocene and Oligocene ages, and these are frequently rather acid in character. Thus, despite the population pressure in this central zone, there is something of a concentration of woodland, heathland and wetland sites because the land is less suitable for agriculture. By contrast, the rolling chalk country of the north-east – the Champagne country – is intensively farmed.

The western part of north France (essentially Brittany, but extending somewhat more widely), is different in character. The underlying rocks are almost all old and hard, such as granites and various Cambrian and Pre-Cambrian rocks. The result is a landscape with much in common with Cornwall or west Wales in Britain, though lacking any substantial highland areas. It is a wilder-feeling landscape, often with wide views across woods, heaths and hills. It is also an area that changed greatly in the 1970s and 1980s, as previously traditional farmers woke up to the potential of intensive co-operative agriculture. Although still an area of interest to the naturalist, especially along the rugged coast, it is undoubtedly changing, and the featureless areas are becoming larger.

Much of the southern central part of France is occupied by hills and mountains (the great Massif Central). This is a general term for a diversity of high-lying land, made up of the volcanic hills of the Auvergne, the limestones of the great Causse plateaus, and the granites and schists of the Cévennes. The highest mountain in this central area is the Puy de Sancy, at 1,886m. Many of France's rivers, such as the Loire, the Lot and the Dordogne rise in this area of hills. Many naturalists travelling south feel that they have only really arrived somewhere special when they reach the Massif Central, and it is undoubtedly true that the natural life suddenly becomes much more diverse and visible as you enter this area. The hilly nature of the country and relatively backward farming techniques have allowed a much more semi-natural habitat to survive, and many meadows and pastures are full of flowers. The

harsh winter works against major agriculture schemes, though it has brought its own recreational activities, such as cross-country skiing, which can be destructive.

The whole of eastern France is taken up with mountains or sizeable hills, stretching in a complex and almost unbroken barrier from the Vosges to the Maritime Alps. Though, at first glance, these areas might be thought to have a broadly similar flora and fauna, in fact the differences are enormous. Although the Vosges and the Maritime Alps share a few species, there are many more that are quite different. Geologically, there are huge differences. The Vosges is made up of rounded Triassic rocks, predominantly acid in character, and lacking the peaks and cliffs that characterize the higher, newer mountains. The Jura is predominantly limestone (after

Wild Tulips in the Maritime Alps.

which the Jurassic limestone is named), with its own special flora and fauna. Then, southwards from here, the Savoy, Cottian, Graian and Maritime Alps vary greatly, with granites, limestones, schists and other rocks. At the same time the climate changes southwards, from the harsh central-European weather found in the Vosges, with relatively damp summers, to the near-Mediterranean climate of the southern slopes of the Maritime Alps. For the naturalist, the whole of eastern France is of supreme interest, and it is barely necessary to pick out key sites – everywhere is likely to hold something of interest to the first-time visitor. This zone also has the highest mountains in France, with many peaks over 3,500m. Indeed, France shares a portion of the highest mountain in Europe – Mont Blanc, which is 4,810m high.

South-western France has a character of its own, seemingly isolated from areas farther south by the Pyrenees or the mountains of Languedoc, yet with a warm, mild climate. It is a more subtle area than the mountain areas, with much of interest, but the visitor must work to find it. The coast is a special glory with endless kilometres of dunes, beaches and lakes, backed inland by the vast forest of les Landes. A little farther inland, towards the Dordogne and Cahors, is an almost forgotten area, with a low population and many fascinating woods and small pastures. The flora and fauna of this border area is very rich, especially in limestone-loving flowers and insects. It is also an area where more southerly birds become more common and there is much to be seen.

The southernmost part of mainland France is dominated by the extraordinary barrier of the Pyrenees. Though lacking the glamour of the Alps, and without the vast area that the Alps cover, the Pyrenees are, nevertheless, one of the most interesting mountain ranges in Europe. Their isolation from other French mountains, and their close links with the Spanish Sierras, have allowed a rather different flora and fauna to evolve. Although many species are shared with the Alps, many others are different, special either to the Pyrenees alone or to the mountains of the Iberian peninsula. As with the Alps, it is hardly necessary to mention individual sites, as everywhere holds something of interest, although it has to be said that some areas are over-grazed, agriculturally improved, or relatively dull by virtue of their geology. For most of their length, the Pyrenees are clearly differentiated from the lowlands, rising like a great wall from the plains. Farther east, though, the position becomes more complicated as the Corbières, the Montagnes Noires, and other low ranges stretch out to meet them. This hilly area, just north of the eastern part of the Pyrenees, is of great interest to the naturalist, well worth exploring whilst on the way to somewhere else.

The landscape of Provence is familiar to almost everyone, whether they have been there or not, through the paintings of artists such as Van Gogh, and through numerous published photographs. The mountains of the Massif Central fade away gradually towards the sea, with increasing areas of intervening fertile plains and wide alluvial areas near the sea. Provence is dominated by a feeling of dry hills separated by fertile valleys and plains, and it is an engaging characteristic that however built-up or intensively farmed the area you are in may be, you can always look out to a nearby hill covered in maquis or woodland. In fact, some of the hills would be considered as major features in most other countries - the Massifs of Maures, St Baumes, Luberon, or L'Esterel, for example, are all superb mountain chains in their own right, each worthy of exploration.

Finally, Corsica, often described as 'a mountain rising from the sea', is one of the great overlooked treasures of the Mediterranean. It is a dramatic island with high mountains, a long, relatively unspoilt coastline, extensive near-natural woodlands, vast gorges, and many species that are peculiarly its own. Access is clearly more difficult than to the mainland, and in many ways it is like going to a separate country from France, but it is certainly worth the effort.

PEOPLE

France has a very long history of settlement and cultivation. The Dordogne and other parts of southern France have superb relics of very early man, dating from long before man became a significant force in shaping the countryside.

After the last ice-age, France, like most of Europe, was dominated by mixed deciduous forests in the lowlands, and by more coniferous forests in the higher areas. From neolithic times onwards, though, man began to clear the forests for cultivation, pasture, and, at first, to attract the animals that he wished to hunt. It is hard to believe that the extensive bare maquis-covered hills of Provence, or the great pastures of the Auvergne were once forested, but all the evidence indicates that this is so.

As the population increased and man's technical capacities were broadened, the pace of clearance accelerated, and gradually forest ceased to be the dominant feature of the landscape. In most cleared areas, cultivated land became dominant, but in other areas semi-natural habitats such as heaths or rough pastures became established, as a result of grazing pressure, producing some of our finest present-day habitats.

Until recently, French agriculture was somewhat backward by north-European standards. Traditional inheritance patterns had tended to keep farms small, and the potential for agricultural change was rarely realized. To the naturalist and casual visitor, this was a great bonus, as the landscape remained intimate and varied, and a great range of species survived in farmed areas. This is changing rapidly, however, and the appearance of larger and larger units, misplaced European Community aid, and greatly increased technical abilities, have caused striking changes in much of the landscape of France recently. Whilst we were researching this book, we found that many of the sites mentioned even in quite recently published books had been ploughed, drained or cleared, and no longer existed.

Today, France has a population of about 54 million with a density of ninety-eight per km^2 (lower than most west-European countries). However, in practice, the population density of the countryside is somewhat lower than one might expect because there is a steady drift towards the major towns, and a depopulation of the countryside. The great distances involved in travel in France mean that huge areas are not subject to commuter pressure, and only the people who make a living from the land actually remain there.

CLIMATE

The size and position of France mean that it has a great range of weather patterns, and it falls into three major climatic zones – Atlantic, central European, and Mediterranean.

The north and western parts of central France are strongly influenced by Atlantic weather patterns, with the effect gradually declining eastwards. Thus, Brittany and

The superb blue spikes of Spiked Speedwell (Veronica spicata).

other western areas have a very mild climate, with regular depressions, and a rainfall of around 1,000mm per year spread through the months. Summers are generally warm, but the temperature can drop quickly when depressions from the west move in; winters are generally mild, though snow and frosts are fairly regular. In this zone, the difference between summer and winter is least marked, and the climate is very close to that of southern and western Britain, if slightly warmer.

Eastern and east-central France are much less influenced by Atlantic weather, and more strongly affected by central European (Continental), high-pressure weather patterns, though of course there is a wide zone that is affected by both systems. These areas tend to have clearer colder winters and hotter summers, though the summers are by no means dry. The difference between summer and winter is much more marked here.

South of the Massif Central, France has a Mediterranean climate. Here, the rain falls mainly in autumn and winter, while late spring and summer are characterized by hot or very hot weather, with little rainfall. The winters are mild, with frost a rarity at sea-level. This particular weather pattern strongly influences the vegetation and wildlife. Most plants, for example, flower in spring or early summer, with a minor burst of activity again after the first rains of autumn. In the hottest and driest parts, there is very little in flower after June. Similarly, birds tend to nest earlier than farther north, and insects peak around June. A few butterflies and other insects are present as adults all year round in favourable areas. Drought-sensitive invertebrates, such as snails, tend to aestivate (rather than hibernate) to avoid the damaging effects of the dry summers. Masses of snails, each thoroughly sealed against water-loss, cover low plants in lime-rich areas in the south through the summer.

The south of France is strongly influenced by the mistral wind from the north, which brings cold air from central Europe, especially down the Rhône valley. It is most persistent in spring, and blows, on average, about 100 days per year. The sirocco wind blows northwards from North Africa, bringing hot dry, often dusty, air into the south. The table gives some indication of the variation between the areas.

REGIONAL DIFFERENCES IN CLIMATE			
	Ave. Jan temp °C	Ave. July temp °C	Ave. annual rainfall (mm)
Brest (W Brittany)	7.5	17	842
Paris	3.5	18	607
Nice	6.5	21.3	805
Ajaccio (Corsica)	8.5	23.5	698

Overlying the general climatic patterns, the effects of the mountains on the weather are considerable. Temperature drops rapidly with altitude increase, and precipitation increases up to all but the highest altitudes. Thus, all the mountain areas are colder and wetter than equivalent lowland areas. For example, the higher parts of the Massif Central and the northern Alps have an annual precipitation in excess of 1,600mm, compared to the lowland average of about 700mm. They may also have a wider effect, such as through the mistral, where cold air from the mountains blows outwards into warmer areas. They may also cause extra-dry areas locally, such as the extreme south-west of France, by taking the bulk of the precipitation from the prevailing winds.

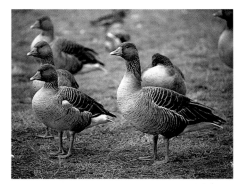

Greylag Geese (Anser Anser) *are regular winter visitors.*

FLORA AND FAUNA

As one might expect from the size, position and variety of the country, France has a very rich flora and fauna. For example, there are around 4,200 species of flower, excluding introductions, known from France; ninety species of mammals; around 400 birds; about sixty reptiles and amphibia; and tens of thousands of insects. To pick out two more specific groups that are of interest to many naturalists, there are over eighty species of orchids in France, and over ninety species of damselfly and dragonfly.

Most of this enormous range of species occurs in other countries around France. Mountain areas tend to develop their own endemic species through isolation, but these are usually shared with adjacent countries in the case of France. For example, there are many flowers and insects peculiar to the Maritime Alps, but most of them occur in the similar parts of adjacent Italy. Similarly, there are many Pyrenean endemics, but most are shared with the Spanish side. Corsica is more isolated than any mainland mountain range, and its isolation has led to the development of many endemic plants and animals. However, it is so close to Sardinia that most are shared with that island and only a few are peculiar to Corsica alone.

Unfortunately, the flora and fauna of France is by no means assured of a safe future, thanks largely to the activities of man. Species such as Monk Seal and Corsican Deer have become extinct relatively recently (though there are current plans to re-introduce both species to appropriate areas), and many others are threatened with extinction. At present, it is believed that about ten bat species, the Brown Bear, Bonelli's Eagle, the Lynx, and around twenty other species of mammal are endangered or vulnerable in France. Amongst plants, one estimate puts sixty-one species (of which fifteen are endemic) in serious danger, and another 342 to be sharply declining. Since 1900, forty plant species, including nine endemics, have become extinct in France.

HABITATS

France, like most countries, no longer has its natural vegetation cover. The present countryside is a mosaic of vegetation ranging from the highly artificial (such as arable fields), through modified semi-natural habitats (like flowery meadows and most woods), to the few barely modified habitats such as cliffs, high mountains, and a few coastal habitats. For the naturalist, the semi-natural habitats, such as woodlands, maquis, heaths, old meadows, and pastures, are likely to be of most interest. The following are the main habitats in France.

WOODLANDS

Woodlands are probably the single most important habitat of France. They occupy over 20 per cent of the country, totalling 14 million hectares in all. The diversity within this amount is extraordinary: the beechwoods of central France such as at Compiègne and around Lyons-la-Forêt, or the mountain beechwoods of the Pyrenees or Vosges; the oak woods of Fontainebleau, the Bourbonnais, Troncais and Reno Valdieu; the vast planted pine woods of les Landes; the chestnut woods of the Massif des Maures or parts of Corsica; or the natural mixed Spruce and Larch forests of the eastern mountain areas, together with many lesser types of woodland.

Most woodlands in France are managed, to a greater or lesser extent. The state directly manages or influences about one-third of the country's woodlands - mainly those marked as 'Forêt Domaniale' (state-owned) or 'Forêt Communale'. Many such forests are superb areas for wildlife, with a rich flora throughout, a good density of breeding birds, and interesting insects, especially in glades and along rides, or in very old compartments. The rotational selection system, and the high proportion of natural hardwoods in these woods ensures considerable natural diversity. Unfortunately, traditional management seems to be declining, whilst straight-line conifer planting is on the

Beech forest in the Loire Valley at dawn.

increase. Such changes will inevitably be detrimental to wildlife, though a few species, such as Siskin, Red Squirrel and Sparrowhawk, may benefit from increased conifer plantations.

In many areas of France, such as the Dordogne and parts of Normandy, coppicing is still widely practiced. If it has been continued over a long period, then this is highly beneficial to wildlife. If passing a recently coppiced area in spring or early summer, it is always worth taking a look to see what flowers, butterflies and other insects are to be observed.

There are also many areas of less-managed woods, in steep or inaccessible areas (though it is surprising how even some steep high-altitude woods are managed); these are often very mixed, since no one tree has been favoured, and common component species include Ash, Elm, Lime, Downy Oak, Wild Cherry, and Hornbeam.

GRASSLANDS

The vegetation that develops where regular grazing or mowing takes place is, on all but the most acid of soils, grassland of some sort. Enclosed grasslands cut for hay are meadows, whereas grazed grasslands, often unenclosed, are pastures. Unfertilized grasslands support masses of flowers, and they are one of the most attractive of all habitats in early summer. Unfortunately, they are also one of the most threatened, as simple applications of fertilizer or herbicides, or ploughing, can quickly destroy this natural variety. Over large areas of France, the meadows have steadily lost their flowers, and such flowery grasslands are a rare site now in most of the north and west. Even the grasslands below orchard trees and

Meadow full of Ox-Eye Daisies in the Pyrenees.

olives have been gradually 'improved', and many of the flowers have gone.

The best places now to see flowery grasslands are in the mountains; they still exist in good measure in the Vosges, Jura, Massif Central, Alps, Pyrenees, and some lesser southern ranges. The meadows are often too steep and small to improve, and up until hay-cut in June-July they are superbly flowery. Above the meadows, interspersed with the forests, there are extensive areas of open pasture which are usually far too rocky and steep to improve, and which therefore retain all their flowers, though they may at times be too heavily grazed to be visible. In the Dordogne and Causse areas, one of the great glories is the roadside grasslands, awash with orchids and butterflies in early summer.

HEATHLANDS

Heathlands are roughly the acid-soil equivalent of unimproved grassland. Although wild and natural in appearance, they are the result of man's clearance of woodlands on acid soil, followed by grazing, mowing or burning over a long period. They tend to develop in areas with higher rainfall, where heathers do well. Their extent in France is rather limited; the best areas are in Brittany (especially towards the coast and in some of the inland forests such as the Forêt de Paimpont – the ancient Broceliande Forest); on the Cherbourg peninsula; in the Sologne area south of Orléans; in patches of les Landes south of Bordeaux, and here and there around Fontainebleau Forest.

Heaths are not obviously species-rich like some habitats, but they do have particular species such as Heath Lobelia, Mossy Stonecrop, Summer Ladies' Tresses (on damper heaths), Sand Lizard and many other reptiles, Stonechat, Nightjar, and numerous specialized insects like sand wasps and tiger beetles.

COASTAL HABITATS

Almost any habitat can occur on the coast, but there are some that are necessarily coastal. The main ones are sand-dunes, shingle, salt-marsh, mudflats, and various rocky intertidal habitats. Coastal cliffs and cliff-top grasslands may also have their own special flora and fauna.

The whole northern and western coast of France, from the Belgian border to Spain, is particularly good for sand-dunes piled up by the strong westerly winds and currents. Good dunes can be found almost anywhere along this coast, though many are heavily used by tourists in summer or motorcycles and other vehicles all year. The west coast, south of Brittany, has particularly well-developed dunes, including the highest in Europe at Dune du Pilat. The flora of semi-stable dunes, where not too damaged, is very rich with specialities like Sea Bindweed, Sand Bedstraw, Everlasting, Sea Holly and Sea Stock as well as many more widespread species of dry grassland. Birds and mammals tend to be much more limited, but insect-life is often rich, ranging from specialist tiger beetles in very open areas, to numerous butterflies and moths in grassier places. Large dune systems may develop damp 'slacks' or larger pools. These are often very rich in flowers, especially

if the sand is calcareous, and permanently wet areas may hold Natterjack Toad and other amphibians. Sand Lizards favour many of these western dunes.

The south coast of France has fewer good dune systems, though those of the Camargue are a notable exception. The coast of Corsica has low dunes scattered all around it, and they are key sites for endemic and special flowers such as the *Silene* species and Sand Crocuses.

Salt-marshes develop in calm waters such as estuaries and bays where silt accumulates. Plants such as *Spartina* grass, Sea Lavender, Glasswort, Sea Aster and others establish and gradually stabilize the area. If left undisturbed, the higher reaches gradually become colonized by other plants and become a transition zone between salt-marsh and dry land. These higher areas may be used for breeding by Redshank, Shelduck, and other coastal birds, and they are feeding grounds for a wider range of species. There are good salt-marshes down the west coast in places like the Golfe du Morbihan, and extensive areas in the Camargue. Mudflats are not vegetated by higher plants, and they occur at lower tide levels; many west-coast bays like Arcachon, Aiguillon and others empty at low-tide to reveal vast areas of mudflats. These are vital

A mass of Sand Crocuses (Romulea revelieri) on the south-eastern coast of Corsica. The spring flowers of the southern coasts of Corsica are staggering in their amount as well as their variety.

feeding grounds for large numbers of waders and wildfowl, especially in winter, as they make use of the high density of invertebrates. Lagoons are often associated with mudflats or salt-marshes, and they are a feature of the Mediterranean coast; they are large lakes very close to the coast and strongly influenced by the sea. The water is brackish and rich in invertebrates and specialized plants. Certain birds, such as Greater Flamingo and Avocet tend to favour these areas.

WETLANDS AND OPEN WATERS

Wetlands are of considerable importance for wildlife. There are many species of birds, amphibians, invertebrates, flowers and mammals that are wholly dependent on water for their survival, in addition, of course, to wholly aquatic species such as fish.

The wetlands of France have declined dramatically in recent years. One recent estimate suggested that almost 10,000ha of wetlands were being destroyed or damaged each year in France. Nevertheless, huge areas of wetland remain, and almost all of them are of enormous interest to the naturalist. On the west coast, areas like the Grand Brière and the Lac du Grand Lieu would be major features of interest in any other country, but are barely known outside France. Elsewhere, there are collections of lakes that are largely artificial in origin, maintained for fishing, hunting, or fish farming, usually on soils that are too poor for much else. The most extensive areas are the Brenne, the Sologne and the Dombes, though there are many smaller such areas, like the low-lying land south of the Argonne, or in the Dordogne around Riberac.

The richest areas for wildlife are always those where there is a combination of unpolluted open water with good marginal habitats, such as fen, wet woodland, and reedbeds. This allows for the survival of the widest range of species from all groups, though admittedly it can sometimes be hard to get into a position to see them!

Other wetland areas, generally on a smaller scale, include fens with calcareous ground-water which are usually very rich in plants, such as those near Berck in the northeast of France, and bogs that often occur in association with heathland, such as those on the Cherbourg peninsula, in the Sologne, or in Fontainebleau Forest. These often support superb collections of insect-eating plants, especially sundews and bladderworts, though they are not generally rich in flowers. They are prime sites for dragonflies, such as the Four-Spotted Chaser, the White-Faced Darter, and several of the large hawkers.

GARRIGUE AND MAQUIS

These two names are used to cover the whole spectrum of dry open vegetation that is so characteristic of Mediterranean France (and other countries bordering the Mediterranean Sea). In fact, the distinction between the two is blurred, and there are many intermediate forms. Garrigue is essentially a low and open community, rich in herbs, whilst maquis is a taller denser scrubby community, up to 4m high. Most other countries manage with one word for both types. Both habitats replace the original woodland cover of the area, and are maintained by grazing and/or burning.

Garrigue is an excellent place for the naturalist, especially on limestone rock. Orchids and other herbaceous flowers are often numerous amongst an open vegetation of French Lavender, shrubby spurges, Honeysuckle, various *Cistus* species, Rosemary and Thyme. Where scattered pines occur, the Violet Limodore is frequent. These are also good places for reptiles, with numerous lizards and snakes, and wild tortoises in a limited area around the Massif des Maures. Birds such as Dartford

Maquis scrub, on the north-western coast of Corsica. Corsica has vast areas of maquis and garrigue, rich in flowers, insects, birds and reptiles. This is mainly due to its low population density and limited tourist industry.

Warbler, Sub-Alpine Warbler, Stonechat and shrikes are frequent. Insect-life is often particularly rich, with numerous mantids, crickets, grasshoppers, butterflies, and various hunting or parasitic wasps.

Maquis is a much denser habitat, less easy to look at, and often poorer in herbaceous flowers. Dominant plants include Myrtle, Strawberry Tree, larger *Cistus* species, Aleppo Pines, *Phillyrea* species, and Tree Heather, frequently draped with Honeysuckle or the spiny *Smilax*. This habitat is generally less good for reptiles, as they like sunny areas, though tortoises will feed throughout the garrigue and maquis where they occur. Birds are frequent, though hard to see. Maquis occurs all along the Mediterranean coast and some way inland, where conditions are right, in all the main *massifs*. It is common in Corsica, as is garrigue; the Desert des Agriates consists of nothing but these two vegetation types.

HIGH MOUNTAINS

France has a large area of mountains, and many of these rise above the tree line. Here, there is a wild, unspoilt area of low woody scrub, open grassland, wet flushed areas, and rocks and cliffs, eventually reaching up to areas of permanent snow or glaciers. Most such areas are to be found in the Alps and Maritime Alps, and the Pyrenees.

Productivity is low in such areas, but the range of flowers is surprisingly great, with gentians, *Primulas*, saxifrages, various *Ranunculus* species, Edelweiss, and many others. Birds are present in low density, but are of great interest, with species such as Alpine Accentor, Snow Finch, Alpine Chough, Raven, Ptarmigan and Golden Eagle. There is also a surprising number of insects, with Apollo, Peak White and Swallowtail butterflies, masses of grasshoppers, and many more.

NATURE CONSERVATION

The conservation of nature in France is a complex business, involving many statutory and voluntary organizations at numerous different levels. Superficially, it appears to be adequate, though in reality the levels of protection and management, specifically for conservation, are poor, and in any serious conflict with an opposing interest, conservation is likely to lose.

At the highest level are the National Parks. At present, there are six of these: The

A general view of the Maritime Alps in spring, the peaks snow-capped for much of the year.

Cévennes, three alpine parks – the crins, Vanoise and Mercantour, the Pyrenees Occidentales, and the small island of Port-Cros. They cover a total of 0.7 per cent of the land surface. With the exception of Port-Cros, the system of protection is based on a 'central zone' free of residents, with greater protection, and a 'peripheral zone' around this. The latter is conceived as a buffer zone, though in practice it often seems to be more of a development zone, with numerous facilities for tourists, skiers and others. The Cévennes are rather different, in that the central zone is also inhabited. Port-Cros differs in being all 'central zone', and is more like a Nature Reserve than a National Park.

Most of the National Parks have Nature Reserves within them, though their selection often seems arbitrary and their management differs little, if at all, from the surroundings. In general, we feel that the parks are inadequate – their boundaries are usually very tightly drawn to exclude any areas that might be used for other purposes, and they do not give adequate protection even within their boundaries. The park authorities vary in their understanding of ecological processes and conservation management, and frequently do not have the powers to take necessary action even when it is perceived. They are better than nothing, though, and all are places of great interest.

There is also an extensive system of Regional Natural Parks, set up under legislation passed in 1967. There are, at present, twenty-six of these, covering around 7 per cent of the surface area of France. Although they sound enticing, they are actually extremely variable and often of no particular interest to the naturalist. The legislation is very loose, and can be interpreted by the local communities that run the parks in many different ways. In general, they are seen as areas in which rural industries are encouraged to keep people within the area. This may be beneficial, but since intensive agriculture, modern forestry, skiing, hunting and fishing are all considered to be appropriate, this frequently conflicts dramatically with nature conservation. A few, by virtue of particular local factors and interests, are more akin to Nature Reserves – the Grand Brière in Brittany is a good example. Others, such as the Volcans d'Auvergne, are more like National Parks in their extent, but without the necessary degree of protection. However, these Regional Natural Parks do share the advantage (to us) of having information centres and displays, which may help to find what you are interested in.

There are also numerous Nature Reserves of one sort or another. These may be run by the state, or by various voluntary organizations. Of these, SNPN (Société Nationale de Protection de la Nature) is the largest general conservation organization, but there are also many regional bodies. The oldest and most effective of these is the SEPNB (Société pour l'Étude et la Protection de la Nature en Bretagne) which runs numerous reserves in Brittany. There are also specialist organizations, such as the LPO (Ligue Française pour la Protection des Oiseaux). In addition, the ONF (Office Nationale des Forêts) runs various reserves in its State forests.

There are many problems with the reserves, stemming partly from different attitudes to conservation, but also from lack of funds. Few are adequately managed or surveyed, and many allow, or tolerate, activities that are incompatible with the aims of the reserve, e.g. hunting and fishing. The lobbies for such pursuits are very strong, up to the highest levels, and they can generally override conservation interests. Although France is a signatory to European conventions on the protection of wildlife, it has failed abysmally to implement them, and hunting of protected species is either authorized or ignored.

It is unfortunate that a country with such exceptional natural history is not protecting it as well as it might. However, it must be acknowledged that hunting and fishing are the primary reason for the survival of some wetland areas such as the Brenne, Sologne and Dombes, and much of these would otherwise be converted to highly farmed agricultural land. Equally, rural traditions of coppicing and other woodland management are still strong in some areas of France, and this tends to maintain a rich and varied wildlife without special conservation management. Hopefully statutory conservation will improve in time.

VISITING FRANCE

France is a very easy country to visit. Roads are good and numerous, and there are frequently tracks into wilder areas. There is little limitation on seasonal travel, except that passes in the mountains are likely to be closed through the winter and into spring. Some higher passes may not open until early June, depending on the weather. Roads into ski resorts are generally kept open, though local people regularly use four-wheel-drive and/or snow-tyres. Finding one's way around is generally easy with the aid of the maps as mentioned on page 21, though the lack of an easy grid reference system, and the French *penchant* for changing road numbers and designations regularly are a nuisance at times.

Finding somewhere to stay is very rarely a problem. Camp-sites are abundant (though mountain ones may not open until after the hay is cut), and there are varying qualities of hotels, Chambres d'Hôte (bed and breakfast), and Gites d'Étape (cheap communal sleeping places) throughout. If walking in the mountains, it is worth considering the use of refuges, where one can sleep and have meals, thus allowing better access to high country the day after. Booking is advisable in high season, especially if you want food – most are on the phone, and they are marked on IGN maps.

Access to the French countryside is generally very easy. Local official footpaths are rare, but unofficial access is nearly always possible if you take care not to cause damage, and there are no signs specifically forbidding it. There is also an excellent network of long-distance footpaths (Grand Randonées), marked on maps as GR, which lead into superb country for the naturalist. Looking at nature in France is almost certain to be a pleasure for all types of naturalist, whatever the preferred area of interest may be.

SECTION II
SITE GUIDE

INTRODUCTION

We have subdivided the country into fifteen regions, which roughly represent natural zones, though we have had to draw firm boundaries where, in reality, no such boundaries exist. This is to allow a more even spread of sites through the country, as well as to facilitate easier planning by the visitor. We hope that the information will assist with planning which regions to visit and look at in detail, and encourage more casual visits to sites *en route* to somewhere else. In either event, it is unlikely that readers will be disappointed.

For the major sites, an information panel gives quick details about finding the site, when best to visit, any restrictions, any special requirements (e.g. Wellington boots), and a summary of the specialities of the site. A longer description gives more information on locating the site, together with more details of what is to be seen there. Clearly, we cannot cover everything that a site has to offer, but, in general, we have chosen places that have a wide range of species from different groups, so there will be much to see besides that which is mentioned. We have avoided mentioning sites that are of value for one species or narrow group of species alone. Below main sites, we frequently mention one or more subsidiary sites that are close by, or comparable. These can be found readily from a good map, though less detail is provided.

Right: a Cattle Egret takes a free ride on one of the well-known white horses of the Camargue.
Opposite: *Tree mallow (Lavatera arborea) at Bonifacio in south Corsica.*

We have referred to two series of maps. The first is the Michelin Motoring Atlas: France, which covers the whole country at 1:200,000. It uses the same scale as the best individual Michelin maps, but is more useful if visiting anything more than a limited area. The second is the IGN, green 1:100,000 series, which is something of a compromise as it does not always have the detail we would like, but it is quite impractical for visitors to buy larger-scale maps in a country the size of France if they are visiting many areas. Altogether, there are seventy-four of these 1:100,000 maps covering France, and relatively few are needed for any one region. However, anyone spending much time in a small area would be well advised to obtain locally the 1:50,000 special maps, or the 1:25,000 (roughly 2.5in to the mile) blue series, to give more detail. The two series will be referred to as MA and IGN respectively in the site information panels. Unfortunately, grid references are not easy to provide or re-find with most French maps, so we have described the location of sites, and marked them on regional and national maps for reference.

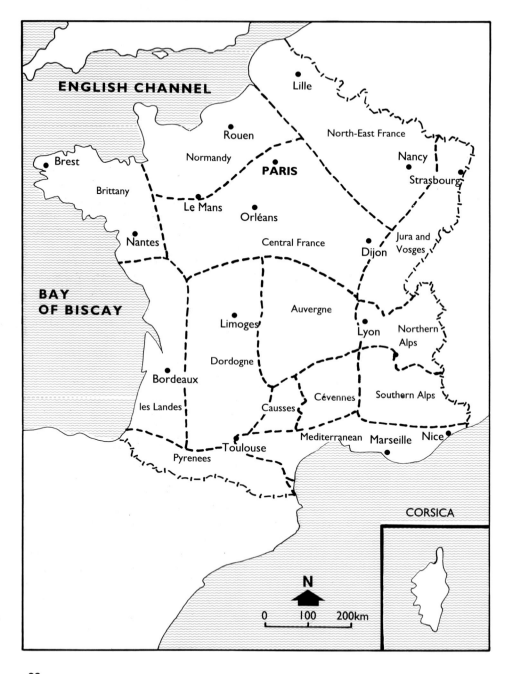

ENGLISH CHANNEL

Lille

Rouen

North-East France

Brest

Normandy

PARIS

Nancy

Strasbourg

Brittany

Le Mans

Orléans

Nantes

Central France

Dijon

Jura and Vosges

BAY OF BISCAY

Limoges

Auvergne

Lyon

Northern Alps

Dordogne

Bordeaux

les Landes

Causses

Cévennes

Southern Alps

Toulouse

Mediterranean

Marseille

Nice

Pyrenees

CORSICA

N

0   100   200km

1. BRITTANY AND ADJACENT AREAS

INTRODUCTION

The region we have defined here, which is essentially Brittany with a small area of land around it, is the most Atlantic in character of the regions. It has a great deal in common with the Celtic fringes of Great Britain, especially Cornwall and west Wales. The climate is similar (though Brittany escapes a few of the Atlantic depressions that sweep through farther north), the geology is similar, and the people and traditions have much in common. Not surprisingly, the natural history has a lot in common, too.

This region is dominated by its immensely long, convoluted, exposed coastline. There are dramatic cliffs here, of hard volcanic and ancient rocks, which provide superb sea-bird nesting sites, and offer shelter to breeding seals on secluded beaches. As with west Wales, there are numerous offshore islands, each with something of interest to the naturalist. Several of these have protection as nature reserves, though this has not saved them from the ravages of several oil disasters. In slightly less exposed places, there are dunes, shingle beaches, salt-marshes, and lagoons, all with a varied natural history.

Opposite: map of France showing the regions as described in the following pages.

Puffins (Fratercula arctica) are common on several offshore islands in Brittany.

Although much reduced in area, this is still a great region for heaths. Today, the best remaining heaths are on the coast, in places such as Cap Fréhel, but there are inland heaths, too, such as in the Broceliande Forest. Unfortunately, the inland ones are becoming overgrown, or are suffering from too many fires.

As one might expect, where there are old woods, they are very 'Atlantic' in character, with slightly stunted old trees, and a rich lichen, bryophyte and fern flora. There are also regional specialities, such as Cornish Moneywort and Ivy-Leaved Bellflower, to be found.

To the south, in the slightly more sheltered waters, are some of the great coastal bird sites of France, and the very best areas of all are to be found where an interesting coast meets a great wetland, such as at the Brière Regional Natural Park.

It is an area that is changing fast, with great strides being made recently in agricultural productivity. This has led directly to many losses for wildlife, as heaths have been 'reclaimed', woodlands felled, and wetlands drained. Fortunately for the naturalist, much remains, partly as a result of areas of poor soil, and partly through the efforts of such organizations as the SEPNB, which owns or manages many sites.

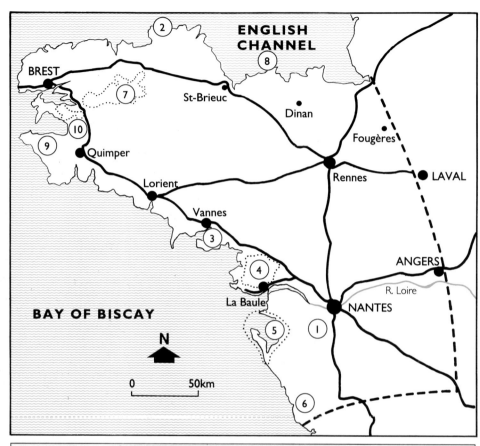

FIFTY INTERESTING SPECIES TO LOOK FOR

Bearded Reedling	Kittiwake	Otter	Tree Mallow
Black-Winged Stilt	Marsh Harrier	Water Vole	Water Violet
Bluethroat	Montagu's Harrier	Wild Boar	White Water-Lily
Brent Goose	Puffin	Cornish Moneywort	Yellow Flag Iris
Cetti's Warbler	Purple Heron	Cottonweed	Yellow Water-Lily
Cirl Bunting	Ruff	Goldilocks Aster	Water Chestnut
Common Tern	Sandwich Tern	Green-Winged Orchid	Marsh Frog
Dunlin	Shag	Heath Lobelia	Sand Lizard
Fulmar	Shelduck	Lax-Flowered Orchid	Grayling Butterfly
Gannet	Woodlark	Plymouth Pear	Hairy Hawker
Grey Heron	Coypu	Sand Bedstraw	Dragonfly
Guillemot	Grey Seal	Sea Holly	Norfolk Hawker
Kentish Plover	Muskrat	Spring Squill	Dragonfly

Maps:	MA pp. 78-9; IGN No. 32
Location:	Just SW of Nantes
Access:	Very limited to lake; peripheral areas easier
Season:	Good at all times for birds; spring and summer for flowers and amphibians
Terrain:	Mainly wet or marshy; dry sand on hilly areas
Specialities:	Huge mixed heronry, Honey Buzzard, Marsh Harrier, Otter

This site is situated 5–6km south-west of the major centre of Nantes, and is easily accessible by road from there. The site itself consists of a very large neutral freshwater lake, varying in size from 4,000ha in summer to 5,600ha in winter, though relatively little of this is open water. It lies ,in a basin surrounded by quaternary sands and gravels. Extensive reed-beds and willow or alder carr surround the lake, and to the south and west lie the grazing marshes of La Marzelle. The open water is well vegetated, with vast areas of Yellow, White and Fringed Water-Lilies, and the rarer Water-Chestnut.

The best point for views of the lake is at Passay, on the north-east corner. Many birds and other features of interest can be seen from here, and boat trips can sometimes be arranged with local fishermen.

The heronries are to be found in the carr and woodland immediately around the lake, though feeding herons and egrets can be seen all around the area, with eel as the most

Opposite: map of Brittany. The sites are numbered as in the text. Only main roads and the major rivers of the region are shown.

A Grey Heron (Ardea cinerea) searching for prey in a marshland ditch.

popular prey. Marsh Harrier are very common, with over forty pairs in the area. Black-Winged Stilt breed on the marshland, at one of their most northerly sites, while breeding Black-Tailed Godwit are at the south of their range. Bluethroat are to be found along the marshland dykes.

Early summer evenings are a good time for seeing more of the area's ten or more species of amphibian, of which the Marsh Frog is probably the noisiest. Evenings and early mornings also offer the best chance of seeing some of the local mammals, which include Otter, Coypu, Genet and Badger and Pine Marten.

2	SEPT-ILES
Maps:	MA p. 27; IGN No.14
Location:	Just off N Brittany coast; N of Lannion
Access:	By boat from Perros-Guirec, in summer only (June onwards); landing on Ile aux Moines, and minor islands
Season:	Major sea-bird breeding colonies, from late spring to summer
Terrain:	Rocky; some grassland
Specialities:	Puffin, Gannet, British Storm-Petrel, Razorbill, Grey Seal

3	GOLFE DU MORBIHAN
Maps:	MA p.62;IGN No.15
Location:	Immediately S of Vannes
Access:	Good roads encircle gulf and many small roads lead to shore; local boat trips
Season:	Wildfowl and waders in winter and on passage
Terrain:	Intertidal areas are very muddy
Specialities:	Brent Goose, Knot, breeding terns

This group of rocky offshore granite islands represents the oldest nature reserve in France, declared in 1912, and now managed by the LPO. They are the finest sea-bird colonies in France, and the southernmost breeding sites for Gannet and Puffin. Numbers of birds have fluctuated considerably over the years, apart from natural fluctuations, as a result of cessation of collection for food, and more recently as a result of several major oil spills, including the Torrey Canyon. Puffins, for example, were reduced to 250 pairs, though now they are steadily climbing. Other birds present in good numbers include Gannet, in their only French colony, now numbering around 5,000 pairs, British Storm-Petrel, Razorbill, Guillemot, Fulmar, Shag, Kittiwake and Sandwich Tern. There are also a few pairs of Raven.

The Islands of Rouzic, Malban and Cerf are probably the most interesting. Landing is forbidden, but excellent views of the cliff colonies, and often Grey Seal, can be had from the boats. A visit to Ile aux Moines is worthwhile for views of Raven and sea-birds.

The Golfe du Morbihan is a huge shallow tidal basin, a 'little sea' at high-tide, emptying at low-tide to reveal a mass of mud, salt-marsh and numerous islands. Its primary importance lies in the huge numbers of waders, wildfowl and other birds that feed and roost there through the winter. It is particularly noted for Brent Geese, Wigeon,

A general view of part of the huge Golfe du Morbihan on the coast of Brittany.

Teal, Pintail, Eider, Merganser, and large numbers of various waders such as Knot.

Its size makes viewing difficult, but good vantage points are to be found on the roads down the east side. North of Sarzeau, there is a Rèserve Ornithologique, which has fine populations of Eel Grass, especially attractive to Brent Geese. The Etang de Noyalo is an excellent area, separated from the tidal basin by the road causeway, while the headlands on either side of the narrow entrance make good general viewing points. Boat trips give the best appreciation of the gulf, though they mainly operate in summer, when bird numbers are lower. The island of Er Lannic has breeding Common and Sandwich Terns.

Although primarily a winter site, from autumn passage to spring passage there are good numbers of breeding terns, Shelduck, and gulls in summer, plus a variety of non-breeding birds.

The Pointe du Grande Mont, some 5km to the south, is an interesting botanical and entomological site, with rarities like Praying Mantis, and Goldilocks Aster.

Brent Goose
Branta bernicla L 56–61

This rather small dark-coloured goose is a familiar feature of the whole northern and western coast of France, from Belgium to Spain, in winter and early spring. They are visitors from the arctic, and French birds are normally the dark-bellied race, subspecies *bernicla*. Their main food is the marine flowering plant Eel Grass, so they tend to congregate in areas where this is abundant. However, they will also move readily to short grass or young cereals if the Eel Grass runs out. The best place to see them is in the great bays and estuaries of the west coast, such as the Golfe du Morbihan, and the Baie de Bourgneuf.

4	BRIERE REGIONAL NATURAL PARK	
Maps:	MA p. 63; IGN ; No. 24	
Location:	Immediately N of St Nazaire, at the Loire estuary	
Access:	Easy by road; boats from Ile de Fédrun; by foot to marsh	
Season:	All year	
Terrain:	Wet marshland	
Specialities:	One of Europe's finest and largest wetlands	

The Regional Natural Park covers some 40,000ha immediately north of the Loire estuary, from la Baule in the south-west corner to la Roche Bernard at the north tip. Within this lies the Grand Brière marsh, which takes up some 7,000ha, and forms one of the largest and best wetlands in Europe. Yet, surprisingly, it is barely known outside the area.

The marsh is made up of reed-beds, canals, lakes, carr woodland and fen, with limited areas of grassland. It is owned by the inhabitants of twenty-one surrounding towns, and is currently managed with the conservation both of its historic and ecological features in mind.

Flat-bottomed marsh boats in the reedbeds of the Grand Brière.

Botanically, the site is rich. The frequent marsh plants occur, such as Yellow Flag, Water-Violet, Ragged Robin, Marsh Mallow, Flowering Rush, White Water-Lily, bladderworts, and numerous pondweed species, all in abundance, together with less frequent species such as Lax-Flowered Orchid. The purplish-blue flowers of Heath Lobelia are abundant in late summer in damp fields.

Mammals include a large and reasonably visible population of Muskrat, together with Otter, Water-Vole, Wild Boar, Brown Hare and much else. Birds are of particular interest during the summer, and breeding species include: Spotted Crake, Marsh Harrier, Montagu's Harrier, Water Rail, Purple Heron, Black Tern, Bluethroat, and numerous more common species. Insects and other invertebrates are still under-recorded, but include numerous dragonflies, and interesting species such as Musk Beetle.

The range of wildlife is best appreciated from a boat. These can be hired (with guide) from numerous locations, especially on the east side of the marsh, with Ile de Fédrun as the centre (the park office is also here).

Altogether, this is a site of exceptional natural history and historical interest. Spring and summer are the best times for visiting, though bird numbers can be very high in winter, especially in bad weather.

5	BAIE DE BOURGNEUF
Maps:	MA p. 78; IGN No. 32
Location:	W coast, about 15km SW of Nantes
Access:	Largely open
Season:	All year; busy July–August
Terrain:	Mudflats, salt-marshes, grazing marshes; likely to be wet
Specialities:	Harriers, Black-Winged Stilt, Avocet; Norfolk Hawker Dragonfly

The site consists of a very large bay, partially enclosed by the Ile de Noirmoutier peninsula. At low-tide, large areas of intertidal muds are exposed, providing rich feeding grounds, especially in winter, for huge numbers of wildfowl and waders. On the mainland side, there are extensive saltings, grading inland into the grazing marshes of

Machecoul. The Ile de Noirmoutier has saltpans and mixed coastal habitats.

In winter, there are normally large numbers of such birds as Brent Goose, Curlew, Wigeon, Teal, Grey Plover, Knot, Oystercatcher, Dunlin and many others. At passage periods, many other species occur including good birds of prey. Breeding birds include Black-Winged Stilt, Marsh Harrier, Black Kite, Bluethroat, Short-Toed Lark, Cetti's Warbler, Kentish Plover, Avocet, Hoopoe, and Woodlark.

The bay itself can easily be reached from numerous roads and tracks all round the periphery, and the two road causeways to the Ile give good views. South of the bay lies an area of forested dunes, the Forêt de Pays de Monts, good for Hoopoe, warblers, Woodlark, and the like, and remnants of the original dune flora exist in places. The grazing marshes to the east have good breeding birds, plus interesting dragonflies such as the Norfolk Hawker and the Hairy Hawker, both to be found in early summer.

6	ILE D'OLONNE	
Maps:	MA pp. 78 and 92; IGN No. 32	
Location:	About 20km NW of la Rochelle, NW of les Sables d'Olonne	
Access:	Generally open	
Season:	Good in summer for flowers, insects, reptiles, breeding birds	
Terrain:	Very mixed; dunes, forest, marshland, open water	
Specialities:	Breeding Avocet, Black-Winged Stilt, Cirl Bunting; Sand Lizard	

The site is easily reached from the D32, running north from les Sables d'Olonne, which bisects the site. Numerous tracks and smaller roads lead into the dunes, which become very busy in summer.

The area comprises a considerable mixture of habitats, mainly sand-dunes, with established pine plantations over most of them; brackish marshlands; and open fresh water with surrounding marshland. The area has been gradually changing, for the worse, as drainage and agricultural improvement nibble away at it.

The remaining open areas of dune have a good flora, though it is well trampled in summer. This includes Sea Bindweed, Sand Bedstraw, Cottonweed, Sea Holly, numerous Evening Primrose species, and much else if you look hard. The woods are rich in some forms of insect-life (though not especially good for butterflies or dragonflies), such as bee hawk moths.

Breeding birds are good throughout, though the old saltpans and marshy areas are best, with Avocet, Black-winged Stilt, Ruff and other species; Cirl Bunting breed in

A Kentish Plover (Charadrius alexandrinus) *in breeding plumage.*

places, though they are declining. At passage times, all the wetland areas are good for migrating birds.

ARMORIQUE REGIONAL NATURAL PARK

This park consists of several discrete sections spread through an area of north-western Brittany. Like many other Regional Natural Parks, its primary aim is not especially the protection of natural habitats, though most parts are of general interest to the naturalist. In total, it covers 65,000ha, which include extensive areas of heathland, woodland, coastal grassland and cliffs, and a number of offshore islands. The Montagnes d'Arrée form an impressive landscape feature running across the park, though the highest point is only 384m. Beavers were re-introduced to the area relatively recently, and they are established on a tributary of the River Aulne.

The following sites have been picked out as being of special interest, though they are by no means the only ones and the area as a whole is well worth further exploration.

7	HUELGOAT FOREST
Maps:	MA p27; IGN No. 14
Location:	c. 25km S of Morlaix
Access:	Open
Season:	Late spring and summer
Terrain:	Woodland; rocky or damp in places
Specialities:	Cornish Moneywort, Redstart, Tunbridge Filmy Fern

The Huelgoat Forest lies north and east of the village of Huelgoat, which is on the B14 off the D769, south of Morlaix. The woodland is a well-used recreational area, and there are good waymarked walks and places of interest.

The woodland is mixed, with Beech, oak, pine and Spruce as the dominant trees. A notable feature of the wood is the abundance of large granite rocks. There are also attractive cascades and steeply falling streams.

An adult Beaver (Castor fiber) feeding on birch foliage.

The attractively delicate flowers of Ivy-leaved Bellflower (Wahlenbergia hederacea).

The wood is good for lichens, bryophytes and ferns, thanks to the high humidity, old trees, and relatively clean air. Tunbridge Filmy Fern is abundant here, and flowering plants of interest include Cornish Moneywort, *Sibthorpia europaea,* Ivy-Leaved Bellflower, Sheep's-Bit, and Royal Fern.

Breeding birds are typical of western deciduous woodland, and include Redstart, Willow Warbler, Wood Warbler, Dipper and other widespread species.

8	CAP FREHEL	
Maps:	MA p.29; IGN No.14	
Location:	N coast, about 20km W of St Malo	
Access:	Open	
Terrain:	Open coastal habitats on cliffs; mainly dry	
Specialities:	Breeding sea-birds; coastal heath plants	

This is a superb headland site, with excellent views. The site lies to the north of the main D786 St Malo to St Brieuc road. Minor roads lead northwards to the headland from between Matignon and Erquy, especially the D34A. It is well signposted. Part of the headland is a reserve run by the SEPNB.

The site consists mainly of high-quality heathland, coastal grassland and spectacular cliffs. Breeding birds include Fulmar, Shag, Kittiwake, Guillemot, Razorbill, and Raven. Cetti's Warbler breeds in the scrub.

The flora is of great interest, and includes most heathland plants, together with Pale Butterwort, sundews, Marsh Gentian, the tiny gentian *Exaculum pusillum,* the rare western species Kerry Lily, and *Ophioglossum azoricum,* Autumn Squill, and Sea Spleenwort, amongst others. Insects are of interest, and includes the Large Marsh Grasshopper.

Large Marsh Grasshoppers (Stethophyma grossum) are locally common on the wet heaths of this area.

All parts of this relatively small site are of interest, and it is easy to see the different habitats from the road. However, it is best appreciated by walking to the cliffs, from where spectacular views can be obtained, particularly in early summer.

31

The stately spikes of Lax-Flowered Orchids (Orchis laxiflora).

9 CAP-SIZUM AND MICHEL-HERVE JULIEN RESERVE	
Maps:	MA p 44; IGN No.13
Location:	On N coast of peninsula W of Quimper
Access:	Open
Season:	Guided tours in summer
Terrain:	Cliffs; coastal grassland and heath; scrub
Specialities:	Breeding sea-birds, Choughs; coast flowers

The reserve lies along the north coast of the peninsula that terminates in the Pointe du Raz, to the west of Quimper. It is marked (without boundaries) on both of the reference maps listed above. From the D7, follow signs to Kergulan and the reserve. There is an information centre here in summer.

The reserve comprises cliffs, cliff-top habitats and offshore waters. It is best known for its breeding birds, which include good numbers of Guillemot, Razorbill, Puffin, Fulmar, Shag, Kittiwake, British Storm-Petrel, and Raven. In one area, with more limited access, there is a colony of Chough, which has been the subject of considerable research here. Selected breeds of sheep have been used in controlled grazing experiments to produce the most suitable turf for the Chough to feed on. More terrestrial birds include Stonechat and Dartford Warbler.

The site is not of special botanical importance, though there are good displays of the more common coast flowers, and heath species such as Western Gorse.

The site is best visited from mid-April onwards, as the birds return to breed and flowers appear in quantity. Guided walks are available from June to August; at other times, the marked footpaths should be followed. The reserve is well run by the SEPNB.

2. NORMANDY

INTRODUCTION

The area covered by this region equates roughly with the area of Normandy. It covers the northern part of France from the Bay of Mont St Michel, stretching eastwards as far as the north of the River Somme, and southwards as far as Le Mans. Not surprisingly, it is reminiscent in many ways of southern England, with a broadly similar geology, climate and agriculture.

The eastern part (roughly east of a line between le Havre and le Mans), is dominated by part of the great chalk massif of north-central France, which encircles the Paris basin. Large areas have been converted to intensive

A female Purple Emperor butterfly (Apatura iris).

agriculture, with little of special natural interest remaining. Hill-tops often have more acid pockets of soil, and have remained wooded. The western part of the region is dominated by older rocks with pre-Cambrian, Cambrian and intruded granite dominating, giving rise to much more acid soils, with pasture as the most prevalent land use. Here and there, especially on the Cherbourg peninsula, patches of heathland, wet heath and bog have survived, though they are steadily declining in both number and area. Good examples are to be found around Lessay.

Between these two major geological zones, there is an area of Jurassic rock in which limestones predominate. This stretches down through Caen, Falaise and Alençon, giving

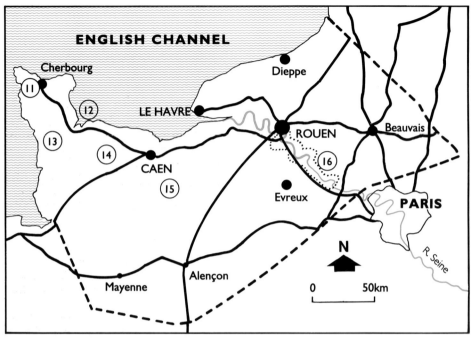

Map of Normandy. The sites are numbered as in the text. Only main roads and major rivers of the region are shown.

rise to attractive countryside, in part, and some interesting botanically rich areas, such as the Monts d'Eraines area.

The coast is long and indented. Although well used both for holiday developments

and, here and there, industry, it nevertheless retains a great deal of biological interest. Soft coasts, such as dunes and salt-marshes, are fre-quent, though there are also rocky coasts and cliffs. The chalk cliffs near Etretat, for

FIFTY INTERESTING SPECIES TO LOOK FOR

Bearded Reedling	Stonechat	Marsh Clubmoss	Tree Frog
Common Crane	Tree Pipit	Marsh Gentian	Clifden Nonpareil
Common Tern	Water Rail	Military Orchid	Moth
Curlew	Woodcock	Rouen Pansy	Adonis Blue
Dunlin	Otter	Spiked Speedwell	Duke of Burgundy
Golden Oriole	Water Vole	St Lucie's Cherry	Lesser Purple Emperor
Kingfisher	Bastard Balm	Summer Ladies' Tresses	Purple Emperor
Lapwing	Cottonweed	Water Germander	Scarce Swallowtail
Marsh Harrier	Fen Orchid	Viper's Grass	Wood White
Nightjar	Fly Orchid	Edible Frog	Ruddy Darter
Oystercatcher	Hare's Tail Grass	Midwife Toad	Scarce Emerald
Redstart	Heath Lobelia	Natterjack Toad	Damselfly
Shelduck	Lady Orchid	Marbled Newt	Emperor Dragonfly

example, are famous for their spectacular height and steepness.

Climatically, the region differs little from southern England, though the summers are slightly warmer. The range of species to be seen is broadly similar to that of southern England, with the addition of a few extra flowers and insects that are absent or extremely rare in England, such as Summer Ladies' Tresses or Camberwell Beauty.

11 MERE DE VAUVILLE	
Maps:	MA p. 12; IGN No. 6
Location:	c. 12km W of Cherbourg
Access:	N section a GONm Reserve, with access restricted to paths; open to S, though firing-range
Season:	Best in summer
Terrain:	Sand-dunes; marshland; open water
Specialities:	Tree Frog, Natterjack Toad, Marbled Newt; Water Germander, Spiked Speedwell

An attractive mixed coastal site, with marshland, reed-beds, open water, dunes up to 80m high, and damp dune slacks. Access is straightforward by car or bus from nearby Cherbourg, on the D118.

The site occupies a flat coastal plain, with extensive development of mature and new dunes across the bay. Behind and amongst the dunes there is a series of freshwater pools and lakes, some of which are surrounded by reed or fen swamp.

The flora is very rich, with most common dune plants, but also specialities (frequently in abundance), like Water Germander, Spiked Speedwell, Wild Asparagus, and Hare's Tail

Bladderworts
Utricularia spp.

The bladderworts are a small group of aquatic, insectivorous, flowering plants. Their underwater parts consist mainly of finely divided leaves with tiny bladders spread along them. These bladders act like little trapdoors – each has a small entrance that is opened when a trigger is touched, and the slight inward rush of water carries the small invertebrate that touched the trigger in with it. It is then digested by the plant. This strange method of nutrition allows the bladderworts to survive in areas that are otherwise poor in nutrients, such as bog pools.

They are quite frequent in France, especially in areas where there is ample open water, like the Sologne and the Brenne, and they are an impressive sight when flowering profusely in midsummer. Besides the Greater Bladderwort, shown here, there are other similar species, and also a much smaller, paler species found generally in the most acid boggy pools.

Grass. Wet areas hold Mudwort, bladderworts, Greater Spearwort, Hornwort, and various pondweeds, amongst other things.

Amphibians include a good population of Common Tree Frog, together with Natterjack Toad, Midwife Toad, and Marbled Newt at their northernmost limit.

Breeding birds include Bearded Reedling and Water Rail, and at passage times almost anything can turn up, with North American birds a speciality after strong westerly gales.

Insect-life includes Bloody-Nosed Beetle, a coastal species of Tiger Beetle, and at least thirty species of dragonfly. All parts of the site are of interest.

12 BANC DU GRAND VEY/ DOMAINE DE BEAUGILLOT	
Maps:	MA pp. 12-13; IGN No. 6
Location:	NE of Carentan
Access:	Limited within the reserve; elsewhere long distances on foot can be involved
Season:	Best in winter or at passage times for birds
Terrain:	Marshland; salt-marsh; mudflats
Specialities:	Huge numbers of Oystercatcher, Dunlin, Lapwing, Curlew, Golden Plover

Access to the site is straightforward by a number of roads and tracks leading northwards or eastwards from the N13 Cherbourg to Bayeux road. The site occupies the whole of the bay around the estuary of the River Vire. It is sheltered by the Cherbourg peninsula, and silts up rapidly in the calm conditions. There are vast areas of sand and mudflats exposed at low tide, and these support enormous numbers of feeding birds. The Domaine de Beaugillot protects one of the high-tide roosts on the west side of the estuary.

Winter brings very large numbers of wildfowl and waders, especially Curlew, Oystercatcher, Dunlin, Lapwing, Knot, Redshank,

A Redshank (Tringa totanus) in breeding plumage, with a ringed leg.

and Golden and Ringed Plovers. Migration periods bring a good selection of other waders. Summer breeding birds include Shelduck in good numbers, Redshank, Water Rail, Garganey, Oystercatcher, and Common Tern.

There are no organized viewing or information facilities, but good views can be had from the shore, especially on the north-east corner of the bay.

13 LES LANDES DE LESSAY AND TOURBIERE DE MATHON	
Maps:	MA p. 12; IGN No. 6
Location:	c. 50km S of Cherbourg
Access:	Generally unrestricted
Season:	Best in summer for flowers and insects
Terrain:	Boggy and heathy; boots needed except in very dry weather
Specialities:	Summer Ladies' Tresses, Heath Lobelia, Viper's Grass; Scarce Emerald Damselfly; Nightjar

South and east of the village of Lessay, there are remnants of a once more extensive tract of heath and bog; the areas of interest have been steadily declining through drainage, agricultural reclamation, building and lack of management. Thus, the remaining areas are scattered, and sometimes difficult to find. There is a station at Lessay, but a car is useful for the more scattered sites.

The predominant habitats are heath and bog, with considerable areas of wet heath, some cut for peat, and much of it reverting to woodland. Open wet areas are the best for flowers and insects. The Tourbière de Mathon (immediately east of Lessay, between the D900 and the River Ay) is a reserve of 16ha run by the National Natural History Museum.

*The rare orchid Summer Ladies' Tresses (*Spiranthes aestivalis*) occurs in several sites within this region.*

Plants of interest include substantial populations of Summer Ladies' Tresses, Heath Lobelia, Viper's Grass, two species of sundew, Marsh Clubmoss, and many other wet heath and bog plants. Insects include the Scarce Emerald Damselfly (*Lestes dryas*) and other bog species such as the Keeled Skimmer. The area is not renowned for birds, but Nightjar, Tree Pipit and Stonechat, amongst others, are present.

There are other areas not far away which may be of interest, such as the Tourbière de Baupte, 10km north-east of Lessay.

14 LA FORET DE CERISY	
Maps:	MA p. 13; IGN No. 6
Location:	14km SW of Bayeux
Access:	Unrestricted, on foot
Season:	Best in spring and summer for flowers, insects, birds
Terrain:	Woodland; generally dry
Specialities:	Purple Emperor, Lesser Purple Emperor, Clifden Nonpareil Moth; rare woodland beetles

The forest is bisected by the main Bayeux to St Lô road, and numerous minor roads and tracks enter it. As with most forests in this area, Beech is the dominant tree, providing a good general woodland environment. The wood is particularly noted for its woodland fauna, and has been described as a reserve on account of a race of the ground beetle *Chrysocarabus auronitens* that is found almost nowhere else in the world. More interesting to the general naturalist is the woodland butterfly fauna which includes the Lesser Purple Emperor, Brimstone, White-Letter Hairstreak, and Camberwell Beauty. Moths include the superb Clifden Nonpareil, and the

Lobster Moth with its bizarre caterpillar. There are also various other beetles, such as the two distinctive longhorns, *Rhagium bifasciatus* and *Strangalia maculata*.

15 LES COTEAUX DE MESNIL-SOLEIL	
Maps:	MA p.32; IGN No.18
Location:	c. 25km SE of Caen, just NE of Falaise
Access:	Limited on the reserve
Season:	Late spring and summer for flowers and insects
Terrain:	Dry limestone grassland; scrub; woodland edge
Specialities:	Bee Orchid, Dark-Red Helleborine, Lady Orchid, Adonis Blue, Duke of Burgundy

The area comprises species-rich dry limestone grassland on the sunny southern slopes of Mont d'Eraines, partially surrounded and sheltered by woodland. Minor roads leading east from Falaise, especially the D248, run close to the site.

Its primary significance is botanical. Dry calcareous grassland is rare in France from here westwards, and the assemblage of species is of considerable regional importance. Flowers of interest include Large-Flowered Self-Heal, Pasque Flower, Bee, Fly, and Lady Orchids, Dark-Red Helleborine, White Helleborine, Mountain Germander, St Lucie's Cherry, Chiltern Gentian, and many others. Not surprisingly, butterflies are worthy of note, with Adonis and Chalkhill Blues, Duke of Burgundy Fritillary, and Scarce Swallowtail. This site is also a northerly outpost for the mainly southern Faust's Burnet Moth.

The best times for a visit are from May to August. The whole area is of interest, and will repay exploration along the southern slopes of the hill, and into the woods.

16 SEINE VALLEY CHALK DOWNLANDS: ROUEN TO MANTES	
Maps:	MA pp. 16 and 34-5; IGN map No. 8
Location:	The scarps of the Seine valley, scattered along both sides, from Rouen up-river to Mantes
Access:	Unrestricted on most sites
Season:	Flowers and insects, from spring to autumn
Terrain:	Dry grassland, scrub, woodland
Specialities:	Rouen Pansy, numerous orchids, Hepatica, White Rock-Rose; Scarce Swallowtail

This section of the River Seine cuts through a major chalk massif, and the steep slopes of the valley have a number of chalk grassland areas remaining on them. These are tending to decline, through lack of management (allowing scrub invasion), over use by motorcycle scrambling and other activities, and agricultural improvement. However, the best of those that remain are rich in species, and varied in character.

Botanically, they are of special interest. Orchids are present in abundance, and they include Monkey, Military, Lady (and hybrids), Bee, Early Purple, Pyramidal, Fragrant, and others. Other flowering plants of special note are the Rouen Pansy, *Viola hispida*, (found only in this area), White Rock-Rose, St Lucie's Cherry, Hepatica, Bastard Balm, Large Speedwell, and several broomrapes. On some areas of downland Laburnum, Locust Tree,

A spike of the beautiful Military Orchid (Orchis militaris) in calcareous grassland.

and Manna Ash are naturalized and invading rapidly.

Insect-life is rich, especially among the butterflies, particularly where sunny slopes back up to woodland. Species include Wood White, Scarce Swallowtail, Duke of Burgundy Fritillary, Brown Argus, Adonis Blue, Brimstone and many others. Field Crickets are common on the sunnier slopes.

Birds are not of particular interest, but include Tree Pipit, Turtle Dove, and Redstart.

Sites are easily found by driving along the roads that follow the floodplain and scanning either bank. However, good sites are to be found at the following locations (working upstream from Rouen; W = west bank, E = east bank):

1. Roches d'Orival, backing onto the Forêt de la Londe Rouvray. An exceptional and very varied site (W).
2. Two patches of downland above Amfreville (E).
3. Two downland areas just north and south of Les Andelys (E).
4. A small semi-wooded area with Hepatica, opposite Bennecourt (W).
5. Downland above La Roche Guyon; invaded heavily by Laburnum, etc., but still species-rich in parts.

A bonus of the area is Monet's restored garden at Giverny, near Vernon, which is superb, and well worth a visit, though always busy.

Chalk downland at the Roche d' Orival, Seine valley near Rouen. Most of the remaining grasslands in this part of the Seine valley are steep enough to avoid ploughing, though motor-cycle scrambling is affecting a number of them.

3. NORTH-EAST FRANCE: PICARDY AND CHAMPAGNE

INTRODUCTION

This region extends across almost the whole of north-eastern France, from the coast around Boulogne and Calais, eastwards to the Vosges mountains. It is bordered to the north by Belgium and Luxembourg. Overall, it is one of the least rich areas of France for the naturalist, with huge expanses of featureless arable land all too prevalent. However, it is by no means without interest, and it is in these huge intensively farmed parts that some guidance is most useful.

Chalk is the dominant underlying rock over most of the area. Here it outcrops as an

Opposite: the Source du Lison.
Below: May-lily (Maianthemum bifolium) is locally frequent in old woods, usually on acid soil.

undulating landscape which has proved easy to farm, giving rise to the huge hedgeless fields which dominate much of the area. For anything of more than patchy interest, we need to look at the coastal fringe, the river valleys, and the areas of older, harder rock. South of Laon, and south of Reims, Eocene and Oligocene rocks outcrop, and there is a modestly hilly area, known as the Mountain of Reims, declared as a Regional Natural Park.

Farther north, the southern part of the hilly Ardennes comes into France, to the north of Charlevilles-Mézières. Although not highlighted as a site, this area is attractive, hilly and wooded, and is worth a visit for its general natural history interest and its landscape. Monthermé, on the River Meuse, is useful as a base for exploration.

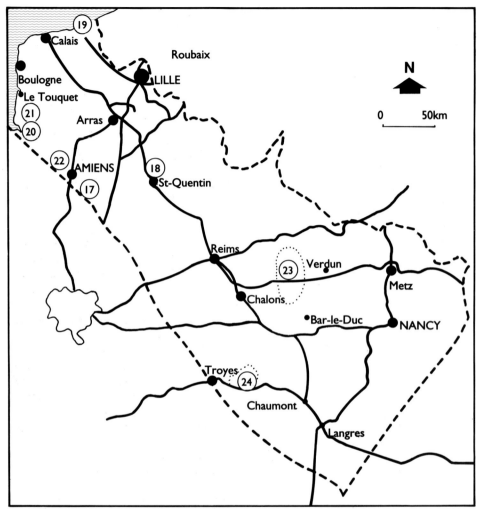

Map of North-East France: Picardy and Champagne. The sites are numbered as in the text. Only main roads of the region are shown.

Climatically, the region is dominated by central European weather systems, progressively more so to the east. The western coastal areas are very similar to extreme south-east England in their weather, though the eastern areas are more Continental in character with hotter summers and colder winters.

The natural history highlights are not very different from equivalent areas of England, though it is noticeable that new species appear as you go eastwards. Birds such as White Stork, wintering Crane, Little Bustard, all three harrier species, Honey Buzzard and Bonelli's Warbler begin to appear more

FIFTY INTERESTING SPECIES TO LOOK FOR

Avocet	Melodious Warbler	Candytuft	Wild Service Tree
Cetti's Warbler	Montagu's Harrier	Common Spotted	Edible frog
Common Crane	Nightingale	Orchid	Grass Snake
Dunlin	Osprey	Cowbane	Adonis Blue
Goshawk	Pintail	Dark Red Helleborine	Brimstone butterfly
Great Grey Shrike	Red Kite	Fen Orchid	Emperor Dragonfly
Grey-Headed	Redshank	Grass of Parnassus	Map Butterfly
Woodpecker	Shelduck	Greater Bladderwort	Purple Emperor
Honey Buzzard	Sparrowhawk	Green-Winged orchid	Scarlet Tiger moth
Kentish Plover	Spoonbill	Marsh Gentian	White Admiral
Kingfisher	Wigeon	Marsh Helleborine	White-Legged
Lapwing	Badger	Pasque flower	Damselfly
Little Bittern	Cambridge Milk	Sea Bindweed	
Marsh Harrier	Parsley	Tufted Loosestrife	

commonly along with various flowers, amphibia and insects which are unfamiliar to British eyes. The Argonne and the Forêt d'Orient Regional Natural Park are particularly good in this respect.

17 AVRE VALLEY FENS/ETANG DE SAINT-LADRE

Maps:	MA p. 17. IGN No. 4
Location:	5km SE of Amiens, between Cagny and Boves
Access:	Restricted in places
Season:	Best in summer for flowers, breeding birds
Terrain:	Wet and boggy generally; boots useful
Specialities:	Marsh Gentian, Fir Clubmoss; Great Grey Shrike, Little Bittern, Melodious Warbler

The site lies in the floodplain of the River Avre, and can easily be reached from the road that runs along the floodplain or the footpath that follows the river. Much of the floodplain of the Avre is of interest, with a mass of fen,

reed-bed, and lakes (used mostly for fishing), and the valley of the River Somme itself is of similar interest, though rather more improved agriculturally. A local reserve occupies a small area of the River Avre floodplain just upstream from Fortmanoir Farm, between Boves and Cagny.

The vegetation consists mainly of fen, bog and open water, with reed-beds and invading scrub woodland. The ground-water is calcareous, allowing an interesting fen flora to develop, though parts are acid. The flora includes several species of Stonewort, nine species of bogmoss *Sphagnum*, Marsh Gentian, Fir Clubmoss (not seen recently), Least Bur-Reed, Greater Bladderwort and various ferns.

A *Snipe* (Gallinago gallinago) *probing the mud for food with its long beak.*

43

Invertebrates are not fully studied, but species such as Scarlet Tiger Moth, Emperor Dragonfly, and numerous damselflies and mayflies occur.

Breeding birds of note include Little Bittern, Great Grey Shrike, Melodious Warbler, and numerous other wetland warblers, together with large numbers of breeding nightingales. Winter brings large numbers of thrushes, together with Snipe, Woodcock, and wildfowl.

The most rewarding time to visit is during the period May to July. More information about the reserve can be obtained from the Mairie in Boves.

18 LE MARAIS D'ISLE

Maps:	MA p. 8; IGN No. 4
Location:	Within St Quentin
Access:	Restricted to paths; closed at night
Season:	Best in spring–summer for flowers, insects, breeding birds, but interesting at all times
Terrain:	Wet; paths satisfactory in drier weather
Specialities:	Marsh Harrier, Cetti's Warbler, Kingfisher, Cowbane, Tufted Loosestrife

This is a rather similar habitat to the Avre valley. Although it is surrounded by urban development, it is run as a nature reserve, such that it retains a surprising amount of interest, and is generally well managed. Habitats include open water (in the form of lakes, waterways and canals), wet woodland and scrub, and fen.

Botanically, there is a good range of typical wetland plants in abundance, with specialities such as Cowbane and the rare Tufted

The main waterway in the Marais d' Isle reserve, in St. Quentin.

Loosestrife. Invertebrates are undoubtedly rich, though poorly studied, and include Scarlet Tiger Moth in abundance, Water Spider, and dragonflies and damselflies tolerant of lime-rich water like White-Legged Damselfly, Variable Damselfly and Emperor Dragonfly.

Marsh Harrier have nested on the reserve irregularly, while numerous wetland warbler species, such as Cetti's Warbler, breed there now. Kingfishers are resident, and Nightingales are abundant. The open water areas attract large numbers of wildfowl in winter, and the Somme Valley is a significant migration route.

Down-river from St Quentin, the floodplain marshes and lakes towards Seraucourt-le-Grand are also worth investigating.

19 LA DUNE MARCHAND

Maps:	MA p. 3; IGN Nos 1 & 2
Location:	Extreme N coast; close to Belgian border
Access:	Limited to paths
Season:	Best in late spring–summer
Terrain:	Mainly sandy; damp slack areas
Specialities:	Fen Orchid, Marsh Helleborine, Grass of Parnassus, Sea Bindweed, Dune Pansy

The site comprises an area of dunes and dune slacks on the extreme north-east coast of France, between the two spreading developments of Bray Dunes and Zuydcoote, just east of Dunkerque. The once-frequent dunes of this north coast have steadily disappeared under development, or been degraded, and this local reserve protects one of the few remnants.

The flora is rich with such species as Sea Bindweed, Musk Orchid, the perennial form of wild pansy *Viola tricolor ssp. curtisii*, Sea Spurge, Storksbill, and various grasses in the drier areas; damp slacks have Fen Orchid, Marsh Helleborine, Creeping Willow, Grass of Parnassus and many other species. Other groups are not well known, though they include common species such as Skylark, Small Heath Butterfly, Poplar Leaf-Beetle and others. In winter, small flocks of Snow Bunting may appear (though the Somme Estuary is a better area for these).

Access is straightforward into the site from either end, though limited in some sections of the reserve. The whole area around the reserve is protected from development, though not managed. It is most interesting during spring and summer.

A Poplar Leaf-Beetle (Chrysomela populi) feeding on Creeping Willow (Salix repens).

20 SOMME ESTUARY

Maps:	MA p. 6; IGN No. 1
Location:	Coast NW of Abbeville
Access:	Straightforward from fringing roads; fee payable for park (open April–November only)
Season:	Best in winter for birds
Terrain:	Variable; wet in places
Specialities:	Spoonbill, Kentish Plover, Fan-Tailed Warbler, Avocet, Muskrat

At the mouth of the River Somme, there is a sizeable sheltered bay, which empties at low-tide to reveal extensive areas of mudflats. A main road encircles much of the bay, with access by minor roads to some of the northern sections, and the reserve and park at Marquenterre. The Parc Ornithologique is most like the Wildfowl Trust in Britain, and provides opportunities for seeing both wild and tame birds at close range.

Habitats include mudflats, marshes, lagoons, salt-marsh, and dunes. The primary importance of the area is for birds in winter, though the park/reserve area remains of interest all year round. Unfortunately, the rest of the bay is too heavily shot over, which reduces numbers considerably. In winter, there are large numbers of Dunlin, Curlew, Bar-Tailed Godwit, Wigeon, Pintail, and Greylag Goose. Snow Bunting and Shore Lark occur in small flocks. At migration times, there are sizeable flocks of Whimbrel, Diver, Shelduck, Whooper Swan, Grey Plover, Scaup and many others, with less frequent visitors such as Osprey, Spoonbill, Little Egret, and Peregrine. Breeding birds include Greylag Goose, Shoveler, Kentish Plover, Oystercatcher, Fan-tailed Warbler and Shelduck.

The dunes north of Le Crotoy have a reasonable flora, though better areas are to be found north of the Bay, towards Fort-Mahon-Plage. It is possible to see most of the common dune plants such as Sea Holly, Sea Bindweed, Yellow Horned Poppy, several species of Evening Primrose and much else besides, though sites 19 (*see* page 45) and 21 (*see* above) are much better in this respect.

21 COASTAL HABITATS AROUND ETAPLES	
Maps:	MA p. 2 and 6; IGN No. 1
Location:	Coast from Boulogne to Berck
Access:	Generally open, though fen areas tend to be private shooting zones
Season:	Best for flowers from late spring to mid-summer;
Terrain:	Sand; marsh; fen; mudflats; woodland
Specialities:	Fen Orchid, Dense-Flowered Fragrant Orchid; Water Germander

The coast running southwards from Boulogne, eventually reaching the borders of the Somme Estuary, has an impressive mixture of habitats. Unfortunately, the basis of most of them is the sand that blows inshore from the English Channel, and this is also the basis of a thriving and spreading tourist industry. Numerous good sites have been built over, planted up or drained in recent years, leaving a scattered string of remnant habitats, some of which are still of very high quality.

The dunes have a rich flora which includes most species typical of neutral sand, such as Sea Holly, Yellow Horned Poppy, storksbills, numerous evening primrose species, Sea Bindweed, pansies, Seaside Centaury, Sand Catchfly, Brooklime and Lesser Water Plantain. Dune slacks may contain species such as Fen Orchid, Marsh Helleborine and Water Germander. Slightly inland, rich fen habitats have developed, and some have a particularly rich flora which includes large numbers of Fen Orchid, Dense-Flowered Fragrant Orchid, three species of bladderwort, Grass of Parnassus, and much else. The Marais de Balançon has been described as 'one of the best fens in Western Europe'.

Many of the wet areas should be good for amphibians such as Natterjack Toad, but these have not been looked at adequately.

The salt-marshes and mudflats at the mouth of the River Canche are good for birds, and winter and passage periods bring relatively large numbers of waders and wildfowl. Species are broadly similar to those of the Somme Estuary, though not as good.

Good areas include (working southwards from Boulogne):

1. The Etang de la Claire Eau, and associated marshland.
2. Dunes and pools south of Hardelot-Plage.
3. Estuary of la Canche.
4. Fen and marsh immediately east of Cucq, between the D940 and the D143.
5. The Marais de Balançon, east of Merlimont, a major fen and marsh complex, though access is rather limited.
6. Dunes between Merlimont-Plage and Berck. These have a rich flora and some good wet areas, though parts are also an unofficial nudist colony.

7. Dunes les Blancs, south of Fort Mahon-Plage; a large relatively unspoilt area.

Above: *a clump of the autumn-flowering Grass of Parnassus (Parnassia palustris).*
Left: *an area of sand dunes near Berck.*

22 SAMARA	
Maps:	MA p. 7; IGN No. 3
Location:	10km NW of Amiens; in the Somme valley
Access:	Only open through holiday season
Season:	Spring and summer for flowers, birds, insects
Terrain:	Generally good paths, some wet areas
Specialities:	Pasque Flower, Cambridge Milk Parsley

The Somme valley below Amiens, together with the valley sides, has a number of semi-natural habitats of interest, especially chalk grassland, fens, and open water. At Samara, between St Sauveur and Picguiny, there is an unusual centre, which comprises exhibitions relating to the history and ecology of the area; a botanic garden and arboretum; demonstration of prehistoric techniques; and reserve areas of marshland and chalk grassland. It provides a relatively quick way of seeing a cross-section of the habitats and species of the Somme Valley, as well as finding out a little extra background information, though a fair amount of habitat seems to have been lost in the construction process! Guided tours of the marshes are on offer here, with information on natural history.

Just upstream from Samara, there is an area of rich fen adjacent to where the D97 crosses the valley; this has Cambridge Milk Parsley, and good wetland warblers amongst other species. The dry valleys south-west of Ailly-sur-Somme have good chalk downland with typical species including Pasque Flower.

Access to the undesignated sites is reasonably easy. Samara is open from 9a.m. to 8p.m. throughout the summer, on payment of entry fee.

The whole chalk area south of here is worth exploring for its patches of remnant downland on steep slopes, often visible from the road. There are several good areas around Molliens-Dreuil.

23 FORET D'ARGONNE	
Maps:	MA p. 39; IGN No. 10
Location:	E of Reims, N of Bar-le-Duc
Access:	Generally free to the wooded areas; some lakes to south more limited
Season:	Best in late spring–summer
Terrain:	Wooded rocky slopes; lakes and marshland
Specialities:	Osprey, Honey Buzzard, Red Kite, Goshawk

The Argonne lies in 'Champagne' country, which is generally intensively agricultural land over calcareous soils. The Argonne ridge is quite different, being hard impermeable acid rock, and it stands out clearly as an ecological haven in this part of France. Access is very easy to the forested ridge, with several minor roads between Beaulieu, Clermont, Lachalade, etc. and many forest tracks from Clermont and elsewhere.

The ridge is covered with Beech and Oak forest, and, despite a maximum height of only 308m, has a mountainous appearance with several ravines. To the south-west of the ridge, around Givry-en-Argonne, there is a superb area of lakes and marshes.

This is best known as a bird site, with a marvellous range of species, especially birds of prey – Osprey, Buzzard, Red and Black Kites, Honey Buzzard, Goshawk, Hobby and all three harriers occur regularly. There are also many other exotic species, such as Golden Oriole, Grey-Headed Woodpecker, and Wryneck. The marshes and lakes are good for Marsh Harrier, Great Reed Warbler and many others.

Botanically, it is not particularly rich, being too acid, though May Lily and Lily-of-the-Valley occur. Many of the forested rides have a good mixture of common flowers which is excellent for butterflies, longhorn beetles, and other groups.

Forêt de Lisle, to the south, near Balval-en-Argonne, is a good Oak forest.

*A close view of a Black Kite (*Milvus migrans*), not infrequent in the south and east of this region.*

24 FORET D'ORIENT REGIONAL NATURAL PARK	
Maps:	MA pp. 56–7; IGN No. 22
Location:	c. 12km E of Troyes
Access:	Mostly open; limited in reserves
Season:	Good at all times for birds; late spring–summer for flowers
Terrain:	Mixed, damp grassland; woodland; lakeside; reed-beds
Specialities:	Common Crane, White-Tailed Eagle, Hen Harrier, Bean Goose

The park covers a sizeable area of forested land around the huge (2,300ha) lake – Lac de la Forêt d'Orient – that acts as a reservoir for Paris. Access is well sign posted and easy, and the west side of the lake is a popular recreation area.

The lake is now well known as a bird site, especially in winter. Several White-Tailed Eagles are regular every year, and Common Crane stop over for long periods and over winter. Large numbers of wildfowl winter here, also. Summer birds are less spectacular, though they include abundant Grey Heron, Marsh Harrier, Great Crested Grebe, and many warblers.

The forests, especially to the east, are on clay and have a good ancient woodland flora, with such species as Wild Service Tree abundant, and numerous Marsh and Spotted Orchids in damp grassy areas. Butterflies include Purple Emperor, Purple Hairstreak, White Admiral, and Brimstone.

The marshy and reedy margins of the lake on the east side (where there is a reserve) are good for amphibians, and Edible Frog are abundant. There is a hide in the reserve,

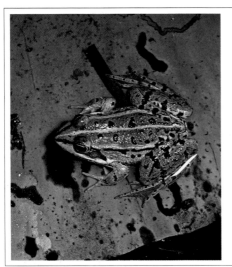

Edible Frog
Rana esculenta L 7.5–9.0
The waters of France are full of frogs, and one of the most common and most visible is the Edible Frog. They are more diurnal (day-active) than most frogs, and their calls can be heard from quite a distance. The populations of Edible Frog are actually more complicated, because two other species, the Marsh Frog and the Pool Frog, are very similar, and they may interbreed to produce offspring that look just like Edible Frog. Without detailed examination or special expertise, it can be very difficult to say exactly which species is present. Edible Frog and Pool Frog occur in water-bodies of all types, often in abundance, throughout France, while Marsh Frogs are more local in the south. Edible Frogs are not the only species that are eaten – all of this group are.

though on such a huge lake, close views are difficult.

About 30km to the north-east lies the even larger lake of Der-Chantecoq, also a reservoir, which is equally well known for its winter birds, and probably better for cranes. Good view-points at the south-west corner.

Part of the eastern section of the Lac de Forêt d' Orient, designated as a nature reserve. In summer, the reedy margins of the lake are home to Marsh Harrier, Great Crested Grebe, and Grey Heron. In winter, the specialities are White-Tailed Eagle and Common Crane.

4. CENTRAL FRANCE

INTRODUCTION

This region comprises the central part of France southwards as far as the Massif Central – essentially the Paris basin, including the areas known as Brie, Beauce, Sologne, Touraine, and Bourgogne (Burgundy).

It is a varied region with complex geology, and both hilly and flat areas, The southern part of the great ring of chalk that encircles Paris comes into the area, but it is a much less dominant feature here than in Normandy or Picardy and Champagne. Most of the region is dominated by more recent sedimentary rocks of the Miocene, Ecocene and Oligocene eras, and these are generally more acid in character, though there are more lime-rich areas here and there.

Although the area is intensively farmed in general, there are many areas that have escaped this. Some large forests remain, such as Fontainebleau, Rambouillet, Chambord, and others. The acidic soils of the Sologne area, south of Orléans, still support a reasonable amount of heathland as well as woodland, and a few areas (most notably la Brenne and

Pasque Flowers (Pulsatilla vulgaris) in heathland in Fontainebleau forest.

the Sologne), have a very high density of wetlands and open water, though much of it is artificial in origin and maintained for fishing or shooting.

For the naturalist coming south, the habitats of this area represent the first taste of the species of southern Europe. Species that are rare in Britain and elsewhere in northern Europe, such as Military Orchid, Red Helleborine, Golden Oriole, or many dragonflies, begin to appear much more frequently. Species that occur in this region, but are wholly absent from Britain, include European Mink, Wild Boar, Pond Terrapin, Black-Crowned Night Heron, Baillon's Crake and Little Crake.

Climatically, the effects of being part of Continental Europe are felt throughout the region, though the westerly parts are considerably affected by Atlantic weather systems. In general, winters are cold and summers hot, though this is ameliorated by westerly winds, and it varies through the region. The southerly parts of the area can become extremely hot and windless, with occasional thunderstorms, in mid- to late summer.

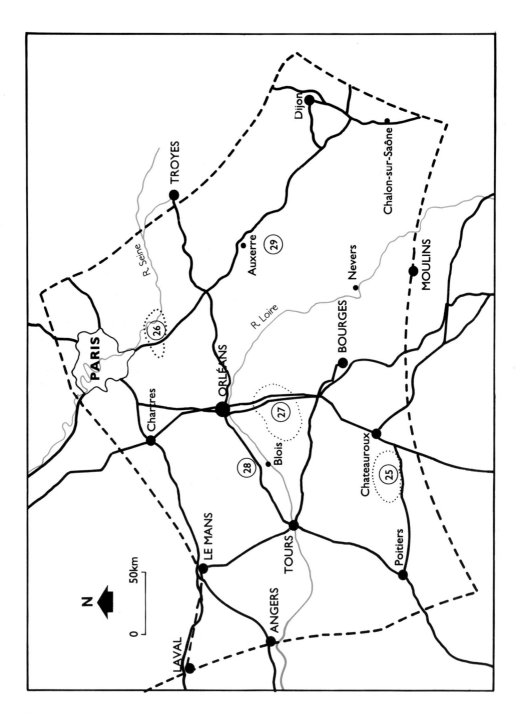

N

50km

0

PARIS

TROYES

R. Seine

Auxerre (29)

Dijon

Chalon-sur-Saône

MOULINS

Nevers

BOURGES

(26)

ORLÉANS

R. Loire

Chartres

(27)

Blois

(28)

Chateauroux

(25)

LE MANS

TOURS

Poitiers

ANGERS

LAVAL

Above: *one of the many small lakes in the Brenne area. This is a typical example of a good dragonfly habitat.*
Opposite: *map of Central France. The sites are numbered as in the text. Only main roads and the major rivers of the region are shown.*

25 LA BRENNE	
Maps:	MA pp. 82–3. IGN No. 34
Location:	Midway between Chateauroux and Chatellerault
Access:	Some areas open; some limited
Season:	Best in late spring and summer for flowers, birds, insects, amphibians; quite good for autumn passage birds
Specialities:	Exceptional breeding birds, dragonflies, amphibia; European Mink

A quite exceptional area of interest, lying between the Rivers Creuse and Indre. The Brenne consists of a vast area of low-lying rough country, mainly on acidic impermeable soil, within which literally hundreds of lakes have been created over several centuries for fishing and shooting. The present-day result is a mosaic of old, new, large, small, vegetated and unvegetated lakes set in a matrix of partly wooded and generally unimproved countryside occupying about 500km². Access

FIFTY INTERESTING SPECIES TO LOOK FOR

Bittern	Hen Harrier	Burnt-Tip Orchid	Pool Frog
Black-Necked Grebe	Little Crake	Cypress Spurge	Sand Lizard
Black Woodpecker	Night Heron	Fly Honeysuckle	Spadefoot Toad
Bonelli's Warbler	Purple Heron	Lady Orchid	Terrapin
Golden Oriole	Redstart	Lizard Orchid	Western Whip Snake
Great Reed Warbler	Short-Toed Eagle	Military Orchid	Adonis Blue
Great Crested Grebe	Whiskered Tern	Pasque Flower	Camberwell Beauty
Grey-Headed Woodpecker	Wryneck	Red Helleborine	Purple Emperor
Hawfinch	Red Squirrel	Swallow-Wort	White Admiral
Little Bittern	Wild Boar	Aesculapian Snake	Norfolk Hawker
Marsh Harrier	European Mink	Agile Frog	Orange-Spotted Emerald
Montagu's Harrier	Alpine Squill	Great-Crested Newt	Praying Mantis
	Angular Solomon's Seal	Green Lizard	

is difficult without a car, since rail links are poor and the area is so vast. Mézières-en-Brenne or La Gabrière make good centres. A good map is essential, and it is worth buying the IGN 1:25,000 blue maps locally.

The range of species to be found in the area is too vast for detailed coverage, though we can give some idea of what to expect. Breeding wetland birds are extremely good, with, amongst others, Purple Heron (declining), Bittern, Little Bittern, all three harriers, Spotted, Baillon's and Little Crakes, Black-crowned Night Heron, Black Tern, Whiskered Tern, Great Reed Warbler, Savi's Warbler, Great Crested Grebe, and Black-Necked Grebe.

Dragonflies and damselflies are exceptional, and an extraordinary total of fifty-seven species has been recorded – just about everything one might expect in this area. These include *Onychogomphus forcipatus* and *O. uncatus*, Orange-Spotted Emerald, *Anax*

The powder blue dragonfly, Orthetrum brunneum, *is frequent in the Brenne area.*

parthenope, Norfolk Hawker and many others. Butterflies are good, though not exceptional, and include numerous fritillaries, and Large Copper amongst others.

The list of resident amphibians includes four species of newt, Tree Frog, several toads (including Spadefoot and Natterjack), Pool Common and Agile Frogs, and European Pond Terrapin at one of its northernmost localities. Mammals are of interest, too, with most lowland wetland species, and an isolated outpost of the little-known European Mink, which has undoubtedly declined greatly but has been confirmed recently in the area. Wild Boar are common.

Flowers are also good, though they take a little more searching for. Thirty species of orchid are recorded; southern plants like the shrubby heather *Erica scoparia* or Parnassus-Leaved Water-Plantain reach close to their northern limits here; and marsh and water plants are abundant, except for those requiring calcareous conditions.

Almost anywhere within the Brenne area is good, but some sites of special interest include:

Domaine de Chérine – A Nature Reserve of 145ha, which includes a lake, L'Etang Ricot. The water of this lake is more calcareous than most, and has a good flora. There are two hides, one public and one for guided tours (information from the Mairie in Mézières).

Gabrière – A very large lake, with good duck, grebes; dragonflies; amphibians.

Gabriau – Superb White Water-Lily; breeding tern; dragonflies.

La Mer Rouge – Very large lake, with good waterfowl and tern.

Areas with reeds are best for warblers and marsh harriers, for example Couvent, but they tend to be difficult to access. Small sheltered lakes with marginal fen and ditches tend to be best for dragonflies.

26 FONTAINEBLEAU FOREST

Maps:	MA p. 54; IGN No. 21
Location:	c. 60km SE of Paris
Access:	Open, except for a few areas
Season:	Best in spring and summer for flowers, birds, insects
Terrain:	Mixed, but mainly dry; rocky in parts
Specialities:	Golden Oriole, Black Woodpecker, Honey Buzzard, Pasque Flower, orchids

This is a major site that defies adequate description. The forest is immensely popular as a recreational area for Parisians, and acts as an important forest resource, yet still retains an enormous range of natural history. It has become well known in Britain both as an ornithological and a botanical site. Access is extremely easy by bus, train or car to Fontainebleau town, and there are endless roads and tracks into the forest. Walking is necessary to reach many of the best sites. (We recommend the purchase of an IGN 1:25,000 No. 401, which exactly covers the forest.)

Car owners should be warned that car thieves are very active in the area, especially during summer weekends.

The Forest now covers about 170km², a remnant of former royal hunting forest. Apart from its history, much of its interest derives from the geology. Sandstone ridges are capped by hard blocks, impossible to farm, that have weathered into a jumble, while in a few places Brie limestone outcrops to give an added dimension to the habitat. In some depressions, there are bogs and pools. Most of the area is wooded, with Oak, Beech and Hornbeam in more natural areas, but there are large areas of plantations now. The ONF, who run the whole forest, manage a series of nature reserves within it, protecting some of the best areas.

Bird-life is very rich, with a number of rare species, and uncommon species in abundance. These include Black, Middle Spotted and Grey-Headed Woodpeckers, Wryneck, Hawfinch, Short-Toed Treecreeper, Honey Buzzard, Buzzard, Golden Oriole (there is a camp-site at La Musardiére where their singing wakes you up!) Crested Tit, Redstart, Wood and Bonelli's Warblers and many, many more.

Old Beech woodland – one of the many superb habitats in Fontainebleau forest. The Beech areas tend to be rich in attractive flowers such as Lady Orchid, Military Orchid, Angular Solomon's Seal, Wintergreen, Bird's Nest Orchid and Yellow Bird's Nest.

The flowers of the area are exceptionally rich, with a remarkable variety, including bog plants, 'Breckland' species, woodland species, and limestone grassland plants. Species to be seen include Red Helleborine Military, Monkey, Lady and Lizard Orchids, Pasque Flower, Swallow-Wort, Perennial Knawel, Spring Speedwell, Spiked Speedwell, Angular Solomon's Seal, Yellow Bird's-Nest, Blue Bugle, Cypress Spurge, several species of broomrape and hundreds more.

Insect-life includes most woodland species, with longhorn beetles, moths, butterflies, and many others common. Camberwell Beauty and numerous fritillaries are abundant. Wild Boar are still common in parts of the forest. The exotic-looking Green Lizard is frequent in some heathy areas.

Most parts of the forest have something to offer. Some key areas include (working southwards):

1. Rocher Cuvier Chatillon, north of the N7, is a good botanical area, especially at the eastern end.
2. The Gorge et Platières de Apremont is an impressive area, good for seeing the geology, and a chance of Wild Boar.
3. The higher ground east of the Carrefour (Crossroads) de la Croix du Grand Veneor on the N7 is botanically rich, and good for birds and Green Lizard.
4. The Gorges de Franchard and the area to the north-east of it is good for birds, and general interest.
5. The Plaine de Chanfroy, just east of the A6, is good for its Breckland flora, for heath plants, lizards, and butterflies.
6. The route of the east-west aqueduct that runs south of Fontainebleau town is of interest for plants, birds, butterflies, especially around where it crosses the N152, the N7, and for 2km east of the D58.
7. The Marais de Couleuvreux in the southwest of the forest, just east of the A6, is a good area for bog and wet heath species.
8. The Vallée Jauberton, just west of Bourron-Marlotte, is of interest for flowers and birds.

27 THE SOLOGNE	
Maps:	MA p. 69; IGN Nos 27 & 26
Location:	S of Orléans
Access:	Road network good
Season:	Late spring–summer for birds, insects and flowers
Terrain:	Heathland; marsh; woodland; open water
Specialities:	Purple Heron, Night Heron, harriers, dragonflies; heath insects

This is an enormous area of land, with immense interest and potential, but too scattered to define clearly as one site. It consists

Opposite: a lake in the Sologne, with Yellow Water Lily.

of a mosaic of woodland and heathland, with hundreds of lakes scattered throughout. Many of the features of interest overlap with the Brenne, but this is a more acidic area, with heaths instead of marshes, and generally smaller, more acid lakes, with less extensive reed-beds. This is hunting country *par excellence*, and access can be difficult in many areas as a result, though, at the same time, this is largely the reason for the site's existence. Access by road is via the N20 or D922, both of which pass through the area. Trains stop at Nouan-le-Fuzelier, which is convenient for the east side of the Sologne.

Breeding birds include Purple and Night Heron, Bittern, Little Bittern, all three harriers, Black-Necked Grebe, Black and Whiskered Terns, Black-Tailed Godwit, Baillon's Crake, Black-Winged Stilt, Nightjar, and Red-Backed Shrike. Autumn passage includes Common Crane, Osprey and others.

*The highly active predatory wasp (*Bembix rostrata*) at its nest hole in sandy heathland.*

Insect-life is interesting, especially for heathland and wetland species. Dragonflies are abundant, with at least thirty-five species, though no full list is available. The heaths are excellent for groups such as robber-flies, empids, grasshoppers, sand wasps, tiger beetles, and predatory *Hymenoptera* like the striking wasp *Bembix rostrata* which is frequent.

*Black-Tailed Godwit (*Limosa limosa*) incubating its eggs at a nest in a wet meadowland.*

Butterflies are good, but not exceptional, perhaps because the area is too acid.

Amphibians include Edible Frog, Agile Frog, Tree Frog, Spadefoot Toad, and Midwife Toad, while reptiles include Green Lizard, Wall Lizard, Sand Lizard, Western Whip Snake, and Smooth Snake. Plant-life tends to be specialized rather than striking; there are impressive displays of White and Yellow Water-Lilies on many small lakes, while heaths and sandy tracks hold many of the rarer heath species such as cudweeds, and Mossy Stonecrop.

It is difficult to pick out key areas of interest in such an extensive and varied area. In general, the northern section is more heathy, whilst the southern is more wooded; the former is better for specialized insects, the latter for birds. Any of the northern heaths will be of interest to a British naturalist. Some good areas include:

1. Etang de Marguilliers for birds.
2. Parc de Chambord, 10km east of Blois, is a National Hunting Reserve, and is a good place for seeing various native wild mammals; some areas of woodland with a rich ungrazed flora, and good woodland birds.
3. La Ferté St Cyr, in the north-west of the Sologne, has a local Nature Reserve on the Etang nearby.

Alpine Squill (Scilla bifolia) is abundant in the woods at Bois du Parc (see overleaf).

28 LES VALLEES DE LA GRAND PIERRE ET VITAIN	
Maps:	MA p. 68; IGN No. 26
Location:	10km N of Blois
Access:	Limited to footpaths
Season:	Best in late spring–summer
Terrain:	Mainly dry grassland and coppice woodland
Specialities:	Mountain Germander; Germander Broomrape, *Coronilla minima*; downland insects

The site is easily accessible from minor roads, off the D924, just north of Blois. The site consists of two valleys in hard limestone – one dry, and one with the River Cisse running through it. The key habitat is one of dry limestone grassland and rock outcrops, but there is also coppiced and standard woodland, and a small amount of floodplain marsh. The site has been a reserve since 1979, run locally from Blois.

The primary interest of the site is botanical. Species of interest include Lax Cinquefoil (*Potentilla caulescens*), Mountain Germander, Germander Broomrape, numerous orchids such as Burnt-Tip, Lizard, Military and Green-Winged. Pasque Flower, *Coronilla minima*, a flax *Linum tenuifolium*, and a Mediterranean-type scrub of Box, Downy Oak, Juniper and St Lucie's Cherry. In all, about 400 species of flower have been recorded to date. Insects are of interest, but still inadequately recorded. They include a good selection of chalkland butterflies such as Adonis Blue and Brown Argus. Birds and mammals are good though not exceptional; at least fifty-three species of bird are known to breed on the site.

The best downland is close to where the two valleys meet, and up the dry, southernmost valley.

29 BOIS DU PARC	
Maps:	MA p.72; IGN No. 28
Location:	c. 20km S of Auxerre, in the valley of the Yonne
Access:	Open on foot
Season:	Spring and summer
Terrain:	Dry rocky and grassy, with cliffs and caves
Specialities:	Snowdrop Windflower, White Rock-Rose, Alpine Squill, St Bernard's Lily; Cicada; Short-Toed Eagle

The site is easily accessible by footpath, off the D130, just south-west of Mailly-le-Château. It comprises the cliffs and grasslands of the east bank of the River Yonne at this point.

The lias limestone gives rise to an eroded Karstic scenery, with numerous caves (in which prehistoric human remains have been found), which supports a dry species-rich grassland, with much in common with Mediterranean vegetation. The site is best known for its flowers, which are extremely rich. Species of interest include Snowdrop Windflower, Crown Vetch, (*Anemone sylvestris*), Bloody Cranesbill, Snowy Mespil, White Rock-Rose, Alpine Squill (*see* previous page), Crested Cow-Wheat, the attractive bindweed *Convolvulus cantabrica*, Lizard Orchid, and Asarabacca, plus many more.

Insect-life includes the 'New Forest' Cicada and Praying Mantis, and good downland butterflies. Amongst the reptiles, the Aesculapian Snake and Asp Viper occur. Breeding birds are not exceptional, though both Honey Buzzard and Short-Toed Eagle hunt over the area regularly in summer, and breed nearby.

A few kilometres to the east, there is some fine woodland on the west bank of the River

Honey Buzzard
Pernis apivorus L 51–58

The beautiful Honey Buzzard is a summer visitor to France, breeding locally throughout the whole country. They favour large areas of woodland, usually broad-leaved. Despite their wide distribution, they are rarely seen in the breeding season, due to secretive habits, and a mainly ground-based way of life. At passage times they are more frequently seen, though unfortunately they are also highly vulnerable to shooting pressure at such times. Their main food items include the larvae and adults of bees and wasps, and (with luck) you may occasionally disturb one from a wasps' nest. In early summer, they have an early-morning aerial display that can be seen from vantage-points over suitable woodland.

Cure, opposite Voutenay-sur-Cure, which is also a good centre to stay at. The D950, from Voutenay to Mailly, passes through beautiful woodland and grassland on limestone.

5. JURA AND VOSGES

INTRODUCTION

The Jura to the south and the Vosges to the north form France's natural borders with Switzerland and Germany respectively. The Jura continues into Germany where it forms the underlying rocks for the Swabian Alps and Black Forest.

The Vosges originated in that same great upheaval that forced the Massif Central and the Armoricaine massif sky-wards in the Primary era some 600 million years ago. Although ancient crystalline rocks form the base of the Vosges, limestone occurs where marine deposits were forced upwards. Unfortunately much of the pasture land has been thoroughly grazed and otherwise improved, though there are remnants rich in flowers. The forests of the region are remarkable in extent and diversity of wildlife, particularly woodland birds (Capercaillie, Hazelhen, owls, woodpeckers) and raptors. Although hunting has taken its toll of larger mammals, as it has everywhere in France, there have been successful re-introductions, not only of deer (Red, Roe and Sika) and Wild Boar, but also of Chamois and even Lynx.

The Jura chain runs through the departments of Jura, Doubs and Ain, the major part of the territory of the ancient Franche-

A male Common Pochard (Aythya ferina), roosting by the lake.

Comte. Taking the shape of a crescent, it extends for some 300km, from the Rivers Rhône to Rhine, with a maximum width of 70km. The highest point is the Crêt de la Neige (1,718m) compared with the Vosges (1,424m).

Although the Jura is not high mountain country, the scenery is dramatic with folded almost pleated mountains and steep rocky cliffs. The chain has given its name to a period in the earth's geological history, the Jurassic. There are numerous lakes and rivers and extensive forests both of Pines and broad-leaved trees. Grazing and clearing has created pasturelands which carry a flora rich in orchids and lime-loving plants. Sub-alpine flowers often follow the path of the melting snow; even late in the year (August–September) roadsides and banks in the Jura are still flower-filled, and supporting large numbers of butterflies. Apollos are frequent, obvious by their size and flight.

As well as resident bird species (many of them characteristic of mountain regions) migratory routes either follow the length of the Jura or cross it – any body of open water during spring, or autumn, will allow one to spot numerous waders, ducks, raptors and passerines. Parts of the area are wild and isolated enough to provide refuges for rare mammal species such as Otter and Wildcat.

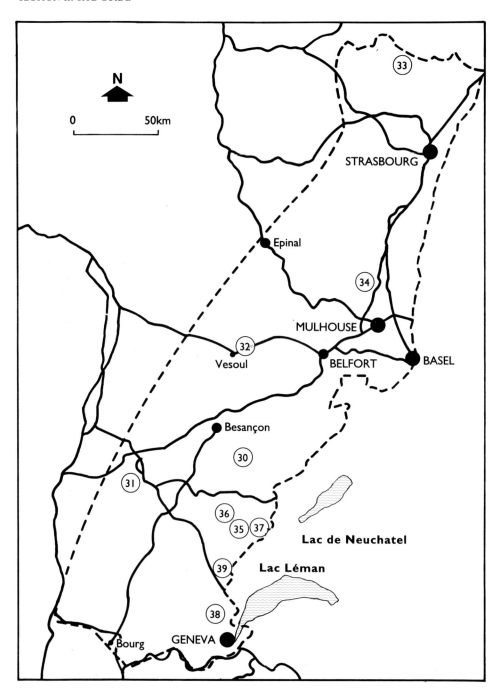

FIFTY INTERESTING SPECIES TO LOOK FOR

Black Kite	Ring Ouzel	Smooth Snake	Globeflower
Black-Necked Grebe	Siskin	Praying Mantis	Late Spider Orchid
Bluethroat	Spotted Crake	Apollo	Lizard Orchid
Bonelli's Warbler	Black Stork	Clouded Yellow	Martagon Lily
Capercaillie	Tengmalm's Owl	High Brown Fritillary	Monkshood
Crag Martin	Woodcock	Queen of Spain	Pasque Flower
Goshawk	Wood Warbler	Fritillary	Small White Orchid
Hazelhen	Lynx	Silver-Washed Fritillary	Soldanella
Hobby	Otter	Purple Emperor	Sowbread
Kingfisher	Red Deer	Scarce Swallowtail	Vanilla Orchid
Little Ringed Plover	Wild Boar	Large Tiger Moth	
Nutcracker	Wild Cat	(Pericallia matronula)	
Red Kite	Fire Salamander	Alpine Sowthistle	
Redpoll	Montpellier Snake	Dark Red Helleborine	

30 LE RAVIN DE VALBOIS

Maps:	MA p. 89–90; IGN No. 38
Location:	20km S of Besançon
Access:	Open part restricted to paths; 178 out of 335ha privately owned (permit needed)
Terrain:	Scrub-filled calcareous valley
Specialities:	Calcicole flora; warblers, Peregrine, Red Kite, Hazelhen; Apollo; rare insects

This is a hidden valley reached from Ornans via the D241 to Chassagne-St-Denis. Part of the site is privately owned and access is by permit only. Information is available from Federation Departementale de Protection de la Nature de Doubs, rue Beauregard, 25000 Besançon (tel: 81 80 22 74). Sculpted by river-flow over a plateau formed from Jurassic limestone some 140 million years old, it

Opposite: map of Jura and Vosges. The sites are numbered as in the text. Only main roads and the major rivers are shown.

is bounded by cliffs 50m high at its edges. Beneath these, the floor and sides are clothed with dense vegetation. Nowadays, the river enters the valley via a waterfall (Cascade de Valbois) and the bed is dry for much of the year. Sharp-thorned bushes of Burnet Rose cover much of the north-eastern slopes, but some scrub clearance to allow cattle grazing has produced meadows with an interesting collection of plants, many of which are at their northern limits – Mountain Kidney Vetch, Hoary Rock-Rose, Moon Carrot, Spignel, Creeping Sun-Rose and Haller's Sedge.

The corniche opposite has not been cut for grazing and the reddish-brown soil sustains woodlands which extend well beyond the reserve limits – Yew grows everywhere; Sycamore and Norway Maple predominate in the shade; Large-Leaved Lime on drier slopes. The diverse vegetation supports a rich insect fauna (over 700 species of butterflies and moths): butterflies include the Apollo; moths, a rare burnet, *Zygaena fausta, Hypocalcia bruandella*, and the largest European tiger moth, *Pericallia matronula*. Careful searching might reveal a pretty jumping spider, *Philaeux chrysops*, less than 1cm long – the male having a scarlet abdomen with black central stripe; the female is a white or fawn one.

Protected by the dense cover, Hazelhen regularly nest in the gorge, and a pair of Peregrines, with a number of eyries locally, use a site in the gorge every two years or so on average. Warblers abound – in spring-time the songs of leaf warblers (Chiffchaff, Wood, Willow and Bonelli's warblers) can be heard with those of *Sylvia* warblers (Whitethroat, Lesser Whitethroat Blackcap, and Garden). Ravens nest in the Reserve. Red Kites are frequent visitors and in winter Wallcreeper arrive to search for food in the nooks and crannies of the cliffs.

Mont Poupet, in the limestone Jura, with Mountain Kidney Vetch (Anthyllis montana) in the foreground.

The Reserve is an excellent place to look for birds of prey during spring and autumn migrations.

31 L'ILE DU GIRARD	
Maps:	MA p. 89; IGN No. 37
Location:	S of Dole
Access:	Marked footpaths
Season:	All year
Terrain:	Alluvial forest
Specialities:	Water birds (Little Bittern, Black-Necked Grebe), Black Kite, Bluethroat, Little Ringed Plover; fish; wetland flora

L'Ile du Girard is a Nature Reserve of some 94.3ha formed from alluvial deposits at the confluence of the Rivers Loue and Doubs. The build-up of mud and silt has led to the formation of a network of channels where pools form when the water-level falls. Higher areas owe their existence to the build-up of coarser alluvial materials, such as sand and gravel, and the central portion is almost an island.

The nature of the vegetation largely depends on the height of the ground above the water – Osier and other willows on more recent (and unstable) deposits; Black Poplar and Elder higher up; dense vegetation where the humus has built up, coloured in spring with Red Campion. An impressive variety of fungi grow on damp rotten wood. Some of the banks are clothed in summer with Common Amaranth (an introduction from America). Flowering Rush and Frogbit are two of the more interesting water plants.

The Reserve is best known for its bird life, whether resident or visiting migrants. Black Kite, Nightingale and Willow Tit nest regularly in the wooded areas. Kingfishers occasionally

A Kingfisher (Alcedo atthis) *perching with its recently caught prey.*

32 LE SABOT DE FROTEY	
Maps:	MA p. 76; IGN No. 30
Location:	Directly E of Vesoul
Access:	Several paths cross the reserve
Season:	All year
Terrain:	Calcareous grasslands and rocks
Specialities:	Calcicole flora (twenty orchid species); Praying Mantis; Grey-Headed Woodpecker, Wryneck, Montagu's Harrier

nest in the banks of the River Doubs and Little Ringed Plovers on the gravel; both can fall victim to unpredictable water-levels. The wet woodlands provide nesting sites for two other birds – Cetti's Warbler and Bluethroat.

The rivers are rich in fish and other aquatic life forms and, as a result, attract a number of interesting migrants, Osprey, Cormorant, Little Bittern and Black-Necked Grebe among them. Fishing is allowed in parts of the reserve and stocks of Pike, Trout and Burbot are substantial.

There are two theories as to the origin of the curious boot-shaped rock formation on the hill immediately to the north-east of Vesoul and to which the name Sabot de Frotey refers. One concerns the devil leaving behind a shoe whilst fleeing from an assignation with a lady of the manor, on the sudden return of her husband. The other, more prosaic and certainly more accurate, is the erosion of compacted Jurassic limestones by water over countless millennia. Surface soils altered with weathering and decomposing vegetation to produce clays containing numbers of blunted pebbles. It was only in anticlinal valleys that this meagre 'humus' could build up in layers of sufficient thickness to sustain further growth of vegetation. On the summit, the soil thickness is no more than 5–15cm and perhaps illustrates the hazards of overgrazing, even in times past when vegetation disappeared and left the soil exposed to the erosive forces of the elements.

On the part of the summit facing towards Vesoul, Austrian Pines were planted about seventy years ago to replace Turkey Oak. Areas where brome grass predominated have been invaded by Shrubby Box and Berberis as part of the succession process and Appennine

Endemic bee orchids *Ophrys aveyronensis*

The familiar Bee Orchid is abundant on the limestones of France. It is one of a family of insect-mimics (*Ophrys*), most of whose members prefer the warmer climes of southern Europe and the Mediterranean.

In the Causse region of the Massif Central there are two endemic *Ophrys* which, although growing in some numbers, do so over a very limited area: Aymonini's Ophrys (*Ophrys insectifera ssp. aymoninii*) is basically a Fly Orchid with a slightly broader lip carrying an obvious yellow margin. It is at home under light pine cover in the woods of the higher Causse. The Aveyron Ophrys (*Ophrys aveyronensis*) is arguably one of the finest of all Bee Orchids. It has bright rose-pink petals and sepals and a rich chestnut-brown lip on which the pattern can vary from a well-ordered 'H'-shape to a marbled 'shield' covering almost the whole of the surface. No two plants seem to have the same pattern and plants grow almost abundantly in a limited area of countryside centred on St Rome du Tarn, disappearing abruptly outside some invisible boundaries.

Sun-Rose and Bladder Senna grow there. The under storey has an interesting flora with White Helleborine flowering some months before two other orchids – Broad-Leaved and Narrow-Lipped Helleborine.

In the grassy areas, the insect mimics (*Ophrys*) are some of the twenty or more orchids recorded for the reserve – Bee, Fly, Late Spider and Woodcock.

The presence of a large population of Praying Mantids bears witness to the warm microclimate of the summit and the conditions suit numerous other insects, among them Mountain Cicada and two species of the nerve-winged ascalaphids.

Reptiles found include the Green Lizard and three snakes – Grass, Montpellier and Smooth.

Hazelhen were known from the reserve until 1975 but have now disappeared completely from the region. Birds of note still nesting in the reserve include Grey-Headed Woodpecker, Wryneck, Nightjar, Woodlark and Montagu's Harrier.

33 VOSGES NORD	
Maps:	MA p. 42–3; IGN No. 12
Location:	N of Strasbourg
Access:	Unrestricted; centres for deep-snow skiing in winter
Terrain:	Diverse
Specialities:	Flora; insects; large mammals; raptors; Hazelhen, Capercaillie

Established in 1976, the Vosge du Nord Regional Natural Park covers an enormous area of 1,175km^2 and it comes as no surprise that there is great diversity in the landscape within its boundaries. To the east lie the hills of the Piedmont Vosges separated from the

Lorraine plateau in the west by a hilly region of Tertiary rocks. Large areas within the park are cultivated. Megalithic monuments testify to the fact that the region has been inhabited for a long time. Extensive managed forests occupy some 60,000ha at the park's centre but their character is changing as conifers replace felled deciduous trees. Red Deer, Roe Deer and Wild Boar are among the larger forest mammals, and since 1983 attempts have been made to re-establish Lynx by releasing animals brought from Czechoslovakia. Similarly, Chamois have been introduced into the higher regions of the Vosges around the massifs of Donon and Hohneck. An animal park established at Schwartzbach, near Neunhoffen, allows visitors to see some of the more elusive mammals.

Over 150 species of birds have been recorded within the park region; birds of prey are increasing in numbers with Buzzard being numerous. Numbers of Hazelhen and Capercaillie are decreasing.

Sunny woodland rides are excellent for butterflies. High-Brown and Silver-Washed Fritillaries, Cardinal, White Admiral, Purple Emperor, Large Tortoiseshell, Scarce and Common Swallowtails, hairstreaks and Wood White are all to be found.

The orchid flora is rich in the beech forests on calcareous soils where large numbers of different helleborines (Sword-Leaved, Red, Broad-Leaved, Narrow-Lipped, White, Violet and Dark-Red) grow. Other orchids such as Lizard, Military, Lady, Bee, Fly and Late Spider are found on calcareous grassland but much of this has been improved for agricultural purposes.

Several good areas remain with their limestone flora largely intact. One of these lies on Bastberg, which is otherwise famous for a trail designed to show off the rich fossil deposits in the rocks.

In the Schwartzbach valley, running from Neunhoffen to Niederbronn, extensive bogs have formed where a lake has become silted up and a rich bog flora (sundews, butterworts) has developed.

34 BOLLENBERG AND SAVERNE	
Maps:	MA p. 42 and 61; IGN No. 31
Location:	Near Rouffach, S of Colmar
Access:	By road
Season:	Spring and summer for flowers and butterflies
Terrain:	Limestone grassland on rolling hills
Specialities:	Orchids and other chalk grassland flowers

Bollenberg

To reach the area of low hills known as the Bollenberg, leave the N83 south of Rouffach and take the road that winds up into the hills. Although some of the natural grassland has disappeared because of agriculture and the establishment of a golf course, there is a very rich limestone flora.

Around Whitsuntide orchids are at their best with Green-Winged, Greater Butterfly, Lizard, Man, Burnt-Tip and Military growing close to the paths that cross the undulating territory. Without doubt, the most numerous are the Late Spider Orchids with an astonishing variety of lip patterns. It is usually the rarest of the insect-mimics in central France.

Other plants of interest include several species of the parasitic broomrape and around Easter-time there are Pasque Flowers. From late May there is a procession of butterflies associated with chalk and limestone grassland

– coppers, Silver-Studded, Adonis, Chalkhill and Small Blues, Duke of Burgundy Fritillary, several true fritillaries (including Dark-Green, Pearl-Bordered and Glanville), graylings, Wall Brown and Marbled White.

Saverne

For the naturalist with a particular interest in orchids, a visit to Bollenberg can be combined with a trip to the Botanical Garden at Saverne (north-east of Strasbourg). Well over 2,000 plant species of various origins are grown there, but of special note are the temperate slipper orchids. There is the chance to see, not only the European Lady's Slipper, but also several American relations, as well as other European orchids. The garden is open from the beginning of May to the end of September every weekday but it closes on Saturdays and Sunday afternoons.

The Lac de Remoray Nature Reserve, with fringing reed-beds.

35 LAC DE REMORAY

Maps:	MA p. 90; IGN No. 38
Location:	S of Pontarlier
Access:	Paths around lake
Terrain:	Bog
Specialities:	Bog flora: rare sedges and mosses, Rannoch Rush, Bog Rosemary; Red and Black Kite, Hobby, Little Ringed Plover; heronry

Established in a glacial basin sculpted out of limestone, the lake was formed by a build-up, first of sedge peat, which then provided the conditions for growth of *Sphagnum* mosses and the subsequent formation of a *Sphagnum* peat. Nowadays, the Lac de Remoray is fed by two streams – the Haut and the Drezin – but, unfortunately, one of these carries outflow from Remoray village. A third stream drains into the River Doubs at

such a slow rate that it is estimated the water change takes over thirty years. At either end the lake extends into stagnant boggy areas. On the eastern slope, the reserve takes in part of the Forêt de Grand'Cote established on calcareous clays and which houses a sizeable heronry. Precipitation in the area can be as much as 1,600mm per annum.

The bog flora includes a range of rare sedges and mosses, Rannoch Rush, Bog Rosemary, Grass of Parnassus, Cranberry, and Round-Leaved Sundew; in less acid areas, Greater Spearwort grows with abundant Reedmace.

Tufted Duck nest in the reeds around the lake; Red Kite and Black Kite nest in the wood. Peregrine and Hobby hunt around the lake. Little Ringed Plover, Redpoll and Fieldfare have also been recorded as nesting birds within the area of the reserve.

Little Ringed Plover (Charadrius dubius) on its breeding ground.

36 ETANG DE FRASNE	
Maps:	MA p. 90; IGN No. 38
Location:	SW of Pontarlier
Access:	Via marked paths in the reserve
Terrain:	Marsh
Specialities:	Spring, summer and autumn migrants

The D49 from Frasne (south-west of Pontarlier on the D471) passes to the east of the large Étang de Frasne. Outflow from this lake feeds an extensive area of marsh and open water (created in 1960 by the flooding of the marsh, and rarely more than 1m deep). This flooded area forms the Reserve with its extensive raised and floating peat bogs, Birch and pine woodland. The open water is a stopover for migrating ducks in spring and autumn: Mallard, Red-Crested Pochard, Pochard, Teal, Garganey, Tufted Duck as well as gulls (including Little Gull) and terns (Common, Whiskered and Black). The peat bog provides nesting sites for many species. A network of paths permits access to observation points for all the more interesting areas without creating an intolerable disturbance for numerous species which choose their nesting sites in this reserve.

In spring, birds to look out for, in addition to those mentioned above, include numbers of raptors – Buzzard, Hobby, Red-Footed Falcon, Osprey, Red and Black Kites. Waders are also abundant, with Redshank, Spotted Redshank, Greenshank, Marsh, Wood and Common Sandpipers, Curlew and Whimbrel. Amongst the smaller migrants are Swallow, Sand and House Martins, Yellow Wagtail and Wheatear. In autumn, the same list of migrants is augmented by Black Stork, Dunlin, Little and Teminck's Stints, and Ringed and Little Ringed Plovers.

Lac de Bouverans

This lies about 3.5km south-west of the Frasné reserve. Extensive Beech and fir plantations house a colony of Grey Heron and provide nesting sites for Raven, and Black and Red Kites. In the damp pastures and marsh to the north-west of the Lac de Bouverans there are Spotted Crake, Curlew, Lapwing, Moorhen, a colony of Fieldfare, a few Great Grey Shrike and nesting Hobby.

37 MASSIF DE MONT D'OR	
Maps:	MA p. 90; IGN No. 38
Location:	S of Pontarlier
Season:	All year, snow permitting
Terrain:	Mountain woodland and subalpine pasture
Specialities:	Subalpine plants; mountain and woodland birds including Tengmalm's Owl, Nutcracker, Hazelhen, Capercaillie and Black Woodpecker

Mont d'Or lies directly south of Pontarlier and, at 1,463m, is the highest ridge in that part of the Jura. On the western side, there are extensive woodlands of Beech and fir together with more open areas of subalpine pasture, bushes and thickets. To the east, the ridge ends with a steep cliff dropping some 250m to a large area of huge boulders and rocky screes.

The flora in the pastures, at the woodland edges and within the woods, is similar to that of the Forêt du Massacre – Martagon Lily, aconites, Alpine Sow Thistle, centauries and Yellow Gentian, Dark-Red Helleborine, Bird's Nest Orchid and Narrow-Lipped Helleborine. In summer, insects abound, and butterflies in particular – Apollos are

A Silver-Washed Fritillary (Argynnis paphia) feeding on nectar from bramble flowers.

common; Clouded Yellows, skippers and browns (Mountain Argus relatives) fly in the meadows with Silver-Washed and High Brown Fritillaries in woodland rides.

The area boasts a variety of uncommon, rare nesting birds characteristic of mountain areas. Raptors present in the summer months include Sparrowhawk, Goshawk, Peregrine and Kestrel. Capercaillie, Hazelhen, Woodcock and Tengmalm's Owl can also be seen. Other birds include Crag Martin, Wood and Bonelli's Warblers, Rock Pipit, Wheatear, Ring Ouzel, Fieldfare, Treecreeper, Siskin and Nutcracker.

To reach Mt d'Or, take the N57 south of Pontarlier, turn at Les Hôpitaux-Neufs on to the D45, and then follow the signs to the summit from Longevilles. Paths lead from the parking area. One, offering a breathtaking view over the cliff, leads to Belvedere des Chamois; another goes to the woodlands beyond la Grangette-Chalet to the west. Le Morond (1,419m), just to the north of Mont d'Or, can be reached via a minor road and offers superb views.

38 FORET DU MASSACRE

Maps:	MA p. 104; IGN Nos 44 & 45
Location:	S of Morez
Access:	Free
Season:	All year, snow permitting
Terrain:	Mountain woodland; alpine pasture
Specialities:	Subalpine and alpine flowers; birds

Roadsides and woodland edges in the Jura are well known for being flower-filled well into late August and September. The Forêt du Massacre is no exception. As one of the high-level forests in the Jura, it culminates in the Crêt Pela at 1,495m. Whether one travels along the D25 Combe-du-Lac or cuts into the forest on one of the narrow roads eventually leading to the Crêt Pela, the tall plants of the understorey make a remarkable summer display – Martagon Lily, aconites, Alpine Sow Thistle, centaures and Yellow Gentian; Globeflowers are common in damp places. Much of the forest is mixed conifer but there are also extensive areas of Beech and Oak. Here, where the overhead cover thins out and especially where the ground is stony, there are clumps of Dark-Red Helleborine, while farther into the gloom there are spikes of Bird's Nest Orchid and Narrow-Lipped Helleborine. The profusion of flowers attracts butterflies in large numbers, especially the large woodland fritillaries like Silver-Washed and High Brown; Apollos are also frequent.

The forest is close to the Col de La Faucille and Mt Ronde and the arrival of spring in high pastures sees the appearance of a carpet of flowers at the edges of the receding snow: White or Purple Crocus, Alpine Snowbell, Spring Gentian and Yellow Anemone. In July, two alpine orchids appear – Small White Orchid and Vanilla Orchid – together with numerous other flowers including gentians and Alpine Rose.

From the Forêt du Massacre it is worth travelling to the Gorge du Flumen just

A flower-rich hay meadow in the Jura showing mainly Greater Yellow Rattle (Rhinanthus alectorolophus).

south-east of St Claude where, in late August, the sweet-flowered pink Cyclamen (Sowbread) appears in abundance, although, sadly, it is an attraction for 'pickers'.

39 FRENCH–SWISS BORDER	
Maps:	MA pp. 90 & 104; IGN Nos 44 & 45
Location:	French–Swiss border near Morez
Access:	Unrestricted
Season:	Spring–summer for flowers; birds all year
Terrain:	Wooded valleys; scree; wet meadows
Specialities:	Orchids, sub-alpine flora; Fire Salamander; Red Kite, Peregrine; Otter, Wildcat

Vallée de Doubs

The River Doubs follows a curious path. It rises south-east of Pontarlier then flows roughly north-east to form the French–Swiss border in part. It meanders north-west to Montbéliard and then south-west to Besançon and beyond. From Morteau, it runs along a valley with steeply wooded slopes and screes on either side. There are lakes at St Point and Chaillexon and waterfalls at the Saut du Doubs (reached from Morteau).

The marshy areas along the valley bottom are good for orchids – Southern Marsh and Broad-Leaved where it is wet; Military, Greater Butterfly, Sweet-Scented and Pyramidal in drier places; and Dark-Red Helleborine on the screes. Fritillaries grow in some profusion where grasslands have been moistened by winter floodwaters. Birds that breed in the region include Peregrine, Red Kite, Raven and Kingfisher. Wildcat and Otter are

The dramatically coloured Fire Salamander (Salamandra salamandra), making a rare appearance in daylight.

reported from the area and the curious Fire Salamander has one of its few Jura sites here.

Forêt du Risoux

The Forêt du Risoux lies east of Morez but only about one-third of its area lies in France. The rest lies in Switzerland and comes within the protected area of the Vallée de Joux. The Lac des Rousses connects, via the River Orbe, with the much larger Lac de Joux. Both lakes have reedy areas which provide breeding sites for numerous waders. Passage migrants include Honey Buzzard, Marsh Harrier, Wood Sandpiper, Marsh Sandpiper, Bluethroat and Red-Necked Phalarope; Black Kite and Hobby are resident. In the mountainous parts on either side of the border, there is a rich limestone flora with a number of species of purple or blue gentians, (Willow-Leaved and Clusius's), the tall Yellow Gentian, fragrant pink Garland Flower, primulae, saxifrages, and Mountain Pansy.

6. LES LANDES

INTRODUCTION

This is a relatively homogenous naturally defined region, stretching along the Atlantic seaboard, from near La Rochelle, south to the Pyrenees. This is a wider area than that covered simply by les Landes, and it includes sites to the north that have more in common with Brittany. It is an area dominated by its coastline, where much of the human activity is focused, but where much of natural history interest is also to be found.

The Gironde river is a major natural history and geological boundary. North from here, the rocks are largley calcareous Upper Cretaceous and Jurassic, though with extensive coastal alluvial marshlands. South of the Gironde estuary lies one of the strangest areas of France – les Landes proper. Here, there is a huge area of blown

*An Oystercatcher (*Haematopus ostralegus*) at its nest on a sandy beach.*

sand, in a triangle with sides of over 200km long. Once, this was a vast area of shifting sand-dunes, marshes and lakes marching westwards from the Atlantic shore, barely productive, with endemic fevers, and hardly settled. However, from the late 18th century onwards, ambitious plans were made, and ultimately realized, to turn the area into productive land by draining the marshes and planting the sand with pines. This area is now classed as the largest forest in Europe, although the loss of biological richness has probably been huge. Today, the area is still dominated by regimented pine forest, but there are increasing areas of arable land, together with relatively small semi-natural areas of heathland, deciduous woods and lakes. The coast itself is dominated by developing sand-dunes, though the pressure

Dune du Pilat, south of the bay of Arcachon, the highest sand dune in Europe at over 100m. This is part of the immense dune area south of the Gironde river which is now planted with pines. It is the largest forest in Europe.

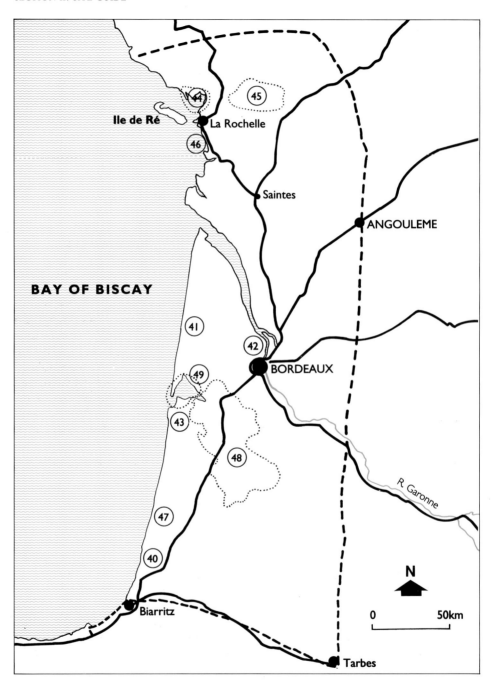

of summer visitors causes much damage to these. The highest dune in Europe is at Dune du Pilat, south of the bay of Arcachon.

Climatically, the area is dominated by the Atlantic, with moist westerly winds frequent, but it is also a warm area, and spring comes early, to be followed by generally hot summers. However, it is not a Mediterranean climate, and the spread of rain through the year keeps vegetation green and plants in flower well into the summer. Its natural history is a blend of Atlantic and Mediterranean species, with many that are familiar, but it also has numerous species with a predominantly south European distribution, as well as a few that are special to the area. Birds like White Stork, Black-Winged Stilt, Bluethroat, and Kentish Plover breed up the coast, and plants like Dune Bedstraw, everlastings (*Helichrysum spp.*), and Cotton Weed are frequent. Sand Lizards are not uncommon, and Red Squirrels are a feature of many of the pine woods. Altogether, it is a good place to mix a holiday with some natural history observation.

Opposite: map of les Landes. The sites are numbered as in the text. Only main roads and the major rivers are shown.

40 L'ETANG NOIR	
Maps:	MA p. 148; IGN No. 62
Location:	About 25km N of Bayonne
Access:	By footpaths only
Season:	Spring and summer for flowers, insects, amphibians; some breeding birds.
Terrain:	Marshy with raised walkways; mosquitoes common in summer
Specialities:	Water Chestnut, Hampshire Purslane, Royal Fern, Lax-Flowered Orchid; Edible Frog

The reserve consists of a moderately sized shallow lake, surrounded by carr woodland, wet heathland and reed-bed. It lies just north of Seignosse, a few kilometres from the coast, and there is a helpful and informative exhibition centre near the south-west corner of the site. From here, marked paths, mainly on raised walkways, lead through the various habitats of the reserve.

FIFTY INTERESTING SPECIES TO LOOK FOR

Black Tern	Night Heron	Red Squirrel	Sea Holly
Black-Winged Stilt	Nightjar	South-Western Water	Star-Fruit
Crested Lark	Red-Backed Shrike	Vole	Spotted Rock-rose
Crested Tit	Ruff	Bayonne Astragalus	Water Chestnut
Dartford Warbler	Sandwich Tern	Bug Orchid	Edible Frog
Goshawk	Stonechat	Butterfly Iris	Ocellated Lizard
Great Crested Grebe	Short-Toed Eagle	Flowering Rush	Pond Terrapin
Hobby	Tawny Pipit	Immortelle	Southern Smooth Snake
Hoopoe	Water Rail	Jersey Pink	Downy Emerald
Kentish Plover	White Stork	Lax-Flowered Orchid	Hairy Hawker Dragonfly
Little Bittern	Wryneck	Hampshire Purslane	Norfolk Hawker
Marsh Harrier	Genet	Sand Bedstraw	Orange-Spotted Emerald
Montagu's Harrier	Otter	Sea Bindweed	

41 L'ETANG DE COUSSEAU	
Map:	MA p. 120; IGN No. 46 or 55
Location:	35km NW of Bordeaux, close to Lacanau
Access:	On foot or by bicycle
Season:	Summer for flowers, insects, birds, reptiles and amphibia
Terrain:	Wet and marshy; sandy in places
Specialities:	Aldrovanda; Southern Smooth Snake; Short-Toed Eagle, Goshawk; Otter

Swampy woodland around the reserve of Etang Noir, in the extreme south-west of France.

The primary importance is botanical, with 430 species (including some lower plants) recorded to date. Higher plants of interest include Water Chestnut, White and Yellow Water-Lilies, Saw Sedge, Royal Fern in abundance, Hampshire Purslane, sundew, Lax-Flowered Orchid, and various pond-weed species. There are also rare mosses and liverworts. The exhibition centre shows botanical specimens that have been collected.

Amphibians include Edible Frog, of which some unusual varieties have been the subject of some research here. Dragonflies are good, but not exceptional, and rather hard to get close to. Breeding birds include Great Crested Grebe, Water Rail, Teal and Shoveler. The fish population is a rich mixture of introduced and natural, and fishing (and shooting) appear still to go on here, albeit in a regulated way.

This is an area of lake, marsh and sand, close to Lacanau, representing a remnant of a formerly larger lake. You can reach the area on foot or by bicycle, either by following the marked paths from the le Huga to Carcans road or by walking up the west bank of the Canal de Jonction, from the D6, until directly opposite the marsh. Access is limited to the pathways, but these allow a good inspection of the habitats and species of the site.

The reserve and surrounding area includes marshland, open water, dunes, and Maritime Pine forest, together with a little Oak forest. Botanically it is interesting, with several bladderwort species, a rare insectivorous plant primarily found in south-east Europe called Aldrovandia (*Aldrovandia vesiculosa*), and many of the dune and wetland plants typical of this area.

Reptiles and amphibia that may be seen at this site include the Southern Smooth Snake and the European Pond Terrapin. Birds breeding locally include the Goshawk, and the summer visiting Short-Toed Eagle and Nightjar.

42 LES MARAIS DE BRUGES

Maps:	MA p. 121; IGN No. 46 or 47
Location:	Just N of Bordeaux
Access:	Limited on foot; occasional guided tours
Season:	Good in summer for flowers, birds, amphibians; good autumn passage of birds
Terrain:	Marshy
Specialities:	Angelica heterocarpa, Whorled Caraway; Genet, Red-Backed Shrike, Wryneck

A Pond Terrapin (Emys orbicularis) just after emergence from hibernation.

An area of marsh and open water, representing one of the last relics of a much more extensive marsh system; the site is now a reserve run by the local nature conservation organization. It is remarkably rich considering its position in the industrial outskirts of Bordeaux, and well worth visiting for anyone staying in the city. Access is straightforward via the path leading from the D210 just north of Bruges. This path allows views of a good selection of species.

Plant-life includes, amongst numerous marsh and water plants, the rare angelica, only found in this area, *Angelica heterocarpa*. Amphibia and reptiles are good, and include Pond Terrapin. Mammals of interest include, surprisingly, Genet, and, more predictably, Coypu and South-Western Water-Vole. Breeding birds include a small population of Red-Backed Shrike, Water Rail, Wryneck, various marshland warblers, and, unusually, a pair of White Storks have bred in recent years, well out of their normal range.

White Stork *Ciconia ciconia* L 102
These beautiful and confiding birds were once a feature of the landscape of much of Europe, but they have declined dramatically in recent years. They were virtually extinct in France, but there are definite signs of a come-back and they can now be seen breeding in south-west France, les Dombes, and Alsace-Lorraine (where they are something of a local celebrity).

They are not resident in France, but arrive in late winter to begin building or refurbishing their extraordinary nests which are frequently built in the most visible possible places, such as church towers or telegraph poles. Their various breeding displays are conspicuous and of great interest. In flight, they are distinctive with their white bodies, black and white wings, and extended neck, not to mention their large size.

43 BANC D'ARGUIN AND DUNE DU PILAT

Maps:	MA p. 134; IGN No. 55
Location:	On the coast just S of Cap Ferret and Arcachon
Access:	The offshore bank can be viewed from boat trips from Pyla-sur-Mer or Cap Ferret; the dunes are generally open
Season:	Summer
Terrain:	Offshore sand and mud islands; dunes with woodland on the adjacent mainland
Specialities:	Sandwich Tern, Tawny Pipit; Sand Bedstraw, *Linaria thymifolia*

The site consists of two separate elements: the offshore sand-bank islands called the Banc d'Arguin, which have been a nature reserve since 1972; and the dunes on the mainland around the Dune du Pilat, the highest sand-dune in Europe. Access to the reserve is by boat only from the nearby towns, and landing is strictly forbidden in season – formerly, boat-loads of tourists used to trample the nests and have egg-fights! Access to the dune area is by path from car-parks on the D218 south of Pyla, or through the numerous camp-sites in the area.

The sand-banks are known for their large tern colonies, especially of Sandwich Tern. Since protection, other birds have begun to breed, including Oystercatcher, Kentish Plover, Tawny Pipit, and Crested Lark. The banks are also the southernmost site for seeing Eider Duck. In winter, large numbers of waders feed and roost on and around the sand-banks.

The flora of the banks is primarily that of unstable dunes, and includes Sand Bedstraw, Sea Stock, Sea Holly, the uncommon toadflax *Linaria thymifolia*, and Sea Bindweed. The flora of the mainland dunes is similar, and includes more stable ground species such as Spotted Rock-rose. The Dune du Pilat is actually more impressive for its size than its flora – it reaches 103m. The pine woods around it are good for Red Squirrel, which are often tame, and Crested Tit.

44 BAIE D'AIGUILLON AND POINTE D'ARCAY

Maps:	MA p. 92; IGN No. 39
Location:	A few km N of La Rochelle
Access:	Unrestricted in the bay, limited on the Pointe d'Arçay
Season:	Good at all times, especially winter for birds; summer for flowers
Terrain:	Marshes; mud; sand; forest
Specialities:	Enormous flocks of waders and wildfowl; breeding Hoopoe, Red-Backed Shrike

The huge Bay of L'Aiguillon, as far north as the sandy peninsula at Pointe d'Arçay, forms one of the finest areas for birds in the whole of France, especially in winter and at passage times. It also connects with the inland wetlands of the Marais Poitevin, making this region a superb one to visit at any time of year. La Rochelle is a major centre, and there is easy road access into the area from there.

Winter birds include huge numbers of Knot, Dunlin, Grey Plover, Avocet, Black-

Shelduck
Tadorna tadorna L 61
A large and very distinctive duck, which shares some characteristics with geese. The boldly coloured black, white and reddish plumage, with a bold red beak, is highly conspicuous, and their behaviour is far from secretive, so they tend to get noticed.

They breed commonly down the western seaboard of France, from Belgium to Spain, and less commonly on the Mediterranean coast. Most birds migrate north to moult, then southwards again for the winter. They are almost invariably coastal, feeding on mudflats and salt-marshes, and breeding in holes in coastal grasslands (or occasionally in trees).

Tailed Godwit, Golden Plover, and smaller numbers of Spotted Redshank, Bar-Tailed Godwit and various wildfowl, including Brent Geese. There are good numbers of Whimbrel, Ruff, Little Stint and other less common waders on autumn passage. Breeding birds are of interest, though those occurring on the marshes are mentioned under the next site. Montagu's Harrier, Marsh Harrier, Black Tern, Black-Winged Stilt and Fantailed Warbler are regular around the bay; the woods and sand of the Pointe d'Arçay have a different selection of breeding birds, including Hoopoe and Red-Backed Shrike.

There are various good view-points around the bay, according to the state of the tide, and most are easily accessible by vehicle.

Across the bay, on the Ile de Ré, there is a nature reserve at the north-west corner, called the Lilleau des Niges (marked as a reserve on the Michelin maps). It is another excellent bird site, all year round, and good for flowers.

45 THE REGIONAL NATURAL PARK OF THE MARAIS POITEVIN

Maps:	MA pp. 92–3; IGN Nos 39 (mainly), 33 and 40
Location:	Westwards from Niort, to the coast
Access:	Difficult in places
Season:	Best in spring and summer
Terrain:	Mainly marsh and open water
Specialities:	Breeding Black-Winged Stilt, Black-Tailed Godwit, Ruff, Black Tern; good dragonflies

This is a vast area of low-lying reclaimed marshland, seamed with dykes and canals. Access by road is easy, northwards from La Rochelle, or westwards from Niort. Coulon and La Garette are good centres for excursions, and are the main boat hire centres.

Grazed marshland is the commonest habitat in the Marais (marsh), much of it agriculturally improved, and some converted to arable or poplar plantations. The ditches themselves are of interest, and they are often lined with Tamarisk or willow, which is good for breeding and migrant birds. The main canals have remained relatively pure and, therefore, rich in aquatic life, because there is little intensive agriculture in the catchment area for the canals and boats with engines are largely banned.

A poplar-lined canal in the Marais Poitevin, rich in all forms of natural life.

Purple Loosestrife (Lythum salicaria) by a drainage channel.

Breeding birds include Black-Winged Stilt, Black-Tailed Godwit, Ruff, Black and Whiskered Terns, Yellow Wagtail, Golden Oriole, Kingfisher, Marsh and Montagu's Harriers, Garganey, Redshank, Bluethroat, Whinchat, and many more.

Flowers are generally rich, with an abundance of more common marsh plants such as Yellow Flag, Purple Loosestrife, and Flowering Rush; and a good range of clovers in the damp grazed marshes, such as Strawberry Clover and Reversed Clover. The lovely bluish Butterfly Iris is locally common, while rarities such as Star-Fruit, Hare's Ear and *Centaurium spicatum* occur here and there.

Dragonflies are abundant, with numerous species. Hairy Hawker, Norfolk Hawker, *Gomphus simillimus*, Brilliant Emerald, Downy Emerald, Orange-Spotted Emerald and many others occur, while the attractive orange damselfly, *Platycnemis acutipennis,* are particularly common. Amphibia are generally abundant, with several species each of frog and toad, and Pond Terrapin here and there. Mammals of interest include the Otter.

Most of the marshland is of interest, and much can be seen simply by driving around. However, a few areas of special interest include:

1. Réserve Naturelle Michel Brosselin, near St Denis-du-Payré, has a good cross-section of habitats, and a visitor centre open in the summer. There is also a hunting reserve to the south of here. Access off the D25.
2. The more coastal marshlands south and east of St Michel-en-l'Herm are a good area for breeding waders, often visible from the roads.
3. The area around Coulon and la Garette is good for canals and tree-fringed water-ways, and boats can be hired from both these villages for longer exploratory trips.

46 LE MARAIS D'YVES

Maps:	MA p. 93; IGN No. 39
Location:	c. 10km NW of Rochefort
Access:	On foot only; limited to certain areas; visitor centre open at peak periods
Season:	Good for birds at any time; flowers in summer
Terrain:	Marshy and wet in places
Specialities:	Bug Orchid, Jersey Pink; Little Bittern, Marsh Harrier; passage migrants

This site is directly accessible from the N137, the busy La Rochelle to Rochefort road, where there is a visitor centre and entrance. The Marais represents a relic of a formerly more widespread marsh in this area, favourably placed on the main west-coast bird migration route. The north part of the reserve is a complex of habitats deriving from extraction of sand and salt over the centuries, with hollows and hummocks of varying character. The rest of the reserve consists of pasture, marsh and open water. The site is run by the LPO, based at Rochefort.

Bird life is the speciality of the reserve. Winter numbers of wildfowl are good, and passage migrants come in large numbers, with numerous rare species, such as Scaup, Collared Pratincole, Glossy Ibis, and Broad-Billed Sandpiper. Breeding birds include various duck, Shelduck, Little Bittern, Marsh Harrier, Reed Bunting and various marsh-land warblers.

The flora is quite rich, with a mixture of marsh, water, dune and dry grassland species, including Jersey Pink, Bug Orchid, and a number of other orchids, Butterfly Iris, and various sand-dune flowers. Pond Terrapin occur, and Otters are regularly recorded.

47 LE COURANT D'HUCHET

Maps:	MA p. 148; IGN No.62
Location:	c. 45km N of Bayonne, by the coast
Access:	On foot or by boat only; also, various roads cross the site
Season:	Best in summer for flowers, insects, breeding birds
Terrain:	Various wetland habitats and sand-dunes; mosquitoes in a few areas
Specialities:	Immortelle, Bayonne Astragalus; Night Heron; Otter

A typical area of les Landes coast, with dunes piled up to the seaward side holding back a lake, and water from the lake breaching a passage through the dunes. The reserve here covers 656ha, which includes the western shore of the larger Etang de Léon and the whole of the smaller lake at Huchet, together with the channel that connects them to the sea, and the surrounding vegetation. Much of this type of habitat has been lost or greatly altered through the development of tourism.

Plant life includes a rich dune flora, with species such as Sea Stock, Sea Bindweed, Immortelle, Sand Bedstraw, Sea Holly, and others. The wet woods are good for ferns and mosses, and the local Bayonne Astragalus is recorded for the reserve. Mammals include Otter, Genet, goats and Red Deer. Birds that breed on, or use, the reserve in summer include Kingfisher, Bittern, Water Rail, Night Heron, and Grey Heron.

Several roads and tracks run through or alongside the reserve, such as from Huchet to Moliets, and there are several parking areas. There are good footpaths within the reserve, or one can be taken by punt from Léon. There is a visitor centre on the shore of Etang de Léon.

A few kilometres to the south, there are good dunes with a rich flora just north of Vieux-Boucau. There is a car-park at the north end of the development, with easy access to very extensive dunes. The car-park has several clover species of interest.

48 PARC REGIONAL DES LANDES DE GASCOGNE	
Maps:	MA pp.134–5 and 120–21; IGN No. 55
Location:	Begins a few km S of Bordeaux, and runs S
Access:	By road, through the park
Season:	Good in spring and summer for birds, flowers, insects, amphibia and reptiles
Terrain:	Mainly dry, coniferous woodland, heath, pasture, and coastal habitats; a few wetland areas
Specialities:	Ocellated Lizard, Southern Smooth Snake; Woodchat Shrike, Pine Marten; heathland plants

The main N10 runs through the centre of the park, allowing easy access via minor roads. In fact, this Regional Natural Park is not particularly better than other areas of les Landes,

Left: sand-dunes at Vieux-Boucau, with a rich flora visible in the foreground.
Opposite: a lagoon in the Teich Ornithological Park, Arcachon Bay.

but it does provide a useful starting point for the naturalist.

Breeding birds in the area include Black Kite, Hobby, Marsh Harrier, Hoopoe, Woodchat and Red-Backed Shrikes, Nightjar, Crested Tit, Dartford Warbler, Serin, and Cirl Bunting. Amongst mammals, the Red Squirrel is the most obvious, though many others occur. Reptiles include Ocellated Lizard, Southern Smooth Snake, and Sand Lizard. Plant life is limited except in wetter or more open areas; plants of dry warm sandy areas, such as *Filago* species, are common, as are plants of winter-flooded areas such as Coral Necklace.

Most of the area is covered by planted pine forests. There are various lake areas, such as around Hostens, and the lower valley of the Eyre is of interest. There is little heathland left, and the best is mainly in military hands, just south of Arcachon.

The Ecomusée de Marquèze, north-west of Sabres in the south of the park, is a museum, specializing in the life of les Landes, its people and natural history. It is well worth visiting whilst in the area.

49 BASSIN D'ARCACHON AND THE ORNITHOLOGICAL PARK AT TEICH

Maps:	MA p. 120; IGN Nos 46 and 55
Location:	c. 35km SW of Bordeaux
Access:	By road
Season:	Bay is best in winter and at passage times for birds; park best in spring to summer
Terrain:	Mudflats and salt-marshes; ample dry-land access
Specialities:	Waders and wildfowl in winter; mixed heronry; White Stork

The bay or basin is a major feature on this part of the coast. It is directly accessible from Bordeaux, by the N250 or D106, and there are roads all around it. Minor roads lead down to better access-points and view-points all around the bay. The Ornithological Park at le Teich combines formal collections of local and exotic birds with access to the edge

Cattle Egret
Bubulcus ibis L 51

Elsewhere in the world, the Cattle Egret has been highly successful, with dramatic expansion during the last few decades. In France, it is still virtually confined to the Camargue (where it is quite common), though there are signs of colonization elsewhere in southern France at present, such as at the Ornithological Park at Teich. These birds were photographed at a breeding colony.

Out of the breeding season, the adults are white with dark legs, but as the breeding season approaches they become partially buff in colour. They frequently feed in association with grazing animals, such as cattle (hence the name) and even Camargue horses. Elsewhere, they will frequently follow tractors in appropriate situations. The French birds are largely non-resident and return in spring from Spain or Africa.

---

of the bay. It is open on weekends and holidays throughout the winter until 28th February, then every day through until the end of September, from 10 a.m. until 6 p.m. It is clearly signposted from the D650/N250.

In winter, numbers of waders and wildfowl are good, though shooting pressure and disturbance by oyster fishermen prevents the numbers from reaching their full potential. Passage periods turn up numerous oddities. The park itself has numerous semi-wild local birds that can be photographed, but a key feature is the large mixed heronry visible from a hide and walkway. This contains around 300 Grey Herons, together with a few Night Heron, Cattle Egret and Little Egret in low trees by a lagoon. There are usually good views of feeding birds, too. White Stork breed irregularly on the site, and are probably increasing slowly.

7. DORDOGNE

The Dordogne is one of the four regions that make up the Massif Central. Before looking at this region it is important to explain the nature of the whole Massif Central region.

THE MASSIF CENTRAL

To appreciate the why's and wherefore's of the way in which plants and animals are distributed, it is necessary to have some idea of the types of soil, the terrain, and the aspect – all factors depending on the geology of a region.

The diversity of habitats in the Massif Central points to a chequered geological history, which we find, by putting together the clues from the rocks, began some 600 million years ago in the Primary era when what is now France was covered with water.

Violent action raised the Massif at the same time as the Vosges and Armoricain Massif as part of a vast European mountain system, composed of impermeable crystalline rocks (granite, gneiss and schist). The relentless action of wind, rain, ice and water over countless millennia eroded these mountains, reduced their height considerably, and rounded the tops.

*A Common Tree Frog (*Hyla arborea)*, clinging to a Reedmace stem.*

Around 200 million years ago, during the Secondary era, the mountains of what are now the Rouergue, Aubrac, Margeride and Cévennes formed boundaries to a gulf and the Auvergne with its volcanoes lay to the north of Aubrac and the Margeride. Within the gulf basin, countless billions of minute sea creatures, diatoms, foraminifera and radiolaria lived and died, and their remains built up the calcareous material for what is now the Causse – a sobering thought if you stand at the bottom of the Gorges du Tarn, look up and realize there are marine fossils at the tops of those cliffs! During the same era the sediment was slowly compressed and raised until it formed a plain some 1,500m above sea-level.

The sculpting of rock-forms familiar in todays Causse, began in the Tertiary era, 60 million years ago, when fault-lines developed, the land tilted and slipped, and acidic water dissolved limestone and created caves and underground rivers. Dramatic changes occurred during the Quaternary era when the earth's atmosphere suffered a general cooling and glaciers formed. Acting like gigantic abrasive pads on the land the glaciers gouged out

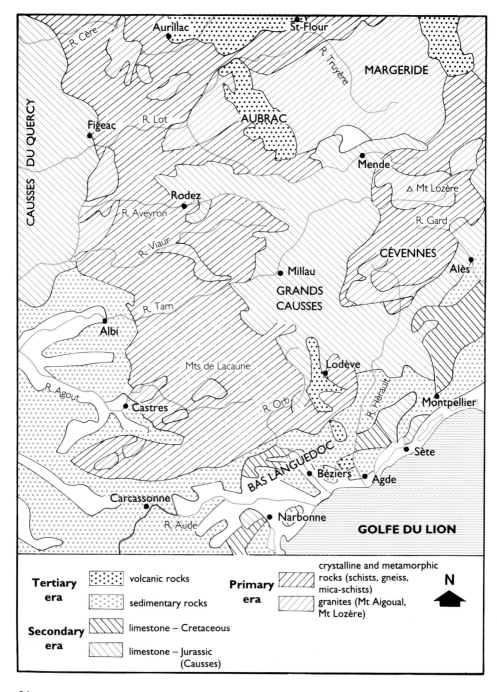

Tertiary era
:::: volcanic rocks
:::: sedimentary rocks

Secondary era
limestone – Cretaceous
limestone – Jurassic (Causses)

Primary era
crystalline and metamorphic rocks (schists, gneiss, mica-schists)
granites (Mt Aigoual, Mt Lozère)

N

canyons and took the sides off mountains. Wind, rain and flowing water washed away the softer rocks leaving bizarre 'sculptures' such as those at the Chaos de Montpellier.

In the following pages, the region is broadly divided into four regions: Dordogne, Auvergne, Causse and Cévennes with boundaries slightly altered to group sites logically. An introduction to features of landscape, climate, extent and diversity of species precedes each region.

INTRODUCTION TO THE DORDOGNE

A broad interpretation of what constitutes the Dordogne region would include territory as far north as Bourges, as far south as Montauban and as far across as from Périgeux to Aurillac. This area takes in many types of countryside: monotonous plains of Berry Champagne in the north, granite plateaus of the Limousin Marche, the high plateaus of the Limousin Montagne with their dense wooded farmland, the limestone plateaus or causse of Périgord and Quercy cut with deep gorges and valleys and finally the rich alluvial plain of the Garonne (the Agenais). The bulk of the sites described within this region fall into the Périgord, Quercy and Agenais locales.

The highest ground in the region occurs in eastern Limousin (Audouze Beacon 953m, Mont Bessou and Puy Pendu both at 977m). This forms the western bastion of the Massif Central formed from eroded crystalline rocks. On the plateaus, the climate is almost as varied as the geology of the soils:
1. Low plateaus (400–500m) west of the

Opposite: map of the Massif Central showing the various rock types.

Water Crowfoot (Ranunculus penicillatus) in the River Lot at Entraygues.

Limousin Montagne where heavy rainfall enables trees and bushes to flourish.
2. South of the Montagne and Monedières Massif, the plateau of Bas-Limousin facing south-west with a comparatively mild climate.
3. The porous limestone plateaus of Périgord (Cretaceous) and Quercy (Jurassic), have caves, underground rivers and can be dry and hot in the summer. The Dordogne, Lot and Vezere have cut deeply into the plateaus and the rich alluvial soil is excellent for crop-growing. The much wider alluvial valley of the Garonne spreads out over the Agenais where the river floods ferilize the soil.

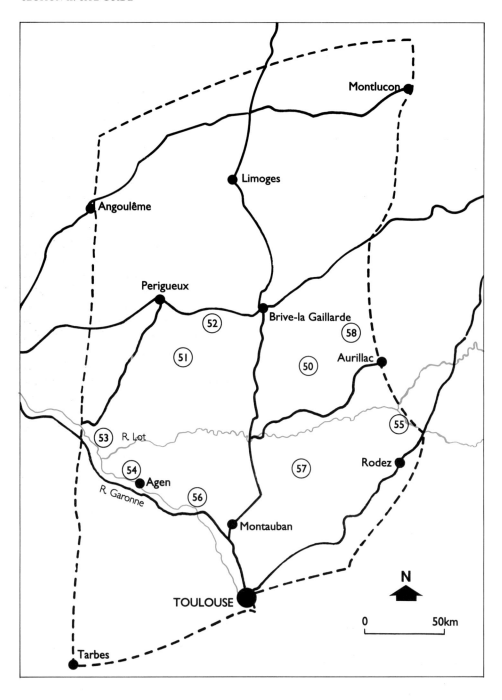

The limestone soils of Quercy and Périgord carry a rich flora – particularly of wild orchids – and a diverse insect population to match. The number of individuals and species of butterfly present in a field of Lucerne is quite staggering to visitors used to the sanitized, intensive culture employed in many agricultural regions. Birds are present in great variety and the Dordogne is often the region in which visitors see their first Hoopoe or Golden Oriole.

The Garonne basin and the regions where it meets with the Rivers Lot and Tarn form extensive wetlands which support large resident bird populations and attract a variety of interesting migrants including numbers of raptors. Fish and amphibian populations are also remarkable. The diversity of landscape and an abundance of hedgerows and woodlands in some regions encourages large populations of smaller mammals, such as shrews, voles, mice, Red Squirrel, Badger, and Fox.

Opposite: map of the Dordogne. Sites are numbered as in the text. Only main roads and the major rivers of the region are shown.

50 CAUSSE GRAMAT	
Maps:	MA p. 124–5; IGN No. 57
Location:	N of Cahors
Access:	Good
Season:	All year for birds; flowers spring – summer
Terrain:	Stony pasture, gorges
Specialities:	Limestone flora, caves, raptors, butterflies

The Causse Gramat forms the largest plateau in Quercy. It lies between the Dordogne valley in the north and the Lot valley to the south with an average altitude of 350m. As with the major causses to the south-east, the limestone plateau is not continuous but is cut by a series of canyons. The cliff-hugging settlement of Rocamadour, with its castle keep, occupies an extraordinary situation, much appreciated by visiting tourists, Crag Martin and Alpine Swift.

Caves at Lacave can be reached from the Dordogne valley and have extensive galleries where the concretions take on bizarre shapes – people, animals, buildings. There are underground rivers, pools and some fluorescent stalactites.

FIFTY INTERESTING SPECIES TO LOOK FOR

Alpine Swift	Melodious Warbler	Green Lizard	Large Blue
Aquatic Warbler	Montagu's Harrier	Sand Lizard	Provence Blue
Bearded Reedling	Penduline Tit	Common Treefrog	Short-Tailed Blue
Black Kite	Peregrine Falcon	Stripeless Treefrog	Cardinal
Booted Eagle	Red-Backed Shrike	Alis Shad	Great Sooty Satyr
Bonelli's Eagle	Scops Owl	Thwaite's Shad	Southern White Admiral
Crag Martin	Subalpine Warbler	Burnt-Tip Orchid	Common Swallowtail
Dartford Warbler	Wallcreeper	Lady Orchid	Scarce Swallowtail
Eagle Owl	Woodchat Shrike	Lizard Orchid	*Argiope* Spider
Golden Oriole	Wryneck	Military Orchid	Strawberry Spider
Hen Harrier	Badger	Red Helleborine	
Hoopoe	Pygmy White-Toothed	Violet Limodore	
Lesser Spotted	Shrew	Ascalaphids	
Woodpecker	Red Squirrel	Carpenter Bee	

The dramatic cliffside town of Rocamadour, set amongst superb country for the naturalist.

Red Helleborine
Cephalanthera rubra H 20–50
This orchid, delicate in appearance with its slightly wavy stem and pink flowers, is a familiar orchid in the Massif Central, growing under light woodland cover provided by Beech or pine. It is certainly the loveliest of the three *Cephalanthera* orchids found in France. The two others, Helleborines, White (*C. damasonium*) and Sword-Leaved (*C. longifolia*), have flowers reluctant to open quite as wide and they are coloured more modestly.

The plants thrive in open woods where the overhead cover allows some shafts of light through. As trees grow and the canopy becomes denser this is one of the orchids that can stop flowering, revert to a vegetative state, and have its food supplies augmented by the actions of mycorrhizal fungi, present, to some extent, in the roots of all European orchids.

Bonelli's and Short-Toed Eagles, Peregrine, Hobby and Black Kite are frequently seen on the Causse and in the canyons; Wallcreepers are winter visitors. The soils derived from the limestone support a very rich orchid population, including Man, Military, Lady, Lizard, and, less frequently, the Monkey Orchid, as well as helleborines (Red, White and Sword-Leaved). Striking patches of colour are provided by flaxes (Yellow, White, Blue), Bugle, Venus' Looking Glass and numerous vetches.

The butterfly fauna in the canyons is particularly rich. Even at the height of summer when parts of the Causse can become arid, Common, Provence and Short-Tailed Blues are particularly numerous. Grasshoppers and crickets occur in abundance, the two most obvious being of the *Oedipoda* species with red (*O. germanica*) and blue (*O. caerulescens*) flash colours on their underwings.

51 LES EYZIE DE TAYAC	
Maps:	MA p. 123; IGN No. 48
Location:	SE of Périgeux at the confluence of Rivers Vezere and Beaune
Season:	All year
Terrain:	Steep cliffs; limestone gorge
Specialities:	Early civilization and human remains

Throughout the millenia, man has influenced the landscape, the plant life and the other animal inhabitants of the Dordogne. The innumerable small fields, the hedges, and most of the woodlands owe their existence to human intervention. Traces of early civilizations abound in the Dordogne with animal remains dug from the floors of caves. Paintings found on the walls show a very different fauna from that of the present day, including Reindeer, Bison and Mammoth. Les Eyzie is justifiably regarded as the 'Capital of Prehistory'; in 1863 work began at the Laugerie and Madeleine sites then, in 1868, workmen building the Périgeux–Agen railway-line unearthed skeletons of Cro-Magnon man.

During the second ice-age animals migrated to the warmer southern areas with man close behind. The bed of the Vezere was some 30m above its present level, with numerous accessible natural caves and a soft, friable limestone that could be hollowed to create new dwellings. The area provided a haven for cave dwellers for tens of thousands of years. Some of the larger caves are open, within restricted times, for much of the year; others only during the summer months. Detailed information on the region can be obtained at the National Museum of Prehistory (Musée National de Prehistoire) and the Musée de la Speleologie, which concerns itself with the history of caving and the formation of caves.

52 HAUTEFORT AND SARLAT	
Maps:	MA p. 124; IGN No. 48
Location:	E of Périgeux
Access:	Good by road
Season:	All year; flowers and butterflies, spring–autumn
Terrain:	Lanes, pastures, small woods, hedges and banks
Specialities:	Orchids, lime-loving plants, insects

Other than being an attractive hill-top town, Hautefort has merit as a useful 'focus' for a network of innumerable, largely deserted roads, leaving and returning to the main D704 running south to Sarlat. These thread a countryside where farming has thrived on a subsistence level for countless centuries on the mineral-rich *'terre rouge'* (the red soil derived from weathered limestone). On roadside banks and in meadows too stony for anything except sparse grazing, a wealth of orchid species can be found. Lizard Orchids are the most obvious with spikes almost a metre tall carrying flowers scented of goat (the French *'Orchis bouc'*); the dried stems persist throughout the summer. Early Purple, Green-Winged, Military, Lady, Burnt-Tip, Bee, Fly and Greater Butterfly Orchids, and Red, Sword-Leaved and White Helleborines are found time and time again. There are numerous species of pea flower, poppies and cornflowers to contribute to the early summer colour.

In summer, thistles and other spiny plants, such as Field Eryngo dominate the dry meadows, but near streams herb growth

*An immature Sand Lizard (*Lacerta agilis*) basking on an old pine stump in the sun.*

can be remarkable in terms of wealth of species and the insects they attract. Lizards, particularly Sand and Green, are frequent and the bird life includes Hoopoe, Golden Oriole and raptors.

Flower-filled roadside banks, woodland clearings and fields full of Lucerne provide food and nectar plants for an astonishing variety of butterflies, in many places in the Dordogne. Just south of Hautefort lies a small lake which, although a 'magnet' for tourists in summer, has paths around its edges. Comma, Southern White Admiral and Silver-Washed Fritillary visit flowering brambles or sun themselves in open rides.

Travelling south, along the D704, roads branch westwards to hamlets such as Granges-d'Ans and St Orse, and eastwards to Nailhac and beyond to Puy d'Yssandon. It is never possible to predict exactly which fields will be used to grow Lucerne as a fodder crop, but it appears over considerable areas away from the roadsides and even in clearings in woods. By visiting at various times throughout a day, it is possible to see quite different sets of species. (Early morning or evening, when butterflies are torpid and can be easily approached, are the best times for photography.)

Open fields will reveal Marbled White, Cleopatra, Clouded Yellow, Black-Veined White, Queen of Spain and Dark-Green Fritillaries. At the edges, White Admiral, Silver-Washed, High-Brown and Cardinal Fritillaries descend from the trees to feed and return. Occasionally, there is an elusive Purple Emperor, a Large Tortoiseshell or even a Camberwell Beauty.

Blues abound, with Common, Chalkhill, Silver-Studded, Long-Tailed, Short-Tailed, Small, and even the occasional Large Blue. (Undersides need to be photographed for positive identification of blues, as with fritillaries.) In wet meadows there are interesting browns such as the Great Sooty Satyr and members of the same family. The graylings (Great-Banded and Woodland), fly towards trees then seemingly disappear. Both swallowtails (Scarce and Common) are frequent and one can look with envy at the numbers of them visiting Buddleia in cottage gardens.

Broad- and Narrow-Bordered Bee Hawkmoths fly by day as do Hummingbird Hawkmoths. At eventide and in the night, Elephant, Convolvulus and sometimes Death's Head Hawkmoths orbit lamps then hurtle into the blackness. During the day you

The extraordinary Death's Head Hawkmoth (Acherontia atropos), with its 'death's head' clearly visible.

53 L'ETANG DE LA MAZIERE-VILLETON	
Maps:	MA p. 136; IGN No. 56
Location:	W of Tonneins
Access:	Strictly regulated
Season:	All year
Terrain:	Lake and reed-beds; paths
Specialities:	Visiting wetland birds: breeding Hoopoe, Bonelli's Warbler, Wryneck, Woodchat Shrike; Common and Stripeless Tree Frogs

Once an extensive marshland extending over more than 5km², the wetlands at Mazière-Villeton now occupy about 68ha. Drainage for land reclamation and so-called 'improvement' have gradually reduced its extent over the decades. By creating a reserve in 1985 it was saved, literally in the nick of time. Work has been carried out to safeguard the area and to set about restoring it to some of its former natural glory. Access is carefully controlled and visitors are restricted to footpaths.

The area can be reached from Tonneins, on the N113, by crossing the River Garonne in the direction of Casteljaloux/Mont-de-Marsan (D120). About 1km after the bridge there is a right turn onto a small track leading to the reserve.

Tree cover is limited in extent with areas of mixed Alder, poplar, willow and Ash. There are reed-beds around the lake margins and flowering plants such as Frogbit, Marsh Woundwort, Tubular Water Dropwort and Fine-Leaved Water Dropwort grow there. In spite of the reduction in size, the site is remarkably rich in birds, fish and amphibia. The breeding list for birds numbers some fifty-eight species including Treecreeper,

can sometimes find hawk moths at rest on tree stumps or cottage walls, with coloured hind-wings hidden by forewings which provide effective camouflage.

Butterflies are not the only insects worth looking for. There are also irridescent Rose Chafer Beetles, red- and black-striped *Graphosoma bugs*, overweight blue-black carpenter bees and lacy-winged ascalaphids. Praying Mantids are often found in summer and the more colourful spiders include the large, tiger-striped *Argiope* spiders and the small scarlet and black Strawberry Spider.

Blackcap, Wryneck, Woodchat Shrike, Bonelli's Warbler, Hoopoe and Cetti's Warbler. Among the regular visitors are Little Grebe, Mallard, Gadwall, Pintail, Shoveler, Teal, Coot, Jack Snipe, Snipe, sandpipers, Bluethroat, Penduline Tit, Bearded Reedling, and Reed Bunting.

Rarer visitors include Cormorant, Black Stork, Greylag Goose, Osprey, Common Crane, Aquatic Warbler, and Spotted Crake. Reed-beds provide important cover for overwintering Reed Bunting. Good numbers of Lapwing and Golden Plover are present each year.

Although not a reserve especially well known for its mammals, Europe's smallest mammal has been recorded here – the Pygmy White-Toothed Shrew.

In the past, both Pond Tortoise and Ocellated Lizard have been found in the area, but they have not been seen recently. However, the marsh can boast both Common and Stripeless Tree Frogs living in the same area, as well as populations of Palmate Newt, Salamander, Grass Snake and Green lizard.

A nearby site which is worth visiting is Forêt de Campet. It is situated south-west of the A62-E72 autoroute, and is a forest of approximately 1600ha, planted mainly with Maritime Pines. Felling and clearing of woodland offers the chance to see Montagu's Harrier, Hen Harrier and Dartford Warbler. Leave the N113 between Aiguillon and Port-Ste-Marie, or the motorway at the Aiguillon exit. Take the D8 for Houeillès.

54 LA FRAYERE D'ALOSES A AGEN	
Maps:	MA p. 137; IGN No. 56
Location:	River Garonne just W of Agen
Season:	All year
Terrain:	River
Specialities:	Spawning ground for migratory fish – Shad

The year 1981 marked an important, but unusual step in the creation of France's network of Nature Reserves with the establishment of

Viperine Snake *Natrix maura*
The Viperine Snake is unusual, though not unique, in the amount of time it spends in water. In summer, it is quite a common sight, if you look carefully, to see several Viperine Snakes poised sinuously in the waters of a river, waiting for fish to pass by. They are most common in the warmer medium-flowing rivers of southern France, though they occur through most of the country. Although they frequent still waters and damp habitats in general as well, we have found that flowing rivers are the best place to see them. If cornered, they may become aggressive and strike, but their preferred method of defence is to move away, and they are unlikely to cause you any harm. Their main food consists of tadpoles, fish, and smaller reptiles and amphibia.

a Reserve at Agen. The purpose was to protect one of the few remaining spawning grounds for the Shad giving the reserve the distinction of being the only one devoted solely to the protection of fish. Of particular importance is the range of the reserve – some 2km of shallow beds of the River Garonne – and also the nature of the species, since the fish is migratory.

The reserve has been set up rather late in the day, for in the last century, migratory fish were still populating most of Europe's rivers: Sturgeon swam in the Seine, the Loire and the Rhône accompanied by both Alis and Thwaite's Shad. Salmon were so common in the 18th century that agricultural workers complained that the fish formed too large a part of their diet (they wanted it reduced to a twice-weekly serving!). Lamprey were also common.

Like Salmon, the Shad is born in rivers and migrates to the sea, returning each year, when mature, to spawn. Eels, on the other hand, are born in the Sargasso and migrate towards estuaries then up-river where they mature, before returning to the Sargasso to spawn. The basins of the Dordogne and the Garonne are the last capable of sustaining these migratory species. The demise of suitable sites has been due to canalization of rivers, construction of dams halting runs (another spawning ground at Lamagistère has a 'lift' to enable fish to get up-river), exploitation of riverine gravel-beds and, of course, pollution. Compared with these over-fishing is a minor worry.

The Agen spawning ground occupies a stretch of river which passes through the town itself.

*A mass of Cornflowers (*Centaurea cyanus*)*
in a Dordogne cornfield.

55 ESPALION AND ESTAING	
Maps:	MA p. 140; IGN No. 58
Location:	On the River Lot, NE of Rodez
Season:	All year; flowers in spring – autumn
Terrain:	River valley; limestone grassland and woodlands above
Specialities:	Limestone flora (orchids)

Both Espalion and Estaing are picturesque towns and good centres for exploration of the Lot valley and its surroundings. Botanically, the Lot valley has limits to what it can offer at this stage in its journey where the river has cut through the limestone to the volcanic rocks beneath. By climbing out of the valley to the north or to the south, limestone and a richer flora come into view. From Estaing, the D22 towards Villecomtal or the D100 to Bessuéjol and then cross-country to Espalion are possible 'escape routes'. Roadside banks and damp meadows offer numerous orchids (especially Military, Lady, and Lizard), Cornflower and Poet's Narcissus. Deserted,

stony vineyards are a treasure house for species which thrive on disturbed soils – countless Bee Orchids (including yellow-lipped variants) and Woodcock Orchid. Adders seem common and the bird life is rich in warblers, raptors and Hoopoe.

From Espalion, it is possible to take narrow alternative roads (D108) to the main D920. Roadside plants include Lizard, Man and Military Orchids, and a few Violet Limodore and Red Helleborine.

The pattern is repeated throughout the area but two journeys are worth taking:

1. By road, south-east over the Causse de Lanhac to the larger Causse du Comtal.
2. By rail, on the local stopping train from Brive to Rodez. Tantalizing glimpses of plants are gained from the train and the answer is to travel in one direction as a reconnoître and then, with plenty of time in hand, and a reliable timetable, get off at tiny stations *en route* and explore.

56 PLAN D'EAU DE ST NICHOLAS DE LA GRAVE	
Maps:	MA pp. 136–7 IGN No. 57
Location:	5km from St Nicholas de la Grave
Access:	Open all year to lake edges; vehicles controlled
Terrain:	Lake edges, paths
Specialities:	Migrant and resident birds, including Wood Sandpiper, Spotted Redshank, Black Tern, Black-Tailed Godwit

An artificial lake was created by the building of a dam downstream from the junction of the Rivers Tarn and Garonne. The surface area amounts to 400ha. The northern part is used for water sports, but the southern part is less frequented by boats and offers a refuge for both passage migrants and overwintering species of ducks and waders. Access to the edges of the lake is unobstructed and there are excellent vantage points from which to use binoculars and telescopes.

Spring visitors include Pintail, Black-Tailed Godwit, Spotted Redshank, Greenshank, Wood Sandpiper, Black-Headed Gull and Black Tern. Autumn migrants are Little Grebe, Lapwing, Golden Plover, and Kingfisher. In winter, visiting birds include Great Crested Grebe, Cormorant, Mallard, Tufted

Limestone Causse country, with masses of flowers.

Duck, Shoveler, Gadwall, Teal, Pochard, and perhaps more exciting the occasional Ferruginous Duck.

Confluence of the Rivers Lot and Garonne
Downstream of the town of Aiguillon, lies the confluence of the Rivers Lot and Garonne. Depending on the season, the area is a haven for numerous species of birds and close by lies the Pech de Beyre, on the calcareous slopes on the right bank of the Garonne where one can see raptors, Little Ringed Plover, Bee-Eater, Orphean Warbler, and Woodlark. It is also a remarkable vantage point for viewing the autumnal migration.

From Aiguillon you can also explore the small valleys of the 'Pays des Serres' on the right bank of the Garonne. The Vallée de la Masse is of particular interest.

57 GORGES DE L'AVEYRON	
Maps:	MA p. 139; IGN No. 57
Location:	On the Aveyron S of Villefranche de Rouergue
Access:	Open
Terrain:	River-bank; limestone cliffs
Specialities:	Wallcreeper, Golden Oriole, Crag Martin, Alpine Swift, Black Kite, Hobby; limestone flora

The Gorge de l'Aveyron stretches over a distance of 12km where it has been cut out of the Causse de Limogne (lower Quercy) over the millennia. There are riverside woodlands with willow, Alder, Ash and poplar and limestone cliffs from 150–200m in height; the plateau above is at an altitude of 350m and has sub-mediterranean vegetation. It can be reached from Montauban taking the

D115, first to Bruniquel and then Penne (parking in both villages). Cross the Aveyron at the bottom end of the bridge and go right on the D173 along the right-hand bank of the river. There are good vantage-points at a number of places, especially Couyrac.

The area is excellent for birds, access is free and the Causse vegetation is rich with an abundance of orchids (Man, Military, Monkey, Lizard, Lady) and other lime-loving plants.

The Wallcreeper regularly overwinters from December to April on the cliffs in the villages of the gorge and on the castles at Penne and Bruniquel. In spring-time the gorge itself has a number of interesting nesting birds including Dipper, Lesser Spotted Woodpecker, Golden Oriole, Black Kite and Hobby. Nesting high on the cliffs and grags are Crag Martin, Alpine Swift, Stock Dove, Kestrel, Peregrine, Eagle Owl, Raven, and Jackdaw. Above the Gorge on the Causse, Subalpine Warbler, Bonelli's Warbler and Red-Backed Shrike nest in the wooded scrub and the area is hunting territory for Short-Toed Eagle.

58 GORGES DE LA DORDOGNE	
Maps:	MA pp. 112 and 126; IGN No. 48
Location:	On the Dordogne SW of la Bourboule
Access:	Open
Season:	All year
Terrain:	River-bank, limestone cliffs, woodlands (scrub)
Specialities:	Raptors (Red and Black Kite, Short-Toed and Booted Eagles, Goshawk, Osprey); cliff nesters; limestone flora

From Madic to St-Projet the valley is deep and narrow, well wooded with broad-leaved and

A Scop's Owl (Otus scops) sleeping in its daytime roost.

Red Kite and Peregrine. Other birds seen here include: Rock Bunting, Dipper, Crag Martin, House Martin, Redstart.

58A FORET DOMANIALE DE GRESIGNE	
Maps:	MA pp. 139 and 153; IGN Nos 57 and 64
Location:	E of Montauban
Access:	Free on foot; limited in car (forest tracks closed during hunting season)
Season:	Late summer; autumn
Terrain:	Woodlan
Specialities:	Raptors, Middle Spotted Woodpecker, Scops Owl, woodland flora, fungi

pine forest, studded in part with cliffs and open heath. Although in the past the Dordogne used to flow through narrow gorges, dams and reservoirs, form a 'stairway' for the water over 100km of the river's length. However, larger expanses of water blend in beautifully with the wildness of the region and the inaccessible cliffs still provide a refuge for numerous breeding raptors – Buzzard, Red Kite, Black Kite, Honey Buzzard, Short-Toed Eagle, Booted Eagle and Goshawk – with Hen Harrier in some places; Osprey are regular passage migrants. Among the numerous species of smaller birds are Melodious Warbler and Whinchat.

Three particularly good sites along the circuit of the river are:
1. Site de St -Nazaire – Offering birds of the woodlands and scrub, raptors; and wonderful views over the valleys of the Dordogne and Diege.
2. Belvedere de Gratte-Bruyere – Excellent for observation of raptors.
3. Barrage de l'Aigle – A dam offering the possibility of good views of Black Kite,

To reach the forest, take the D964 from Gaillac towards Castelnau-de-Montmiral. After 8km take the D15 towards Vaour and, about 1.5km before Vaour, turn left on the D28, then left again at the first crossroads (around 0.5km) to Pas-de-Pontraute (there is a large car-park at the forest entrance).

The whole forest occupies a large south-facing 'basin' of 200–500m altitude. The lower slopes are clothed with Oak and the west- and north-facing slopes tend to be mainly Beech woodland. The area is well worth visiting in spring for the diversity of its forest birds, including raptors – Buzzard, Goshawk, Sparrowhawk, Booted Eagle, and Short-Toed Eagle. In the woods on the south-facing slopes near the ridge there are Middle Spotted Woodpecker; lower down there are Woodcock; and elsewhere, Wood Warbler, Hawfinch and Marsh Tit.

Montoulieu is a good place to observe Honey Buzzard, Hobby and Hen Harrier. On summer evenings Scop's Owls call around Puycelci.

8. AUVERGNE

INTRODUCTION

By far the greatest part of this section concerns sites in the Regional Natural Park of the Auvergne, a scenically dramatic area with numerous old volcanic cones, coniferous and broad-leaved forest and extensive green pastures. By any standards the park is large – 120km from north to south and including an area of 2,815km² – and takes in five regions:

Monts Dôme – The youngest in geological terms with its volcanoes only 'recently' extinct, and Puy de Dôme the highest cone at 1,465m.

Monts Dore – The remains of three cones close together which once soared to over 2,500m. Puy de Sancy (1,886m), though reduced, is still the highest mountain in the Massif Central.

Cezallier – A plateau with immense pastures.

Artenses – Also a plateau.

Monts du Cantal – To the south with the highest point, Plomb du Cantal (1,858m).

Alpine Snowbells (Soldanella alpina) growing close to the snow line.

To the north lie the Monts de la Madeleine, whilst to the east are the granite Monts du Forez. Beyond and separated by the River Loire is Mont Pilat (also considered in this section).

Winters are cold with plenty of snow on higher ground; summers are warm, but the rainfall is appreciable and accounts for the lush pastures and luxuriant woodlands.

Lakes are an important feature of the Auvergne, ranging from large open bodies of water in extensive marsh to lakes in ancient craters and peat bogs on poorly drained soils. The Dordogne is one of numerous rivers that rise in this mountain region.

Much of the land up to a height of 800–1,000m is cultivated or pasture land and above that are forests, often of mixed Beech and Silver Fir. Oaks are dominant at lower altitudes with the Sweet Chestnut in valleys on lower slopes. Beech grow above these and then are replaced by Silver Fir on the summits.

The flora is very distinctive with a very wide range of sub-alpine plants which would normally not be found below 1,500m but, in the Auvergne, occur at lower altitudes because of the combined influence of high summer rainfall and Atlantic-influenced weather. For the visitor in spring or early summer (mid-May to June), one abiding memory is of meadows, yellow with Wild Daffodil and damper hollows white with Poet's Narcissus. Dog's-Tooth Violet is abundant in the woodlands and later there are flowers such as the yellow Provence Orchid, Red Helleborine, Welsh Poppy and Blue Sow Thistle. Another feature is the number and variety of large raptors – one seldom seems to be out of sight of large outstretched soaring wings.

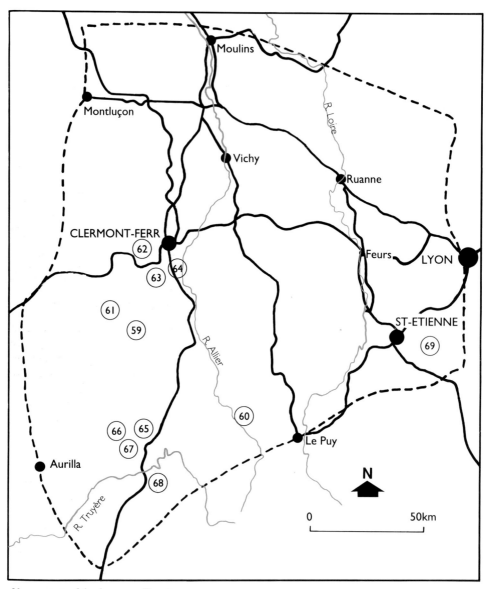

Above: *map of the Auvergne. The sites are numbered as in the text. Only mains roads and the major rivers of the area are shown.*

59 LES SAGNES DE LA GODIVELLE

Maps :	MA p. 113; IGN No. 49
Location :	S of Clermont Ferrand
Access:	On paths from la Godivelle
Terrain :	Wetland
Specialities:	Wetland flora; dragonflies; breeding Coot, Montagu's Harrier, Little Grebe; migrants

The word 'Sagne' means 'marsh' in the Auvergne dialect, though in fact the Sagnes de la Godivelle are high-level peat-bogs. The village of la Godivelle lies close to 1,200m altitude on the Cezallier plateau, which, like the plateau of Aubrac, was formed from fluid lavas which spread outwards rather than piling up into cones. The landscape was sculpted by glacial action. Only the most recent eruptions produced craters such as the one found at Lac d'en Haut, which adjoins the village of Godivelle in the west. This eruption doubtless followed the last glacial era and occurred recently, that is only a few thousand years ago.

The Lac d'en Bas, which is largely

Old hay meadows in the central Auvergne.

surrounded by the reserve (some 24ha), owes its existence to glacial erosion, is only a few metres deep and is becoming slowly silted up. Open water has gradually been invaded by *Sphagnum* which decays to form peat-bogs, several of which lie above the current level of the lake. In places there are deposits of diatomaceous earth resulting from the siliceous skeletons of microscopic plants.

FIFTY INTERESTING SPECIES TO LOOK FOR

Alpine Accentor	Merlin	Water Shrew	Alpine Aster
Alpine Swift	Montagu's Harrier	Wild Boar	Arnica
Black Kite	Nightjar	Apollo	Dog's-Tooth Violet
Crag Martin	Ortolan Bunting	Clouded Apollo	Fringed Pink
Crossbill	Red Kite	Common Swallowtail	Grass of Parnassus
Eagle Owl	Rock Bunting	Scarce Swallowtail	Knautia
Firecrest	Rock Thrush	Banded Agrion	Marsh Andromeda
Golden Eagle	Short-Toed Eagle	Brown Hawker	Poet's Narcissus
Great Grey Shrike	Wallcreeper	Dragonfly	Provence Orchid
Hobby	Woodchat Shrike	Emperor Dragonfly	Round-Leaved Sundew
Honey Buzzard	Red Squirrel	Irish Damselfly	Whorled Solomon's
Hoopoe	Red Deer	Keeled Skimmer	Seal
Long-Eared Owl	Roe Deer	Aconite	Wild Daffodil

Club-Tailed Dragonfly
Gomphus vulgatissimus L 33–37mm
This distinctive dragonfly does well in France. It is one of the relatively few species of dragonfly that live (as larvae) in large rivers, and the great slow-flowing rivers of France suit it perfectly. In May, the aquatic larvae, which may have spent several years growing in the river, crawl out onto the bank or nearby vegetation, and the adults emerge. They fly for about four to six weeks, and are surprisingly sluggish by dragonfly standards. The males have an expanded tip to their abdomens, hence the name 'Club-Tailed'. They also have eyes that are quite distinctly separated from each other, whereas in most other species they touch.

Although the dragonflies emerge from rivers, they may fly for considerable distances and turn up well away from rivers. We have found them high on the dry slopes of the Causse hills, for example.

Amongst the higher plants growing in damp places are Grass of Parnassus, Marsh Andromeda and Daffodil, with Round-Leaved Sundew on the peat. Abundant invertebrates living in the reserve attract and sustain populations of small mammals, such as Common, Pygmy and Water Shrews.

Of the insects, dragonflies are particularly well represented, with nineteen species recorded, among them Irish Damselfly. Bush crickets are unusual in that several genera have a number of species living together which are normally distributed separately – Grasshoppers: *Medioptera brachyptera* (Northern), *M. roeselii* (central European), and *M. saussuriana* (Atlantic). Two rare moths (microlepidoptera) occur – *Elachista abbreviatella* (first time in France) and *Phyllonorycter salicicolella* (first described from Godivelle).

Breeding birds include Montagu's Harrier, Little Grebe, and Coot.

Rocher de la Jaquette

This is a small reserve (18.4ha) established in a valley (Couze d'Ardes) on the edges of the Cezallier plateau just east of Ardes. Occupying a cliff ranging in altitude from 870–1,050m, the reserve carries an interesting flora, including Amelanchier, Orpine, Common Broomrape and Fringed Pink. However, the real purpose for the creation of the reserve was to protect a nesting pair of Eagle Owls. In the 1950s there were about twenty nesting pairs in Puy de Dôme; by the 1970s there were seven and those nested irregularly. There is no public access to this reserve and its precise location is, therefore, not given.

*A female Bog Bush-Cricket (*Metrioptera brachyptera*), common in the Sagnes de la Godivelle.*

60 ROCHERS DE PRADES	
Maps :	MA p. 127; IGN No. 49
Location :	River Allier, E of St Flour
Access:	Free
Season:	All year for birds
Terrain :	River-bank, grasslands, woods
Specialities:	Raptors: Short-Toed Eagle, Red Kite, Black Kite, Honey Buzzard, Sparrowhawk, Hobby and Kestrel; Crag Martin

The site is reached from Langeac by following the course of the Allier on the D585. At St-Arcons-d'Allier take the D48 to Prades. Park in the car-park just before the bridge crossing the Allier. Coming from Puy en Velay, take the D589 as far as St Privat d'Allier and follow the gorge on the D301 with a good view over the valley. Then at Vergues turn towards Prades on the D48.

Rochers de Prades is a basalt rock towering more than 200m above the torrents of the River Allier. Between the granite or volcanic plateaux there are a great number of habitats – gravel beaches, riverine woodlands, gorse scrub, dry grassland and rocky areas. This is an area of refuge for raptors, not only in terms of species, but also good numbers of rarer species preferring rocky areas.

Winter visitors include Raven, Great Grey Shrike, Red-Legged Partridge, numerous Dippers, occasional Wallcreeper and Alpine Accentor. Spring and summer see the mating of numerous raptors, including Short-Toed Eagle, Red Kite, Black Kite, Honey Buzzard, Sparrowhawk, Hobby and Kestrel. On the rock itself there are colonies of Crag Martin, and a few pairs of Alpine Swift, Raven and Rock Bunting. The edges of the River Allier hold Common Sandpiper and Dipper.

Val d'Allier

The most interesting bird life on the River Allier is to be found between Pont du Château and Maringue. Man's activities have created a great number of habitats – riverine woodland of varying age, gravel beaches, meadowland, and gravel pits. Bird life is visible during all seasons of the year. In winter, visitors include Grey Heron, Mallard, Teal, and Black-Headed Gull. In spring Red Kite and Osprey occur as well as numerous species of ducks and small waders. Grey Heron, Night Heron, Black Kite, Stone Curlew, and Common Snipe all mate here, while autumn sees a stop-over by Little Egret and numerous other exciting migrants.

A Stone Curlew (Burhinus oedicnemus).

61 PUY DE SANCY	
Maps:	MA p. 113; IGN No. 49
Location:	SW of Clermont Ferrand
Access:	Free, snow permitting
Season:	Spring and summer
Terrain :	Grasslands, mountain slopes, rock areas
Specialities:	Mountain flowers, Rock Thrush, Alpine Accentor, Crag Martin, Wallcreeper

Although the heights of Puy de Sancy (1,885m) can be reached by a cable car journey from Super-Besse. It is well worth walking down, because the display of mountain flowers is quite superb and offers a wonderful sample of the best that the Auvergne has to offer.

Towards the end of June, slopes and seepages are filled with colour – Yellow Daffodils, White Narcissus and the occasional natural hybrid between them (*Narcissus x incomparabilis*), Wood Anemone, Alpine Pasque Flower, Narcissus-Flowered Anemone, Whorled Solomon's Seal and Bluebells in the woods. On higher ground grow Alpine Clover, Pink Rock-Jasmine, Arnica, Alpine Aster and, at the snow line, Alpine Snowbells.

Vallée de Chaudefour
This valley lies in the Sancy Massif within the parish of Chambon sur Lac. To reach it, take the D36 from le Mont-Dore to Besse; about 15km from le Mont Dore a minor road leads into the valley with Puy Ferrand at its head. It is a site renowned on several counts: flora (many of the plants mentioned above), fauna, and views.

Formed originally by glacial action, it has remained protected from change and is the subject of attempts to create a reserve. When the snows melt is the time to look for Rock Pipit, Treecreeper, Ring Ouzel and Coal Tit (at the bottom of the valley). Similar sites (for flowers) are Puy de Dôme and Plomb de Cantal.

Amongst the rocky outcrops live Crag Martin, Wallcreeper, and Raven, whilst at the head of the valley there are Rock Thrush, Alpine Accentor and hunting Montagu's Harrier.

In autumn soaring birds appear since the valley is on a migratory route. These include Honey Buzzard, Osprey, Marsh Harrier, Hen Harrier, and other passage migrants.

62 PUY DE DOME/ CHAINE DES DOME	
Maps :	MA p. 113; IGN No. 49
Location :	W of Clermont Ferrand
Access:	All year, snow permitting
Season:	Spring and summer best
Terrain :	Mountain pastures, woods, rocky outcrops
Specialities:	Mountain birds, Tengmalm's Owl, Black Woodpecker, Short-Toed Eagle, Crossbill, Goldcrest, Firecrest; mountain flowers

To the west of Clermont Ferrand lies the Chaîne des Dômes, undoubtedly one of the finest of the European volcanic ranges. It is a vast range of peaks covered with scrub and forests. Exploring the area comprising le Puy de la Vache, le Puy de Lassolas, and Cheire d'Aydat allows a good insight into the area and its wildlife.

The area boasts a characteristic mountain-bird fauna: Tengmalm's Owl, Black Woodpecker, Treecreeper, Crossbill, Goldcrest, Firecrest, and as many as six species of tit living close together. Raptors include Short-Toed Eagle, Goshawk, and Red Kite.

Scrubland and heath provide nesting places for Hen Harrier, Nightjar, Meadow Pipit, Whinchat, and Great Grey Shrike. Spring (from mid-May) is the best time for walking here, but in Autumn there are numerous Red Kites and Hen Harriers.

Flowers are very impressive with abundant narcissi and many of the species mentioned in the previous site. In summer, the meadows are full of butterflies including Common and Scarce Swallowtails, Apollo, and, occasionally, Clouded Apollo as well as a range of blues, coppers, fritillaries and skippers.

An old meadow full of Wild Daffodils (Narcissus pseudonarcissus) close to the Puy de Dôme.

63 LAC D'AYDAT

Maps:	MA p. 113; IGN No. 49
Location:	SW of Clermont Ferrand
Access:	By road
Season:	All year, snow permitting, for birds; summer for dragonflies
Terrain:	Wetland
Specialities:	Dragonflies: Brown Hawker, Emperor, Keeled Skimmer, White-Legged Damselfly, Scarce Blue-Tailed Damselfly

Reached either via the N89 south-east of Clermont Ferrand, taking the D901 south to Lac d'Aydat or from the main N9-E11

leaving in the direction of St Amant, taking the D213 towards the lake. The forest surrounding the lake is predominantly coniferous with plenty of open rides and glades. The area is very good for dragonflies and the following species have been recorded: Brown Hawker, Emperor, Keeled Skimmer, White-Legged Damselfly, Banded Agrion, Blue-Tailed Damselfly, Scarce Blue-Tailed Damselfly, and *Onychogomphus forcipatus.*

64 MONTAGNE DE LA SERRE

Maps:	MA p. 113; IGN No. 49
Location:	W of Clermont Ferrand
Access:	By footpaths
Season:	All year, snow permitting
Terrain:	Mountain pastures; woods; rocky outcrops
Specialities:	Mountain birds, Tengmalm's Owl, Black Woodpecker, Tree-creeper, Crossbill, Firecrest; mountain flowers

To reach la Serre, take the N9 from Clermont Ferrand towards Issoire, turning on to the D213 at la Vierge de Monton towards St Saturnin, then the D96 across Chadrat. Carry on for 1.5km to a car-parking area. Access is also possible via the N89, turning off at Theix, then at the entrance to the village of Nadaillat, and continuing for a few kilometres beyond.

A basalt flow, issuing from Mt Vigeral several million years ago, reached what is now the village of Crest, and formed Montagne de la Serre. Erosion shaped its form and, al-though cultivated over millennia it is now only partially farmed, and therefore, is returning to its original form of meadows, wasteland and wooded slopes on the flanks. Sedimentary deposits on the southern end form the Chadrat Plateau which is still cultivated. The tremendous diversity of habitat encourages a correspondingly rich bird life, particularly as far as raptors and small birds are concerned.

The bottom of the Limagne forms a 'funnel' and a visit to la Serre at the right time (from 1st August to 31st October) allows one to see migrants in their hundreds of thousands, Cranes, storks and raptors among them. Numerous paths permit free and easy access.

Spring-nesting birds include Short-Toed Eagle, Buzzard, Honey Buzzard, Red and Black Kites, Sparrowhawk, Kestrel, Hobby, Quail, Hoopoe, Red-Backed Shrike, Woodlark, four species of *Sylvia* warblers, and Hawfinch.

Summer migrants are Black Stork, Honey Buzzard, Black Kite, Montagu's Harrier, Meadow Pipit, and Ortolan Bunting. In autumn, migrants include Osprey, Marsh Harrier, Hen Harrier, and Red Kite. In mid-October there is the passage of pigeons, plus Swallows and martins, Cranes, Greater and Lesser Spotted Woodpeckers, and Great Grey Shrike.

65 ST FLOUR	
Maps:	MA p. 127; IGN No. 49
Location:	S of Clermont Ferrand
Access:	By car
Season:	All year for birds; spring–summer for flowers
Terrain:	Varied, agricultural land; hills; woodland; wet meadows
Specialities:	Elder-Flowered Orchid, Cévennes Pasque Flower, shrikes, Short-Toed Treecreeper, raptors

The N9, when approaching St Flour from Marvéjols to the south, runs for much of its length across wild terrain, which lies at over 1,000m above sea-level. Wet areas away from the road are often white with narcissus and on slopes, the meadows can contain a wealth of interesting plants – both yellow and magenta forms of the Elder-Flowered Orchid, the dark-red Cévennes Pasque Flower and Globeflowers.

Both yellow and magenta forms of Elder-Flowered Orchids (Dactylorhiza sambucina) *in an Auvergne wet meadow. This name is a misnomer, as the elder-flower odour belongs to another yellow-flowered species, the Pale-Flowered Orchid* (Orchis pallens). *The 'error' has never been rectified and the name remains.*

St Flour offers a good base from which to explore the surrounding region, much of which is rolling agricultural land, but there are numerous belts of conifers, hills and small fields. To the south, there is an artificial lake, the Viaduc de Garabit, and in the surrounding pinewood country there are Woodchat and Red-Backed Shrikes, Black Redstart, Firecrest, Short-Toed Treecreeper, and Crested Tit.

To the north, wide open spaces around the Col de la Fageole (1,153m) attract the raptors Buzzards, Red Kite, Montagu's Harrier and Booted Eagle. Farther on towards Clermont Ferrand the route takes in the impressive Gorges de l'Allagon where the same raptors can be seen. Wooded areas along the river offer the chance to look for Wryneck and Cirl Bunting.

The N106 crosses similar wild territory and joins up with the N9 to reach St Flour. From Mende to le Puy, branching either via the D88 or N88 offers many high-level meadows, hills and woods. From the N88, the N102 to Aubenas follows the infant Ardèche River through superb countryside.

In the southern part of the Cantal massif, the traditional summer pastures are extremely rich in terms of flowers and insects. There is an astonishing variety of habitat, with sloping peat-bogs, scrub, low shrubs, sub-alpine pastures and rocky outcrops. Since 1982, this has been one of seven sites for data collection on annual migration as it occupies a unique position on migratory routes through the Massif Central. The Prat de Bouc can be reached directly from Murat on the N122. From August to October there is an exhibition dealing with the migration held at the Centre École et Ski de Fond.

Spring and summer witness numerous mountain birds nesting here. These include Rock Thrush, Ring Ouzel, Rock Pipit, Alpine Accentor, and Crossbill. Also to be seen are Black Kite, Honey Buzzard, Montagu's Harrier, Swift, warblers (in August), White Storks, Osprey, Short-Toed Eagle, Swallows, Peregrine, Merlin, Sparrowhawk, Woodpigeon, Stock Doves, Mistle Thrush, Fieldfare, Redwing, Brambling, Chaffinch, Siskin, Greenfinch, and Goldfinch.

66 PLOMB DU CANTAL AND PRAT DE BOUC

Maps:	MA p. 126; IGN No. 49
Location:	W of St Flour
Access:	Cable from Super Lioran
Season:	All year, snow permitting
Terrain:	Peat bogs; pasture; scrub; rocky outcrops
Specialities:	Mountain flowers (particularly bog species); butterflies; nesting Rock Thrush, Ring Ouzel, Rock Pipit, Alpine Accentor, Crossbill

67 LASCOLS AND CUSSAC

Maps:	MA p. 127; IGN No. 49
Location:	SE of St Flour
Access:	Free, snow permitting
Terrain:	Wetland
Specialities:	Ducks; waders; raptors; nesting Spotted Crake, Lapwing, Snipe, Curlew, Black-Headed Gull

To the west of Lascal, there is a wetland occupying some 110ha where it is possible to see habitats juxtaposed in a manner which is unusual for the Auvergne – open water of variable level; muddy pools; scrubby grazing land; water courses feeding the marsh. The area is of greatest interest during spring, particularly at dawn and dusk. It can be reached from St Flour by taking the D921 towards Chaudes-Aigues then turning at les Ternes on the D57 towards Cussac. Take the minor road to Lascols just before reaching Cussac.

In spring, all the dabbling ducks occur with numerous small waders (Greenshank, Redshank, Spotted Redshank), Curlew, Golden Plover, Black-Tailed Godwit and raptors (Marsh Harrier, Hobby, Merlin). Five of the nesting species occur at their highest limit in Europe: Spotted Crake, Lapwing, Snipe, Curlew and Black-Headed Gull.

From mid-August to mid-September, Cussac becomes a stop-over for Hen and Montagu's Harriers, herons, occasional White Stork, Crane, Yellow Wagtail, Red-Throated Pipit, Whinchat, and Stonechat.

68 GORGES DE LA TRUYERE

Maps:	MA p. 127; IGN No. 49
Location:	S of St Flour
Access:	Free all year
Terrain:	Wooded slopes; cliffs; scrub
Specialities:	Raptors

Over a distance of 35km from Chaliers to Paulhenc, the Gorge de la Truyère has wooded slopes and scrubland bordering reservoirs created for hydroelectric power.

This is an excellent region for viewing raptors which can be seen to advantage from numerous places along the river course, such as Longevialle on the right bank near to Ruynes (good in spring and autumn). Cheyle Belvedere, on the left bank at Fridefont offers ducks in spring, Booted and Short-Toed Eagles, and both kites. Turland-Pony-de-Troubol, on the right bank at Pierrefort sees migrant pigeons and raptors, whilst in spring

and summer Hen and Montagu's Harriers nest in the scrub and the Grey Heron is often seen in the water. Four owls – Little, Tawny, Long-Eared and Eagle are also present.

69 PILAT REGIONAL PARK

Maps:	MA p. 115; IGN No. 51
Location:	SE of St Etienne
Access:	Unrestricted; two 'zones of silence'
Season:	All year
Terrain:	Wooded hills; granite outcrops; heaths
Specialities:	Mountain flora; birds of prey; woodland birds

Rising to 1,432m at the Crêt de la Perdrix, Mt Pilat dominates the central part of the extensive Regional Natural Park, some 600km² in area. To the west, the landscape is a wild mixture of heaths and wooded hills with granite outcrops, while vineyards and orchards predominate where the land falls towards the River Rhône in the east.

At middle levels there is mixed broad-leaved forest of Sweet Chestnut, Downy Oak, Ash and poplar which has a correspondingly rich bird population (owls, woodpeckers, Hoopoe, and Golden Oriole). Forests in the montane zone consist mainly of Beech, pine or fir with a rich flora in the understorey growing on siliceous soils – Aconite, Arnica and Knautia.

Towards the Rhône, the southwards autumn migration is spectacular. Bonelli's Eagle, Citril Finch and Crag Martin have all been recorded and the bird list numbers over 100 species (there is an information centre in the park as well as marked paths). Mammals include Red Squirrel, Badger, and Roe and Red Deer. Wild Boar inhabit the higher regions around Roizey and Pelussan and forest areas such as Pavezin and Terrasse sur Dolay.

9. CAUSSES

INTRODUCTION

The Causses of today are vast limestone plateaux, dotted with bizarre calcareous formations, dissected by deep gorges and here and there clad with pine forest remnants and plantations.

It is a wild region, depopulated in human terms but home to enormous grazing flocks of sheep. In spite of the attentions of these animals, it supports a rich and varied vegetation where familiar mountain flowers such as Alpine Aster grow along-side Mediterranean bee orchids (*Ophrys*).

Unusually for a region of France, the Causses are geographically well defined. To the south they open out towards Bas Languedoc, whilst the higher ground and ancient crystalline rocks of Rouergue, Aubrac, Margeride and Cévennes provide the other boundaries to what, many millions of years ago was a gulf.

Alpine Asters (Aster alpinus) growing in higher altitudes Causse pasture.

The soils of the Causses, originating from calcareous rocks, retain heat longer than the crystalline soils from neighbouring regions, which enables the more tender plants to survive the rigours of winter. For, although summers can be hot and the more southerly Causses du Larzac becomes almost arid, winters are cold. Icy winds descend from Aubrac and Margeride in the north and Mt Lozere in the east, sweep across the plateaux, and bring frequent snow storms until late February.

Early spring flowers appear in April and, by late May the area is ablaze with plants often covering large patches (Yellow, White and Blue Flax, Alpine Aster, pea flowers and pink cushions of Rock Soapwort); side by side grow plants of Mediterranean and alpine origin. Over forty species of wild orchid have been found in the region (including Lady's Slipper) and, for the observant traveller thirty or more can be seen with little difficulty. The dry, sunny Causses provide a home for innumerable lizards and other reptiles, butterflies and other insects, small mammals and, above all, birds. Whenever one looks up there is inevitably some large raptor wheeling overhead, whether, Buzzard, vulture or Golden Eagle. On the Causses, the woodlands are of pine, broad-leaved trees or Box scrub and, although exploited to a certain extent for timber they have a very rich flora and fauna.

Harsh winter living conditions have meant that the area has never been bursting at the seams as far as its population is concerned. Nowadays, further depopulation has occurred as people have moved way into towns to find work.

But the Causses are still used, as they have been for centuries, as the grazing lands for millions of sheep. Some of the flocks are vast,

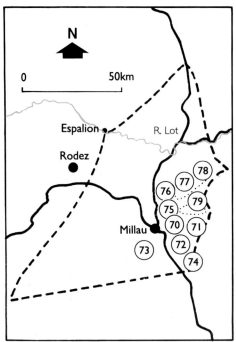

N

| 0 | 50km |

R. Lot

Espalion

Rodez

Millau

78
77
76
79
75
70 71
72
73
74

Map of Causses. The sites are numbered as in the text. Only main roads and the major rivers of the region are shown.

and if you happen on a sea of sheep being moved down from one Causses and up to another (through the village of la Malène in the Gorges du Tarn, for example), the only thing to do is sit and wait! Many of the minor roads across Causses, into valleys and through villages are built on ancient drovers' trails called '*drailles*'. The milk from the sheep is processed at Roquefort into the famous cheese of the same name.

CAUSSE NOIR

70 CHAOS DE MONTPELLIER-LE-VIEUX	
Maps:	MA p. 141; IGN No. 58
Location:	E of Millau, Causse Noir
Access:	Footpaths
Season:	Birds all year; late spring/summer for flowers; reptiles; insects
Terrain:	Rocky limestone with paths and 'steps' to aid ascent/descent on main route
Specialities:	Eroded rocks; limestone plants; woodland orchids; Blue Rock Thrush, Chough, raptors

From a distance, the bizarre shaped, weather-sculpted rocks of the Chaos de Montpellier-le-Vieux once seemed like a ruined city to superstitious shepherds, who avoided the area, believing it to be the home of the devil. The 'attraction' is well marked from Millau and reached via a turn off from the road to the Gorge de la Dourbie above which it lies. For the more adventurous, there is a narrow road from la Roque St Marguerite in the gorge which offers spectacular views.

It is open every day from March to November, from 9 a.m. until nightfall. Maps supplied at the entrance (small fee payable) are well marked with paths – blue and yellow

Grasslands near St Rome-de-Tarn.

The extraordinary weathered rocks of the Chaos de Montpellier-le-Vieux.

represent easy routes; red, the complete circuit (1.5–2hr).

Human imagination has run riot in naming the rock formations encountered along the various routes – Arc de Triomphe, Mycenaean Gate, and Sphinx. A bonus for the naturalist is the number of sheltered areas of rocky damp woodlands which provide species-rich habitats unnoticed by most visitors.

Plants common on the rest of the Causse – Alpine Aster and various flax species – thrive here with tiny flowers of Alpine Erinus, Blue Aphyllanthes, bushes of Amelanchier and carpets of Lily Of The Valley. Mossy, sheltered

FIFTY INTERESTING SPECIES TO LOOK FOR			
Black Redstart	Red-Backed Shrike	Praying Mantis	Aveyron Ophrys
Blue Rock Thrush	Short-Toed Eagle	Glanville Fritillary	Aymoninii's Ophrys
Chough	Sparrowhawk	Provençal Fritillary	Bug Orchid
Cirl Bunting	Stone Curlew	Alpine Aster	Early Spider Orchid
Corn Bunting	Pine Marten	Alpine Erinus	Loose-Flowered
Crag Martin	Red Squirrel	Alpine Rock Rose	Orchid
Crested Tit	Wild Boar	Bastard Balm	Man Orchid
Crossbill	Green Lizard	Blue Aphyllanthes	Military Orchid
Eagle Owl	Sand Lizard	Corncockle	Monkey Orchid
Great Grey Shrike	Montpellier Snake	Cornflower	Rock Soapwort
Golden Eagle	Blue-Winged	Crested Cow-Wheat	St Bernard's Lily
Griffon Vulture	Grasshopper	Perennial Flax	
Orphean Warbler	Red-Winged	Pyrenean Flax	
Ortolan Bunting	Grasshopper	Yellow Flax	

woodlands at the farthest reaches of the main path boast a rich assemblage of woodland orchids: Red Helleborine, Bird's Nest Orchid and the curious Violet Limodore. Numerous lizards scuttle in the rocks with the large Green Lizard being the most instantly recognizable. Crested Tits nest in the pine woods, Blue Rock Thrush and Chough are readily seen and heard while the area is just a glide away from the colony of Griffon Vultures in the Gorges de la Jonte.

71 LANUEJOLS	
Maps:	MA p. 141; IGN No. 58
Location:	On Causse Noir E of Millau, SW of Meyrueis
Access:	Easter-time to late autumn (the caves at Dargilan are open everyday to visitors with a one-hour guided tour from spring to autumn, otherwise on a Wednesday afternoon)
Terrain:	Limestone grassland and open stony ground on Causse; railed paths in cave
Specialities:	Causse-country for lime-loving plants; cave for spectacular stalactites

Lanuéjols is little more than a village, but five roads radiate out over the Causse Noir and it has a Gite d'Etap. When walking or driving on roads that cross any of the Causse allow ample time to cover short distances because likely sites follow one on the other.

The D28/29 meanders roughly northwest until it descends to le Rozier at the junction of the Rivers Tarn and Jonte. By stopping at roadsides and wandering around, a staggering number of orchid species can be

*A single flower of the saprophytic orchid, Violet Limodore (*Limodorum abortivum*).*

discovered around Whitsuntide: Lady, Military, Green-Winged, (Early Purple and Monkey are at their best a few weeks before), Sword-Leaved and White Helleborine, Man Orchid and, a little later, massive spikes of Lizard Orchid. There are two insect-mimicking orchids (*Ophrys*) restricted to the region. One of them – Aymoninii's Ophrys grows here under open pines. It is a fly orchid with a slightly broader lip and distinct yellow edging. Ten and more orchid species will be found growing within a short distance of one another near the crossing with the D110 to Millau or close to the paths that make up the Corniche de Causse Noir. This is reached from a turning off the D29 just beyond la Roujarie. It offers superb views of the Gorges de la Jonte and vultures on the evening thermals in the air above le Truel and le Rozier.

The D474 runs north from Lanuéjols to the caves at Dargilan where cast-iron walkways allow the visitor to view stalactites forming huge curtains, a mosque and even petrified waterfalls. Similar sites are to be found simply by wandering on the Causse Noir.

CAUSSE DU LARZAC

72 MILLAU	
Maps:	MA pp. 141 & 155; IGN No. 58
Location:	SE of Millau
Season:	Mainly spring and summer for plants, reptiles and insects
Terrain:	Open stony pastures; some rock formations
Specialities:	Orchids, Causse flowers; raptors; reptiles; butterflies; grasshoppers

The N9 rises out of Millau, providing spectacular views as one nears the top and the road becomes a dual carriageway. After a few kilometres, large rocky outcrops are visible on the right and parking places (a series of interconnecting dirt roads) allow stops for exploration and an excellent introduction to the Causse flowers.

In late May, the ground is a veritable carpet of Alpine Aster and flaxes: Yellow, White and Blue; pea flowers in yellows and reds: (Mountain Kidney Vetch and Purple Kidney Vetch); Garland Flower; the great dried stars of a large stemless thistle, *Carlina acanthifolia*, Red Salsify, the stately Blue Bugle and numerous rock roses.

There are small populations of *Ophrys* (bee orchids) thriving wherever their particular wasp pollinator lives – Early Spider Orchid, Woodcock Orchid, the occasional Yellow Bee Orchid and the Bee Orchid itself. Spikes of Military and Lady Orchids are easily visible from afar and can be numbered in hundreds as one sets out across the Causse.

By early June, the vegetation has changed and Feather Grass has become dominant. Yet every now and again there is a cultivated field, perhaps with Italian Sainfoin as a fodder crop, where butterflies will thrive on the nectar. The blues and the fritillaries occur in abundance. Make sure you photograph the undersides for identification later as three of the fritillaries found in the area – the Glanville, Heath and Provençal – are remarkably alike on the upper surface. The same goes for the blues with several close relatives of Small, Chalkhill and Adonis to identify.

In summer, grasshoppers are everywhere in evidence, from their strident calls to the numbers hopping out of the way as you walk. Two, in particular, are easily recognized by the 'flash' colours they show on take-off – carmine *Oedipoda germanica* and blue *Oedipoda caerulescens*.

Lizards abound in the rocks and on the dry ground. Snakes are common, but not a hazard if one keeps one's eyes open. They provide a source of food for the Short-Toed Eagles which range far and wide over the ground.

Feather Grass (Stipa pennata) is a common sight on the Causses in June.

73 ST ROME DE CERNON AND TIERGUES	
Maps:	MA pp. 141 & 155; IGN No. 65
Location:	SW of Millau on the D992
Season:	Spring through summer to autumn for plants, insects, and birds
Terrain:	Roadside meadows and banks in cultivated region
Specialities:	Endemic orchids; cornfield weeds; Praying Mantis; Red-Backed Shrike

A very rich collection of plants, birds and insects lives within a triangle which starts with the D31 from St Rome-de-Cernon, takes in the D993 running from St Affrique to St Rome-de-Tarn and is completed by the narrow road that returns from Tiergues (D3) to St Rome-de-Cernon.

Fields next to the junction of the D31 and D993 are usually under cultivation with a scarlet blaze of poppies and blue Cornflower at the edges. By crossing the D993 one can walk along a narrow road which rises through woods where Crested Cow-Wheat, Bastard Balm and Red Helleborine grow. The Aveyron Ophrys grows here too. Discovered a decade or so ago, it is frequent within a small area but unknown outside it. Open spaces farther on provide plants of the Bug Orchid, pink Convolvulus and shrubby Wild Thyme.

Beyond Tiergues the road returns to St Rome-de-Cernon and passes small cultivated fields where poppies, Cornflower and Corn-cockle grow. Pyrenean Golden Drop grows at field-edges, and roadside banks provide a haven for insect-mimicking orchids: Yellow Bee, Woodcock, the Aveyron Bee Orchid,

Bee Orchid and Early Spider (see page 66). These same roadsides have rich insect fauna, the most impressive being the Praying Mantis and, in late evening, glow worms.

Red Kite frequent the area and are a familiar sight towards evening, even on the outskirts of Millau. Red-Backed Shrike sit on top of Hawthorn bushes which are worth searching for their 'larders'.

Also worth visiting are the verges of minor roads near St Affrique.

74 LA BLACQUERIE, LA COUVERTOIRADE AND CANYON DE LA DOURBIE	
Maps:	MA p. 155; IGN Nos. 65 & 59
Location:	SE of Millau
Season:	Spring through to autumn for plants and insects
Terrain:	Rocky pastures and banks; cultivated land

By turning off the dual carriageway onto the D7 which leads to la Blacquerie, the visitor immediately meets with an area of botanical contrasts. On the south side of the road the terrain is undulating grazed pasture land with a rich population of orchids (Ophrys, in particular). But on the north side there is a roughly cultivated area with poppies and Cornflowers, making an immediate impact, and scarlet Pheasant's Eye. Shrubs include Amelanchier, Shrubby Box and white Fly Honeysuckle. The few stone walls provide an inevitable hide-away for small lizards. Birds seen include Orphean Warbler, Red-Backed and Great-Grey Shrikes, Hoopoe, Stone Curlew, Corn and Ortolan Buntings.

La Couvertoirade is worth a detour. It is a medieval walled town rising from the flat plain, now restored for working craftsmen.

A newly emerged Black-Veined White butterfly (Aporia crataegi).

The ancient roofs are encrusted with Stonecrop; one of the 'weeds' round the outer walls is Henbane; and doors are adorned with dried heads of stemless Carline Thistle.

In following the signs to Nant and then the D991 through the Canyon de la Dourbie the soil changes from limestone with Pasque Flowers to volcanic where ancient underlying rocks have been pushed to the surface or exposed via roadcuttings. Here, the rocks can be bright pink with hummocks of a Soapwort. A butterfly to look out for is the Black-Veined White, usually present in some numbers where it occurs, but confined to well-defined territories.

The Canyon de la Dourbie is not as awe-inspiring as the gorges cut by the Rivers Jonte and Tarn, but it is still impressive, with plenty of opportunities to scan crags for birds of prey. Photogenic walled villages, like Cantobre perched on limestone pinacles, fit the landscape well: the narrow road through it offers a route up on to the Causse Noir but better views are obtained by climbing the road through Revens.

CAUSSE DE SAUVETERRE

75 MOSTUEJOLS AND TREBANS	
Maps:	MA p. 141; IGN No. 58
Location:	NE of Millau, before the entrance to the Gorges du Tarn
Season:	Spring through to late autumn for flowers and insects
Terrain:	Grassy and rocky roadside slopes; pine woodland
Specialities:	Hillside seepages with wetland plants and insects

Immediately after the bridge in Mostuéjols lies a left turn to le Massegros. After a short distance the road divides. The lower road follows the River Trebans, while the upper leads to le Massegros (*see* the following site). The attraction is a wet valley, where streamside pastures are a haven for butterflies and flowers alike. Stops along the floor of the valley can be profitable, but the richest meadows begin where the road climbs sharply in a series of bends. Wet flushes in the hay meadows below are purple with tall spikes of the Loose-Flowered Orchid, and white drifts turn out to be Poet's Narcissus. Bug Orchid is abundant, but the diminutive Frog Orchid can take some searching for. Other plants in these flower-filled meadows include Meadow Clary, and Lesser Butterfly and Pyramidal Orchids. There are numerous fritillaries, including Marsh and Pearl-Bordered, browns and blues that thrive on the nectar-rich flowers abundant in this area.

Higher up, roadside seepages provide a habitat for the Robust Marsh Orchid. This is a stately species with deep magenta flowers and stems sheathed with unspotted leaves. Where road widening has created waste ground, there are plants of *Aristolochia pistolochia*, one of the two species of Dutchman's Pipe growing locally. The same open boulder-strewn ground provides a haven for lizards (including the Green) and on, occasions, when taking the road in fading light you can see Eagle Owl gliding silently over the dense woodland below. Just before the road reaches the dual carriageway back to Millau, the ground around the railway-line is rich in the inevitable orchids, other limestone grassland species, and butterflies.

76 BOMBES AND LE MASSEGROS	
Maps:	MA p. 141; IGN No. 58
Location:	Causse de Sauveterre NE of Millau
Season:	Spring through to autumn for flowers, insects, reptiles; all year for birds
Terrain:	Undulating Causse; stony pine woodlands
Specialities:	Woodland plants, animals, insects, birds

Instead of the secondary route along the valley bottom, take the primary road up onto the Causse de Sauveterre. The road climbs through small cherry orchards where the ground can be covered with plants of Birthwort. This name derives from its supposedly foetus-shaped flowers: it was once used in a preparation involved in midwifery. In June, the normally impressive spikes of the Lizard

Orchid, almost a metre tall, are hard to miss growing with Pyramidal Orchids.

From where the road gains the plateau to the intersection of minor roads near Bombes, the open wooded country is exceptionally rich in orchids (Man, Lady, Military, and Monkey). Cleared cultivated land near the intersection has very thin soil but the display of 'common' flowers in some years is quite breathtaking – the authors visited the site one year, after there had been fires a few years earlier, to see a patchwork quilt of deep-blue Bugle, Yellow Vetch, and purple Thyme, punctuated by Stinking Hellebore, light-green Spurge and scarlet poppies. Farther on, the woodlands become denser near le Massegros; they are worked to a certain extent as indicated by the occasional pile of trunks. The endemic Fly Orchid (*Ophrys insectifera ssp. aymoninii*), recognized by the distinct yellow edging to the fly 'body', grows along with Red, White and Sword-Leaved Helleborines, stately Military Orchids, drifts of Alpine Asters, Candytuft, and large areas covered with White and Yellow Rock Roses.

In places the branches of the pines seem almost alive with the busy *si si si* of Crested

A female Siskin (Carduelis spinus).

Tits. Siskin, Crossbill, and Firecrest make use of the pine forests and raptors include Golden and Short-Toed Eagles, Goshawk and Sparrowhawk.

From le Massegros the D995, travelling west to Severac le Château, offers rolling stone-strewn Causses country with large areas covered by Shrubby Box. These bushes shelter innumerable orchids and there are colourful displays of lime-loving plants in open areas.

Alternatively, the visitor has the choice of the D67 which meanders to the main N9, or a longer journey on the D32 across the Causse de Sauveterre. Both trips will take much longer than the distance seems to indicate because of the attractions of the pine and mixed woodland.

To add to a long list of orchids seen elsewhere there are various helleborines – Broad-Leaved, Narrow-Lipped and Dark-Red (at their best in July). Blue Aphyllanthes is abundant and the occasional cultivated field offers tall yellow spikes of Woad as well as other 'weeds'. Deer are more often heard than seen. There is plenty of evidence and occasional sightings of Wild Boar, Pine Marten and Red Squirrel. In late June and July the butterfly fauna is particularly rich with numerous fritillaries (including Marsh, High Brown, Cardinal, Silver-Washed and Queen of Spain), blues, skippers and browns (including the Dryad) and White Admiral. If time permits, a series of small roads eventually leads to the Col de Montmirat.

An added attraction of the D32 is that it offers access to the Gorges du Tarn by way of a spectacular route to les Vigues. Alternatively, the D46 travelling towards Pointe Sublime and then along the top of the gorge to meet the D43 offers stunning views and vertiginous glimpses into the depths below before descending into la Malène.

CAUSSES MEJEAN

77 GORGES DU TARN (FROM BELOW)	
Maps:	MA p. 141; IGN No. 58
Location:	NE of Millau
Season:	All year for birds; plants in spring and summer
Terrain:	Preciptious cliffs; river-banks
Specialities:	Crag-nesting birds; cliff flora; scenery

Stretching for some 50km, the Gorges du Tarn is the best known of all features in the Causses region. The River Tarn rises on Mt Lozère at an altitude of 1,520m and descends in a series of torrents from the slopes of the Cévennes. The course of the river has been determined over the centuries by a system of faults and its flow is fed by the run-off from the Causses Méjean and the Causse de Sauveterre. From above or below, it is hard to comprehend that the cliffs of calcareous and dolomitic limestone were formed at the bottom of the sea by deposition of the shells of marine plankton and larger animals. For the paleontologist, they have provided a rich source of fossils including giant ammonites and a complete plesiosaur skeleton (now exhibited in Millau museum).

Although the gorge can be viewed from the road that runs its length, a more leisurely journey can be made via canoe, hired from la Malène, or by booking a barque in the same village. For a fee, the trip involves a journey from la Malène to Cirques des Baumes and return by taxi. These trips run every day from May to September, except for national holidays.

Dipper and Grey Wagtail are in constant view near the water and Black Redstart are familiar in and around the villages and settlements along the gorge.

The cliffs above provide nesting sites for Kestrel, Peregrine, several pairs of Eagle Owls, Short-Toed Eagle and the occasional Golden Eagle. Blue Rock Thrushes can be seen on the crags as well as Chough and Crag Martin. Around le Rozier, Griffon Vulture have become a familiar sight.

78 GORGES DU TARN (FROM ABOVE)	
Maps:	MA p. 141; IGN No. 58
Location:	NE of Millau
Season:	All year for birds; plants in spring and summer
Terrain:	Preciptious cliffs; river-banks
Specialities:	Crag-nesting birds; cliff flora; scenery

On the northern side it is possible to climb out of the gorge on any one of four roads from: le Rozier, les Vignes, la Malène, or St Enémie. Though narrow roads with hairpin bends are not to everyone's taste the views make them worth the effort and care. Like most French roads they are well surfaced.

Pointe Sublime, above the Cirque des Baumes, is one of the best-known vantage points and on a clear day the view into the gorge is staggering. Pink splashes down below are formed by a soapwort (*Saponaria ocymoides*). Woodlands near the view-point are good for orchids and roadside seepages on roads out of the gorge often have magenta spikes of the Robust Marsh Orchid.

On the southern side, it is worth travelling along the gorge to St Enémie then taking the D986 which climbs slowly out of the gorge and provides exceptional views and a chance to scan the cliffs opposite with binoculars for raptors. For the walker, paths from le Rozier offer a route for climbing high above the gorge. The route lies on the GR6a, one of the long-distance footpaths forming the Grande Randonée network, and leads up to Capluc. To reach this outcrop means climbing for the last part on vertical iron ladders but the view along the Gorge de la Jonte to the limestone pinnacles of the Corniche de Méjean is well worth while, especially with Crag Martin and Chough wheeling around the rock. Below, the view plunges to Peyreleau and the junction of Rivers Tarn and Jonte. By following the GR6a and then branching off on marked paths, a circular tour is possible via Col de Francbouteille, Belvedere, Rocher de Cinglegros and back along the gorge to le Rozier. The route is not for those who suffer from vertigo because

The spectacular Gorges du Tarn from the cliffs above, viewed from the D986 which climbs the south-eastern side of the gorge from St Enémie. The gorge, from Florac to le Rozier extends for about 90km. The most dramatic cliff scenery occurs along the 60km stretch between St Enémie and le Rozier.

Scarce Swallowtail
Iphiclides podalirius W 64–90

Stop at any flower-filled roadside or wander in unspoiled meadows on hillsides or in valleys, and it will not be long before you notice Swallowtail butterflies. Their strong flight, size and colour make them unmistakeable. The so-called Common Swallowtail (*Papilio machaon*) appears to be a much deeper yellow than the Scarce Swallowtail, even in flight. Certainly in France, the name Scarce seems to be a misnomer. It picked up that title by visiting Britain on a handful of occasions over the last couple of centuries. With the vertical black stripes on its pale wings, it is a very handsome creature and, fortunately for the photographer, when it has located a suitable source of nectar it will sit with its wings open. Its eggs are laid on Blackthorn, Hawthorn, Cherry and other fruit trees and the caterpillars are handsomely striped. In France, there are two other closely related species: Southern Swallowtail, and Corsican Swallowtail.

part of the descent into the gorge is via metal stairways and crampons set into rocks. However, the route provides unrivalled opportunities to look at the birds of the gorge, particularly raptors. From Capluc, the path crosses abandoned terraces where Military,

Man and Lady Orchids thrive with rock roses, vetches, and white daisies. Butterflies on the wing at Whitsun include Adonis Blue, Green Hairstreak, Scarce Swallowtail and the Cleopatra (a brimstone with large orange patches on the forewings of the males). Lizards hide in the old walls. Higher up, one meets Shrubby Box forming the underlayer in pine woods. The rocky crevices of the Corniche des Causses Méjean shelter an interesting collection of alpines – Pyrenean Flax, White Rock Rose and Alpine Rock Rose.

79 LE ROZIER: GORGES DE LA JONTE	
Maps:	MA p. 141; IGN No. 58
Location:	From le Rozier, NE of Millau
Season:	All year for birds; spring through to autumn for plants
Terrain:	Rriver-banks; roadsides; cliffs
Specialities:	Griffon Vulture and other birds of prey; cliff-dwelling plants

The Gorges de la Jonte is not quite as dramatic as the Gorges du Tarn, but neither is it as well frequented by visitors. It has a wilder feel which is certainly enhanced by the likelihood of seeing considerable numbers of Griffon Vulture wheeling overhead. The project to re-establish these lords of the air near le Truel has been the subject of televison documentaries, and the efforts of local activists have brought the species from the point of extinction in France to a thriving colony of upwards of seventy birds. To see twenty or thirty of these soaring on thermals in the late afternoon above le Truel or le Rozier is the

The beautiful St Bernard's Lily (Anthericum liliago) is frequent on roadsides in parts of the Causses.

were released into the wild and the population is large enough to be self-sustaining. Elsewhere, the birds of the Gorges de la Jonte are the same as those of the Gorges du Tarn.

From Meyrueis the D986 climbs above the Gorges de la Jonte towards the Aven Armand, a cave which is rated as one of the underground wonders of the world. The formations within are quite amazing and access can be gained from the end of March to the beginning of November via an access tunnel 188m long. This leads into the main chambers, to reveal bizarre concretions formed on boulder materials. Aptly named the Forêt Vierge, the shapes evoke images of Cypress and palm trees from up to 3m in diameter at the base and with some reaching a height of 15–25m. In addition there are about 400 stalagmites with shapes strange enough to rival the 'trees': slender needles, pyramids and mushrooms, all beautifully lit to enhance the impact on the eye.

The road continues over the Causses Méjean, passing through orchid-rich woodland and alongside fields with a patchwork of blue Cornflowers and red poppies bordered by dark pines.

A left turn at Hures-la-Parade onto the D63 brings you down into the gorge via hairpin bends, superb views, and roadsides full of St Bernard's Lily. Again, about 3km along the D63 from Hures-la-Parade, is a right turning via a narrow road that passes through botanically rich woodland. The GR6a crosses it at St Pierres les Tripiers and this affords a way of joining the path. This road too, brings one into the gorge, just above le Truel and the views are, if anything, even better. It is marked on Michelin maps as 'difficult' but with care is worth taking, in the evening, for possible views of vultures.

highlight of any trip to the gorges. From a distance they can look like hangliders, so great is the wingspan (up to 2.8m in a full grown adult).

The vultures are carrion feeders and deaths in the vast flocks of sheep grazing on the Causses provided adequate food supplies. Poisoning to eradicate foxes and other 'vermin', together with hunting, depleted numbers until a stock of captive birds from zoos (including injured birds), were used to establish a breeding centre in le Truel. Birds bred in captivity in the 1970s and early 1980s

10. CEVENNES

INTRODUCTION

Strictly speaking, the Cévennes National Park embraces considerably more than the mountains of the Cévennes which form the south-eastern wall of the Massif Central. The park has a superficial area of 840km² and includes the major limestone Causse within a triangle having Millau, Mende and Alès as its vertices.

The landscape is one of great contrasts, from green hills and lush forests to deep gorges and stony plateaux, barren in summer but a riot of colour with hundreds of species of wildflowers in spring and early summer.

The highest mountains are part of the volcanic wall which originally surrounded the basin in which the limestone, forming the Causses of today, was slowly deposited. Mt Aigoual (1,545m), Mt

A lovely hybrid daffodil, Narcissus poeticus x N. pseudonarcissus, *is frequent in this area.*

Bouges (1,400m), and Mt Lozère (1,700m) are composed of granite or schist and their vegetation differs markedly from that of the limestone Causses which are lower (between 900m and 1,200m). Summers are hot and sudden thunderstorms, clearing the air, are a feature of the region. Winters can be bitterly cold with the chilling effect of the winds which sweep off the peaks across the plateaux. This harshness of climate has never made life in the Causse an easy proposition and what farms there are seem scattered far and wide. Agriculture is 'basic' – something for which the

naturalist can be grateful because many plants rare elsewhere still exist in the Cévennes. There are woods, hundreds of miles of hedgerows, and lush flower-filled meadows. Where else can one still see fields ablaze with scarlet poppies, dotted with blue Cornflowers and occasional pink Corncockles, for example?

There are extensive forests in the Cévennes. In many of the higher areas these are established pine plantations managed for their timber and boasting a rich flora and fauna. Broad-leaved woodlands of Sweet Chestnut, Oak and Beech clothe the slopes and valley bottoms.

Away from the heights and their volcanic soils, expanses of gorse are left behind and on the plateaux and the limestone flanks of the hills there is a bewildering variety of orchids to be found. In fact, the area has become a place of pilgrimage for botanists – amateur and professional alike – who converge on the region in late May and early June, from all over Europe. The sole object is to see an abundance of orchids (Man, Military, Monkey, Lady, Lizard, Fly, and Bee) that may very well have become rare in their home countries.

Likewise, birdwatchers have discovered, in the Cévennes, skies where one is seldom out of vision of some large raptor – Black and Red Kite, Booted, Short-Toed and Golden Eagles, Hen and Montagu's Harriers, Goshawk, Buzzard, Sparrowhawk, and Kestrel.

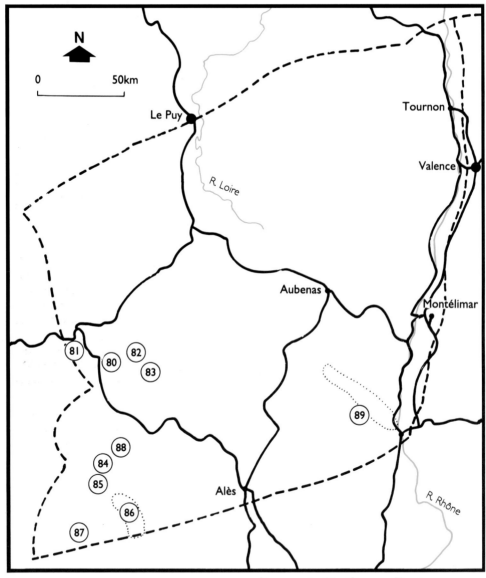

N

0   50km

Tournon

Le Puy

Valence

R. Loire

Aubenas

Montélimar

⑧⑴ ⑧⓪ ⑧② ⑧③

⑧⑨

⑧⑧ ⑧④ ⑧⑤ ⑧⑥

Alès

⑧⑦

R. Rhône

Gorges in particular are the home of vultures – Griffon Vultures as residents (as at le Truel) and Egyptian Vultures as visitors. Other residents include Eagle Owl, Ortolan Bunting, Crested Tit and Little Bustard.

Above: *map of the Cévennes. The sites are numbered as in the text. Only main roads and the major rivers of the region are shown.*

Opposite: *Globeflowers (Trollius europaeus) are common in wet hillside meadows.*

FIFTY INTERESTING SPECIES TO LOOK FOR

Bee-Eater	Griffon Vulture	Two-Tailed Pasha	Cévennes Pasque
Black Redstart	Great Spotted	Ascalaphids	Flower
Bonelli's Eagle	Woodpecker	Carpenter Bee	Common Pasque
Booted Eagle	Lesser Spotted	Bird's Nest Orchid	Flower
Golden Eagle	Woodpecker	Creeping Ladies'	Poet's Narcissus
Short-Toed Eagle	Middle Spotted	Tresses	Sticky Catchfly
Goshawk	Woodpecker	Elder-Flowered Orchid	Violet Limodore
Honey Buzzard	Badger	Globeflower	Whorled Solomon's
Eagle Owl	Genet	Grape Hyacinth	Seal
Long-Eared Owl	Apollo	Red Helleborine	Light-Green
Scop's Owl	Black-Veined White	Sword-Leaved	Wintergreen
Peregrine Falcon	Marbled Fritillary	Helleborine	Nodding Wintergreen
Red Kite	Marbled White	White Helleborine	One-Flowered
Sparrowhawk	Pale Clouded Yellow	Martagon Lily	Wintergreen
Egyptian Vulture	Purple-Shot Copper	Mountain Pansy	

80 COL DE MONTMIRAT

Maps:	MA p. 142; IGN No. 58
Location:	Between Mende and Florac
Season:	Spring to late summer for flowers and insects; birds all year (when col is open)
Terrain:	Steep meadows; wet flushes; pine woodland
Specialities:	Sub-alpine calcicole flora; Golden Eagle

The Col de Montmirat can be reached by travelling south on the N106 from Mende or north on the same road, north, from Florac. As the road descends on the north side of the col there are very different soils on opposite sides of the road – on the west side, brooms and other plants of acid soils; on the east, steep mountain grassland on limestone.

The meadows extend from where the series of sharp road-bends begins up to the col. There is the GR44 path and a hotel at the top. In late May or early June, stately spikes of Yellow Gentian are only just coming into flower as the pasque flowers are at their best. Both Common Pasque Flower and Cévennes Pasque Flower grow on the slopes with Grape Hyacinth. Orchids are inevitable on the limestone in the Cévennes and here the 'assembly' is characteristic of sub-alpine pastures – red and yellow Elder-flowered Orchid; Burnt-Tip, Early Purple, Frog, Green-Winged, and Lesser Butterfly. Globeflowers grow in the wet flushes close to the road with narcissus and Arnica on the slopes. Woodlands begin high on the slopes. They are a mixture of plantations and established pine woodland. Golden Eagle are frequently seen; Buzzard and Long-Eared Owl nest there. In June and later months, the abundance of flowers attracts numerous butterflies including Black-Veined White, Marbled White, Clouded Yellow and Apollo.

**8	TOUR LE CHOIZAL**	
Maps:	MA p. 142; IGN No. 58
Location:	SW of Mende on Causse de Sauveterre
Season:	For flowers, spring to autumn; birds all year depending on snow
Terrain:	Established pine woodland on flat and slopes
Specialities:	Woodland flora and birds

Chanac, on the northern edge of the Causse Noir, is where the D31 begins, continues south-east and then branches west across the Causse. In so doing, it skirts the edges of the forests which plunge down to the Lot valley where soils change from limestone to acidic.

Roughly half-way between the branching from the D44 and where it meets the D986 at Tour le Choizal (a fortified farm), tracks lead into pine forest. Almost immediately, in the half-light clumps of White Helleborine are visible with a dozen and more stems; Bird's Nest Orchid are scattered under the pines. Thick moss cushions adorn the woodland floor together with a deep rich humus. In these woods an unusual number of winter-greens (*Pyrolas*) grow, plants characteristic of long-established pine woods. There is Light-Green Wintergreen, Lesser and Intermediate Wintergreens, Nodding Wintergreen and, where the moss-cushioned slopes begin, One-Flowered Wintergreen, sends up its tiny parasol flowers. Yellow Bird's Nest, a sapro-phyte and close relative of the wintergreens, grows under mixed pine and Beech. Here the moss cushions are also threaded by a tiny or-chid, Creeping Ladies' Tresses, which flowers in late June. Crested Tit, Firecrest and Greater, Middle and Lesser Spotted Wood-peckers inhabit the forest. Red Squirrel, Pine

One-Flowered Wintergreen
Moneses uniflora H 5–10

Wintergreens are plants characteristic of ancient woodlands where there is a rich humus layer on the floor and, above that, a thick cushion of moss. They are all attractive plants with pretty, hanging flowers but *Moneses uniflora* is perhaps the most delicate. As its specific name suggests, it has just one flower, held like a tiny white umbrella on a nodding stalk, no more than a few centimetres long; the style protrudes from the flower forming the 'handle'. In parts of the Cévennes and the woods of the Causses they are a familiar site dotting the ground, their white flowers showing through forest gloom.

Marten and Badger are resident, but seldom seen by the casual observer. Farther along the road to the junction at Tour le Choizal the fields are blue-tinted by Cornflowers. Similar sites occur in many places in the woods on the Causse de Sauveterre.

*Yellow Bird's Nest (*Monotropa hypopitys) *is a saprophyte, found occasionally in pine and Beech woods.*

82 MT LOZERE (ASCENT)	
Maps:	MA p. 142; IGN No. 59
Location:	SE of Mende
Access:	Ski resort in winter; roads clear
Season:	Flowers, spring - autumn
Terrain:	Mountain pastures; woodland; outcrops
Specialities:	Orchids, Wild Tulip, Poet's Narcissus

The route to Mt Lozère is well signposted from Mende as the mountain is a winter ski resort. For the naturalist, the potential interest begins as soon as the D901 leaves the N88 at the Col de la Tourette and begins the climb out of the Lot valley. The rock changes to limestone which flanks the mountain, then back to schist and gneiss higher up. Roadside pastures on limestone boast Military and Lady Orchids as well as a small-flowered form of Early Spider Orchid (*Ophrys araneola*).

There are several photogenic villages *en route*, such as Bagnols-les-Bains, and the roadside cliffs are covered with saxifrages. From le Bleymard, the D20 follows a stream to le Mazel where the the GR68-44 crosses the route. Along this stretch, particularly down near the stream, the flowers (and butterflies) are abundant – Whorled Solomon's Seal, Mountain Pansy, Greater Meadow Rue, Water Aven, Spiked Rampion, Poet's Narcissus and Elder-Flowered Orchid in yellow and magenta.

This picture is repeated in seepages up towards the Col de Finiel (1,541m) but the col, itself is disappointingly bare. Narcissus (both white and yellow) grow with Wood Anemone and the occasional Wild Tulip shelters in the pine plantations. By way of compensation, the views are seemingly end-less, stretching to Mt Aigoual, the Causses, and the Tanargue massif. Paths strike out from the col to the Sommet de Finiels (1,699m) or, via the source of the Tarn, to Pic Cassini, where eagle and buzzard soar.

83 MT LOZERE (DESCENT)	
Maps:	MA p. 142; IGN No. 59
Location:	SE of Mende
Access:	Ski resort in winter, roads clear
Season:	Flowers, spring to autumn
Terrain:	Boulder-strewn scrub; mountain pastures; woodland; outcrops
Specialities:	Wet flushes; woodlands; birds of prey; mountain birds

The road south from the Col de Finiels follows the route taken by Robert Louis

Stephenson on his donkey-trek through the Cévennes. The southern aspect of Mt Lozère presents slopes strewn with giant granite boulders and outcrops, a scrub of Bilberry, and wet flushes where White Narcissi grow in profusion.

You can quickly get away from the road to where the terrain is wild, open and offers the chance of seeing Merlin, Booted, Short-Toed and Golden Eagles and, if lucky, Hen or Montagu's Harriers. Smaller birds abound and one is never far from Wheatear, Whinchat, Stonechat and Rock Pipit. By striking out west from the road and keeping roughly to a contour the terrain suits Rock Sparrows, Rock Bunting, Black Redstart, and Alpine Accentor.

The road follows a stream which becomes a torrent rushing towards le Pont-de-Montvert where it joins the embryonic Tarn. Soon the slopes become clothed with Oak and Sweet Chestnut. Above and below the road west from le Pont-de-Montvert the slopes are densely wooded. These woods have a rich bird population which includes, among others, Lesser Spotted Woodpecker. Nightingales are common and there is a wide range of warblers, tits and finches as well as Buzzard, Goshawk and Sparrowhawk.

The D998 joins the N106 north of Florac and the road leads, via a lengthy series of hairpin bends, through soils of volcanic origin yellow with broom, to the Col de Montmirat where limestone appears again.

84 MT AIGOUAL (ASCENT AND SUMMIT)	
Maps:	MA p. 142; IGN No. 58
Location:	E of Millau
Seasons:	Spring to autumn for flowers; snow-covered in winter
Terrain:	Mountain pastures; woodland; wet flushes
Specialities:	Orchid, narcissi; raptors

The best way of investigating the great rounded bulk of Mt Aigoual is by means of a circular tour. Travelling east from Meyrueis to the Col de Perjuret allows a clockwise circuit; the D986 south from Meyrueis begins the anticlockwise trip. The choice is difficult to make because of the temptation to take other minor roads on the way down.

The road south from Meyrueis climbs initially through mixed chestnut and Beech woodland, but as the altitude increases, pines start to dominate. After the initial climb the road reaches a 'plateau' with the wooded slopes of Aigoual's higher reaches to the east. Drifts of white in fields away from the road turn out to be countless thousands of Poet's Narcissus, whereas roadside verges themselves yield uncommon plants (Bug and Lesser Butterfly Orchids).

Around the beginning of June, the wooded route to the summit offers masses of Elder-Flowered Orchids growing on wet verges and there is also the chance to visit L'Abîme de Bramabiau, the course of an underground river which emerges over an impressive waterfall.

The summit is dominated by a meteorological observatory. (On the northern side the run-off feeds the Rivers Tarn and Lot which eventually run into the Atlantic; the

A female Stonechat (Saxicola torquata) on the way to her nest.

Hérault, rising on the southern slopes, pours into the Mediterranean Sea making the mountain an important watershed.)

About 1.5km below the summit, signs point to the '*Sentier des Botanistes*' which is a circular route of about twenty minutes' walking time. It passes below an arboretum created by Charles Flahault, assistant to Georges Fabre, with the intention of studying exotic essences. Views to the south are superb and large raptors (occasionally Egyptian or Griffon Vultures) can often be seen soaring above and over the landscape below. On exceptionally clear days, the view from the observatory stretches to Mont Blanc in the Haute Savoie, and Maladetta in the Pyrenees.

85 MT AIGOUAL (DESCENT)	
Maps:	MA p. 142; IGN No. 58
Location:	E of Millau
Season:	Spring to autumn for flowers; birds all year
Terrain:	Mountain pastures, woodland and wet flushes; snow-covered in winter
Specialities:	Narcissi, Sticky Catchfly, Purple-Shot Copper

The descent on the D9 leading north from the summit offers the chance to set out on the GR6b, or lower down on the GR66 (the paths meet at the Col del Bes). Yellow Tulips grow in open areas with Martagon Lily at forest edges and in clearings. Herb Paris is found in shadier habitat where pine plantations give way to Beech. Raptors can usually be seen, as can the occasional Red and Roe Deer, and Capercaillie may be heard.

Via the D9, the road leads to the Col de Perjuret where limestone appears again with Military and Lady Orchids. An alternative route involves ignoring the fact that the Michelin map suggests that the route is difficult and turning off from Cabrillac on the D19 to Rousse. Almost immediately, the slopes are white with narcissi and growing amongst them are yellow Daffodils and *Narcissus* x *incomparabilis* an aptly named natural hybrid between them. Globeflower, Aconite-Leaved Buttercup, Marsh Orchid, lousewort and Spiked Rampion complete the picture. The road is narrow but open and soon crosses soils on schist where the roadside boasts Sticky Catchfly and a large-flowered broom, *Cytisus sessilifolius*.

Butterflies include Scarce and Purple-Shot Coppers, Pale Clouded Yellow, Orange Tip, Cleopatra, and Marbled Fritillary, and Hummingbird Hawk Moths hover over warm banks. Buzzard, Short-Toed Eagle, Red Kite, Scop's Owl, and Hoopoe are some of the birds seen and heard in the area.

From Rousse it is possible to travel via the Fraissinet valley, to Meyrueis and then through the Gorges de la Jonte.

86 HERAULT	
Maps:	MA pp. 142 and 156; IGN Nos 58, 59 and 66
Location:	SE of Mt Aigoual
Season:	All year for birds; flowers from spring to autumn
Terrain:	Rocky river valley; woodlands varying from sub-alpine to Mediterranean vegetation
Specialities:	Varied flora and fauna from montane to Mediterranean

Almost from source to sea, the course of the River Hérault is closely followed by easily negotiable roads. The river rises high on the southern slopes of Mt Aigoual near Col de

Prat Peyrot at an altitude of 1,400m, and the changes in flora and fauna over its length make the trip a living 'textbook'.

Close to its source, it plunges in a series of waterfalls – Cascade de l'Hérault – then bursts through a montane landscape with granite outcrops and a ground-cover of Bilberry and low Juniper.

The young river flows through mature Beech forest where Meadow Saxifrage and Wood Anemone cover the floor in spring. The woods provide one of the sites for a rare longhorn beetle (*Rosalia alpina*), which has black spots on a slim blue body, antennae nearly twice its body length, and is protected in most areas where it is known.

Wetlands, where the trees open out, form summer grazing areas but in spring they are white with narcissi. Globeflowers are abundant and there are confusing marsh orchids (broad-leaved with magenta flowers and spotted leaves), and Elder-Flowered Orchids with yellow or magenta flowers and immaculate leaves. From any small bridge Dipper and Grey Wagtail can be watched at leisure. At Vallerague there is Sweet Chestnut but soon the evergreen Holm Oak is the river's companion.

The most dramatic changes in vegetation take place with a change of soils, where schists give way to limestone and Sage-Leaved Cistus makes a first appearance. Here, as throughout much of the southern Cévennes, False Acacia is planted along roads and riversides, recognized by its strings of white 'pea' flowers in spring.

Lush woodlands with White Oak, Holm Oak, Ash and Alder accompany the river from Pont de l'Hérault to Ganges and the bird life is rich, with Hoopoe, Greater and Lesser Spotted Woodpeckers, Buzzard, Sparrowhawk, Goshawk and Nightingale.

Rocky limestone hills beyond Brissac are rich in orchids, especially Monkey, Man, Lady and the insect-mimicking *Ophrys*. Mediterranean shrubs such as Turpentine Bush, *Cistus*, and Holm Oak form a maquis where birds such as Subalpine and Sardinian Warblers are the usual inhabitants, with numerous small lizards.

87 ALZON	
Maps:	MA p. 156; IGN No. 65
Location:	SE of Millau
Season:	All year for birds; insects and flowers, spring to late autumn
Terrain:	Lush woodland; calcareous meadows
Specialities:	Insects: butterflies and Ascalaphids; orchids (woodland and grassland species)

To reach Alzon, take the D7, which lies 8km south-east of la Cavalerie, as far as Saucliere and then the D999 beyond it. About 1.5km before the village of Alzon, the road sweeps into a tight bend under one arch of a viaduct and then out under another. Rough ground between the bends offers a place to park and a choice of routes to the woods and meadows above. Easier access is offered by going farther along the road and climbing up to the long-disued railway track base, but then it is possible to miss the Red Helleborine and Violet Limodore that grow in the woods.

Once through the woods and up on to the meadows above, Man Orchids appear in thousands. They hybridize naturally with Monkey Orchid growing here, with the offspring called x *Orchiaceras bergonii*. Butterflies visit both species and facilitate cross-pollination. The result has flowers with elongated 'legs' of a Man Orchid but with added red to the extremities. Early in the year

The Spotted Fritillary (Melitaea didyma) is probably the most variably patterned butterfly in Europe. It is widely distributed in a variety of habitats throughout much of southern and central Europe, from sea level to 1800m. It is frequent in warm grassy places in parts of the Cévennes and may be seen from May to September.

Early Purple and Green-Winged Orchids flower but they are over by the end of May, when the Lizard Orchid begins to open and the flower-tails uncurl. This is the time to start looking at the butterflies which abound on these slopes. Black-Veined White are present in numbers as are Scarce Swallowtail. Later on, Cleopatra, fritillaries (Cardinal, Silver-Washed and Queen of Spain in summer), and Marbled White appear. There are Lesser Purple Emperor and Southern White Admiral in the woodlands with the occasional Camberwell Beauty and Large Tortoiseshell. Day-flying moths include Hummingbird Hawk, both Broad- and Narrow-Bordered Bee Hawks, Cream Spot and Jersey Tigers.

Ascalaphids (*Libelloides coccajus*), relations of the ant lion resembling dragonflies at first sight, are one of the unusual insects in the meadows; another is the large blue-black carpenter bee, *Xylocopa violacea*. Plants of Henbane and Deadly Nightshade grow around the ruined settlement on the hill-top and cracks in the walls are home to lizards.

Other sites for butterflies and orchids exist at many points along the route from Alzon to le Vigan. Detours to the north (D231 to le Villaret and D189 to Peyraube) bring you right into the wild south of the Cévennes.

88 CORNICHE DES CEVENNES	
Maps:	MA p. 142; IGN No. 59
Location:	SE of Florac
Season:	All year (snow permitting) for views and birds; spring through to autumn for flowers and insects
Terrain:	Limestone plateau giving way to schist ridge
Specialities:	Dinosaur footprints; scenery; calcicole flora; raptors

The route between Florac and St Jean-du-Gard follows the top of a long ridge which starts on limestone but gives way to schist near le Pompidou. With valleys on either side, it offers outstanding views. It is essential to choose a fine day, perhaps with the clarity of late-afternoon light, when the low sun brings the landscape into sharp relief.

The road first climbs to St Laurent-de-Trèves where dinosaur footprints have been found on the limestone promontary near the village. Dating from some 180 million years ago, they are thought to belong to bipedal dinosaurs, around 4m tall, tramping around the shallow lagoon that existed there. This site offers some idea of the vastness of the Cévennes National Park with views over Mts Aigoual and Lozere and, from north to south, three of the Grandes Causse – Sauveterre, Méjean and Noir.

For the botanical purist, the road from St Laurent via the Col du Rey to Barre-des-Cévennes and then on the D20 to the N106, offers a potentially more attractive route via limestone country, rich in orchids, where roadside stops can reveal Frog, Fragrant, Twayblade, Lesser Butterfly, Early Purple, Green-Winged, Bug, Burnt-Tip and Elder-Flowered Orchids.

There are plenty of opportunities to see birds just by stopping at view-points to drink in the spectacle afforded by the Corniche des Cévennes – Crag Martin, Alpine Swift, Buzzard, Red Kite, and the occasional eagle.

89 GORGES DE L'ARDECHE	
Maps:	MA p. 143; IGN No. 59
Location:	NW of Orange
Season:	All year for birds; spring and summer for flowers and insects
Terrain:	Gorge; cliffs; alluvial banks
Specialities:	Egyptian Vulture, Bonelli's Eagle, Genet; rich flora; insects

The fast-flowing waters of the River Ardèche have, over countless millennia, sculpted deep gorges in the limestone plateaus of Bas Vivarais. In 1980 this portion of the Ardèche and surrounding territory was declared as a Nature Reserve (1,520ha). At points within the reserve the river is around 350m below the plateaux and its meanderings have created pebble deposits on which alluvial soils have built up banks.

Plateaux, terraces and 'beaches' have a luxuriant plant cover which, in terms of species, owes much to the proximity of the Mediterranean Sea. Yet there is a marked difference in species growing in shady or open parts of the gorges: Holm Oak, Montpellier Maple, Strawberry Tree and Juniper occupy the open spots, while Downy Oak and Shrubby Box thrive in the shade. The Mediterranean influence is strongly evident in the flora of the gorge bottom – Kermes Oak, Grey-Leaved Cistus, Blue Aphyllanthe and Lavender.

The effect of a variety of climatic influences over the history of the gorges has meant that particular plant genera are represented by several species of northern, Atlantic or Mediterranean origin. For example, there are three junipers (*Juniperus communis, J. phoenicea* and *J. oxycedrus*) and three honeysuckles (*Lonicera periclymenum, L. etrusca* and *L. implexa*)

The Strawberry Tree is the foodplant of the Two-Tailed Pasha, a large, magnificent butterfly that flies in the gorge. Praying Mantids feed healthily on an abundance of butterflies and other insects. Badger and Genet are the most important of the larger mammals known in the park, though visitors will be lucky to see either of them.

Although Golden Eagle and Peregrine Falcon have disappeared from the gorge in comparatively recent times, Egyptian Vulture

A general view in the Ardèche valley.

and Bonelli's Eagle still nest there – alone enough to justify special status for the area. Other birds of prey to be seen within the reserve include Short-Toed Eagle, Sparrow-hawk, Goshawk, Honey Buzzard, Hobby and at least two owls – Scop's Owl and the Eagle Owl (known aptly as *le Petit Duc* and *le Grand Duc* respectively). Alpine Swift and Crag Martin nest as neighbours on the cliffs. Bee-Eaters visit to feed and three shrikes are recorded – Red-Backed, Woodchat and Great Grey.

The gorge has been inhabited since pre-historic times and remains show that Auroch and rhinoceros were hunted there. (Man's activities have helped shape the diversity of habitats.) But nowadays the problem for the gorge is tourism. In high summer, up to 2,000 canoes negotiate the river each day, there are numerous other visitors, and in spring people are certainly not averse to pick-ing bunches of a dwarf iris, *Iris lutescens*, and paeonies. The pressure on the natural in-habitants is almost unbearable.

Overleaf: *the beautiful Grey-Leaved Cistus (Cistus albidus) in flower in spring.*

131

11. NORTHERN FRENCH ALPS

INTRODUCTION

The French Alps are so rich in natural life and undisturbed habitats that it hardly seems necessary to pick out sites of interest at all. Almost anywhere in the mountains will prove to be of interest to the naturalist. Three out of the six French National Parks lie within the Alpine region, as well as two major Regional Natural Parks. Indeed, many areas outside these protected zones are of equal interest. For convenience on describing sites we have divided the Alpine area of France into two sections – north and south – though there is no clear physical divide between the two.

Although the Alps only occupy a very small proportion of France, they actually cover a huge area, stretching some 250km from Lake Geneva to the coast. The region described here includes the area north of Grenoble and Briançon, westwards as far as the Rhône valley, and it therefore includes an extensive area of Pre-Alps and some flatter land north of Lyons.

The climate is essentially Continental, but strongly modified by the presence of the mountains. The weather is generally unpredictable, as in most mountain regions, and the relatively warm summers may be broken by periods of rain. Winters are very cold over most of the region, and spring comes extremely late to the higher parts.

Mountains are an irresistible lure to naturalists, and these are no exception. The loss of so much natural habitat throughout the lowlands of Europe, including France, has emphasized the already-rich mountains, where so much more has survived. The steep slopes, long winters and generally difficult conditions have prevented intensive agriculture from becoming pervasive, allowing a more traditional form of agriculture to persist. This has produced some of the most attractive and species-rich of mountain habitats – enclosed meadows and high pastures, both a mass of flowers in summer, especially on lime-rich soils. Forests are widespread, too, as a convenient way of making use of difficult land, and many of these are managed descendants of natural forest, rich in species. Generally, there has been much less mass-coniferization of upland forests than in the lowland counterparts. There are also numerous lakes in the uplands, many of them natural, but, increasingly, some man-made, created specially in association with hydroelectric power schemes, or as reservoirs. In this area, there are very large natural lakes – Geneva, d'Annecy, du Bourget – and numerous

Marsh Gentian (Gentiana pneumonanthe), flowering in autumn.

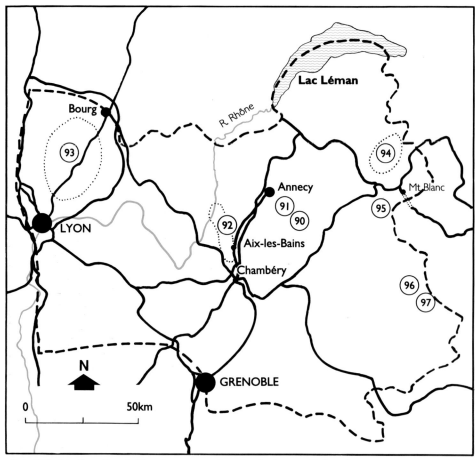

Map of the Northern French Alps. Sites are numbered as in the text. Only main roads and the major rivers of the region are shown.

smaller ones scattered throughout. Preeminently, though, this is the region of high peaks, and it includes the highest mountain in Europe, Mt Blanc (4,807m), as well as many others over 3,000m.

There is a tendency to ignore lower-lying areas near high mountains, because sights become set on the peaks as they are approached. However, the lower-lying areas west of the Alps in this region are of enormous interest, with superb forested hills, meadows, lakes and areas of limestone. Close to the Rhône valley, north of Lyon, the extraordinary area of the Dombes is a paradise for ornithologists.

Hay meadows on the Alpine slopes near Chamonix. Fortunately, the French Alps are still full of such sights, though they have disappeared from much of the rest of Europe.

FIFTY INTERESTING SPECIES TO LOOK FOR

Alpine Accentor	Red-Crested Pochard	Lady's Slipper Orchid	Sword-Leaved
Alpine Chough	Red Kite	Lily of the Valley	Helleborine
Alpine Swift	Ring Ouzel	May Lily	Vanilla Orchid
Black Kite	Rock Bunting	Military Orchid	Yellow Gentian
Black-Necked Grebe	Rock Partridge	Monkey Orchid	Aesculapian Snake
Buzzard	Short-Toed Eagle	Mont Cenis Bellflower	Alpine Salamander
Corncrake	Snow Finch	Queen-of-the-Alps	Green Lizard
Crag Martin	Wallcreeper	Sowbread	Apollo Butterfly
Golden Eagle	Alpine Marmot	Snowbells	Cynthia's Fritillary
Honey Buzzard	Chamois	Snowy Mespilus	Mountain Clouded
Little Bittern	Ibex	Spring Gentian	Yellow
Little Grebe	Alpine Clematis	Summer Ladies'	Peak White
Marsh Harrier	Alpine Columbine	Tresses	
Ptarmigan	Edelweiss		

90 LAKE ANNECY MARSH

Maps:	MA p. 118; IGN No. 45
Location:	The S end of Lac d'Annecy
Access:	Limited to paths
Season:	Best in spring and summer for flowers, insects, birds; winter birds good
Terrain:	Marshy
Specialities:	Pugsley's Marsh Orchid, Marsh Gentian, Sowbread; Corncrake

At the southern end of the superb Lac d'Annecy, two small rivers have formed a marshy delta (partially colonized by woodland) of largely calcareous alluvium. Although the shores of the lake are well developed generally for housing, this area is protected as a nature reserve. The site is encircled by roads, and access is straightforward from the N508.

The plant life is very rich, with numerous fen species such as Marsh Helleborine, Pugsley's Marsh Orchid, Marsh Gentian, Parsley Water Dropwort and numerous sedges, whilst the local sowbread (*Cyclamen purpurascens*) occurs in damp woodland areas.

Breeding birds include various marsh and reed-bed warblers, Great Crested and Little Grebes, Little Bittern, and possibly Corncrake. Winter and passage times are good for wildfowl, though these are hard to see; they include Red-Crested Pochard, Goldeneye and Eider Duck.

Beaver have been successfully re-introduced on one of the contributing rivers, and are surviving there.

Although not very close, there is a very similar type of site on Lake Geneva (Lac Léman) at the delta of the Dranse, just north-east of Thonon-les Bains. Access is open from the minor road running north from Thonon.

91 ROC DE CHERE	
Maps:	MA p. 118; IGN No. 45
Location:	On the Lac d'Annecy, north of Talloires
Access:	Numerous footpaths through the area
Season:	Best in late spring and summer for flowers, insects, reptiles
Terrain:	Mainly dry rocky, partly wooded; also an area of bog
Specialities:	Numerous orchids, Yellow Gentian, clubmosses, Maidenhair Fern; Aesculapian Snake

A superb headland of limestone jutting out into Lac d'Annecy from the east side, with exceptional views over the lake and mountains. Access is easy from the D909a and parking is available at Talloires or at the Echarvines golf club area to the north, from where a path leads into the reserve.

The underlying rock is limestone, so the

Spring Crocus (Crocus vernus) on the Col des Aravis, French Alps.

woods and slopes of much of the rock have a calcareous flora. However, on top of the rock, there is a more acid area, with a modest peat bog, and more Alpine species. The area is very rich in plants, with an odd mixture of geographical and habitat associations.

Orchids such as Military and Monkey, and Sword-Leaved Helleborine and many others are common in the southern areas. The woodland is good for limestone woodland species such as Lily of the Valley, uncommon whitebeams, Box, a mossy sandwort (*Moehringia muscosa*), Amelanchier, and Montpelier Maple. The boggy area contains sundews, several clubmosses, and creeping willow. Elsewhere on the top, there is Yellow Gentian, Alpine Spurge Laurel and, very locally, Maidenhair Fern.

Reptiles include the Aesculapian Snake and Green Lizard, and there are two newt species recorded. Breeding birds of the woods are good, but not exceptional, though Peregrine sometimes nest on the cliffs.

Nearby, the woods above Talloires, especially between Ermitage de St Germain and the Col des Nantets are rich in flowers.

92 LAC DU BOURGET AND LE MARAIS DE LAVOUR	
Maps:	MA p. 117; IGN No. 53
Location:	Just N of Chambéry
Access:	Generally open
Season:	Best in summer and passage times for birds
Terrain:	Marshy; cliffs; open water; woodland
Specialities:	Kite, Little Bittern, Short-Toed Eagle, Great Reed Warbler, Alpine Swift

Lac du Bourget is a sizeable lake, some 18km long, lying midway between the mountains and the plains, at an altitude of about 230m. It is a well-known birdwatching site, though its value has declined somewhat as towns around it have enlarged. An airport occupies much of the marshland, and agriculture has intensified. None-the-less, the combination of semi-natural habitats is of great value, and bird life is still rich.

Breeding birds include Little Bittern, Great Crested Grebe, Curlew, Hobby and Great Reed, Savi's, Marsh, and other warblers around the marshes and lake shore; Alpine Swift and Crag Martin on the cliffs; Black Kite, Honey Buzzard, Short-Toed Eagle, Quail, and Rock Bunting breed in the area generally. Wallcreepers are said to frequent the area in winter.

The Marais de Lavours is the marshland at the north end of the lake, towards the Rhône, and, in particular, west of the Rhône. Apart from birds such as Marsh Harrier, these marhses are very rich botanically and parts are protected as a reserve. Flowers include Fen Orchid, Summer Ladies' Tresses, Marsh Pea, Marsh Gentian, and several sundew species. There is access to the main part of the reserve from the D37, close to where it crosses the River Rousses.

93 THE DOMBES	
Maps:	MA pp. 102 and 116; IGN No. 44
Location:	NE of Lyon
Access:	Generally open
Season:	Best in spring–summer for birds, flowers, insects, amphibia
Terrain:	Marshland; open water; meadow; woodland
Specialities:	Black-Necked Grebe, Night Heron, Squacco Heron, Little Egret, Whiskered Tern

The Dombes is an extraordinary area of land lying north-east of Lyon, between the valleys of the Rhône and Saône, in which lie literally hundreds of lakes and ponds. Some, like those of the Brenne, are artificial, whilst others are of natural glacial origin. Collectively, they form an extremely important natural resource, though they are barely protected by any reserve or other designation. Villars-les-Dombes lies at the centre of the region, easily reached by road (the N83), or rail, with buses from Lyon and Bourg-en-Bresse.

The best-known feature of the area is its breeding wetland birds. These include Black-Necked Grebe, Purple, Night and Squacco Herons, Little Egret, Bittern and Little

One of the hundreds of lakes in the Dombe area, rich in all forms of aquatic life.

Red-Crested Pochard
Netta rufina L 56

This beautiful duck breeds very locally in scattered areas of wetland and open water through France, though it has a primarily southern distribution. It is a summer visitor to most of the country, but is resident throughout the year only in the extreme south. The male has a striking red head with a crest that can be erected; the female is much duller in colour.

They breed in areas of well-vegetated water, and good places to see them include the Camargue, and Lake Biguglia in Corsica. They are also frequent in wildfowl collections, such as those in the Ornithological Parks at Villars-les-Dombes, or le Teich.

Bittern, Red-Crested Pochard, Black-Winged Stilt, Marsh and Montagu's Harriers, Black Kite, Black Tern, Whiskered Tern, Bee- Eater, and Fan-Tailed and numerous other warblers.

Although less well-known and significant, the area is of great interest for the flowers, amphibia and dragonflies. The fish fauna is extensive and varied, though highly managed in a unique system of rotational flooding.

The area is so densely packed with lakes and marshes that finding sites of interest is not difficult with the aid of the 1:100,000 map, or a larger scale (available locally). There is a Parc Ornithologique south of Villars, open to the public, with displays and further information, and access to the Nature Reserve nearby. It is open every day from 8.30 a.m. until evening, and a suggested route around the lakes is provided, though this seems to be designed more to get you into local restaurants than to see birds! The large lakes, Etang de Birieux and Etang de Glareins, south of Villars, are both good sites, though many other areas would repay exploration.

THE MOUNTAINS OF HAUTE-SAVOIE

The mountains around Chamonix include the highest in France and Europe, and the scenery is superb. Everywhere here is good, though some areas are subject to more ski disturbance than others. A number of areas have been set aside as nature reserves, on a grand scale, offering protection from de-velopment. There are four reserves, with Chamonix at their centre (and the ideal base for their exploration), though the northerly three abut each other and are considered together. All of these sites need walking to see them adequately.

94 THE AIGUILLES-ROUGE AND SIXT-PASSY RESERVES	
Maps:	MA p.105; IGN No. 45
Location:	The high mountains N of Chamonix
Access:	Open
Season:	Summer for flowers, birds, mammals
Terrain:	Very mountainous; high cliffs in places; serious mountain walking required for the core of the reserve
Specialities:	High mountain flowers, birds and insects

Chamois
Rupicapra rupicapra
H 70–80 (at shoulder)

Chamois are small goat-like mountain animals. In France, they occur throughout the Alps and in the Pyrenees, often in good numbers. They are rich brown in summer, darker and shaggier in winter, and both males and females have horns when mature. They occur in groups, generally living around the tree line, moving up into high pastures in summer, or down into woodland in winter. They are most easily seen in the early morning or towards evening, when they emerge from day-time resting places to begin feeding. They may feed all day on rocky inaccessible slopes, and it is always worth scanning such areas with binoculars.

A major high-mountain area, with dramatic scenery, protected (more or less) from ski and other developments. Access into the area is from various minor roads running north from the N205, from the Col des Montets, north-east of Chamonix, near where there is an information centre, or from the north via the village of Sixt-Fer-à-Cheval.

Geologically, the area is varied, with both acid and calcareous rocks. The Aiguilles (Needles) are mainly of granite, with schists and gneiss, while the western areas and the Belvedère are of sedimentary lime-rich rocks. Collectively, the flora is extremely rich, though it takes a while to see it all; this is one of the best areas of Alpine France to see flowers.

Queen-of-the-Alps, Alpine Columbine, thirteen species of gentian, twenty species of orchid (including Lady's Slipper Orchid), several *Primula* species, and a rich variety of high-altitude lichens occur, among many others.

Specialist high-altitude birds are of interest, with Golden Eagle, Ptarmigan, Rock Partridge, Rock Thrush, Black Grouse, Pygmy Owl, Ring Ouzel, and many others present. This is also a site for the Alpine Salamander.

95 LES CONTAMINES-MONTJOIE/MONT BLANC	
Maps:	MA p. 119; IGN No. 53
Location:	SW of Mt Blanc; S of Chamonix
Access:	Open
Season:	Late spring and summer for flowers, birds, insects
Terrain:	Woodland; pastures; cliffs and glaciers; must be treated with respect and needs preparation for higher areas
Specialities:	High-altitude flowers and birds

The reserve area of Contamines-Montjoie includes or abuts the highest mountain land in Europe, and includes glacier scenery. Naturally, the scenery is superb – this is all wonderful walking country and one does not need to be a serious naturalist to appreciate it. Access is via the Contamines-Montjoie valley, or by ski lift, when open, from les Houches. Walking is required to reach most areas of interest.

The flora is not as rich as the Aiguilles Rouge area, as the rocks are mainly acidic, but there are superb examples of the widespread flora of the Alps, and some specialized high-Alpine species. Plants of interest include Alpine Rock-Jasmine, Simple-Leaved Milfoil, Alpine Saussurea, Blue Arabis, and many more common species.

Birds and reptiles are generally similar to those of the previous site. The insect life includes numerous Alpine butterflies and grasshoppers.

Other sites of interest abound in this area. Possibilities include the Chaîne des Aravis (crossed by the Col des Aravis), and the Col du Petit St Bernard above Bourg-St Maurice (on the way into Italy).

THE VANOISE NATIONAL PARK

The Parc National de la Vanoise was France's first National Park, and is still one of the best known. It is a superb high-mountain area, between the valleys of the Arc and L'Isère, comprising a wonderful mixture of higher-altitude habitats (including lakes, forests, meadows, pastures, torrents), and high-altitude habitat, culminating in peaks of up to 3,852m. Altogether, the park covers 529km^2 of largely unspoilt scenery.

Geologically, it is mixed, with areas of calcareous rocks, especially around the Col de la Vanoise in the centre, whilst elsewhere there are harder metamorphic rocks. This adds to the interest and variety of the park. Mountain National Parks in the French Alps are not necessarily more interesting than surrounding areas, but they are at least partially protected from the skiing, hunting and general development pressure experienced elsewhere in the mountains. Within the park, there are three large nature reserves, of which one is split into two separate blocks. These have an added degree of protection and management, in theory at least.

Access into the park area is easy enough, weather permitting, from the south or north, from around Lanslebourg, on the N6, or from the Moûtiers direction, on the N90. The Col de l'Iseran, on the D902, passes through the park and one of the reserves, and, at a height of 2,769m, gives exceptional access to some high country; however, it is liable to be closed during much of the winter and spring.

96 THE TIGNES NATURAL RESERVES	
Maps:	MA p. 119; IGN No. 53
Location:	The N of the Vanoise Park, W and S of Tignes
Access:	Open; ski lifts run into reserves; dogs must be on leash
Season:	Summer for flowers
Terrain:	Rocky, high-mountain terrain; needs considerable care
Specialities:	High-mountain and glacier flowers; insects; birds

This reserve is split into two sections. The southern one comprises the Glacier de la Grande Motte, which is superb to look at, and of interest as a geographical feature, though it has relatively limited flora and fauna. The northern section lies just west of Tignes, and has a more varied mixture of habitats and species, though really, there is little difference between the reserve and the surroundings, and it is by no means necessary to stay within the reserve.

Flowers of interest include sheets of Rock Jasmine, Spring Gentian, Vanilla Orchid, *Corydalis solida*, mountain bellflowers such as *Campanula thyrsoides* and *C. rhomboidalis*, and many others. Butterflies include Apollo, Peak White, Scarce Copper, and there are numerous high-altitude grasshoppers such as *Arcyptera fusca* and *Podisma pedestris*. Breeding birds include Ptarmigan, Snow Finch, Alpine Accentor and both chough species.

A view in the Vanoise National Park, with masses of Arnica (Arnica montana) in the foreground.

Yellow Bellflower (Campanula thyrsoides) is not uncommon at middle altitudes in the Alps.

97 NATURE RESERVES OF LA GRANDE SASSIERE AND L'ISSERAN	
Maps:	MA p. 119; IGN No. 53
Location:	The E side of the Vanoise National Park
Access:	Open; limited only by snow
Season:	Best in summer for flowers, birds, insects
Terrain:	High mountain with rocks and cliffs; numerous trails
Specialities:	Alpine Bells, Large-Flowered Bellflower; Ibex, Marmot; Wallcreeper

*A female Ibex (*Capra ibex*) resting on an alpine pasture.*

These two reserves occupy an extensive area of land on the east side of the park, extending almost to the Italian border, over which the Gran Paradiso National Park lies – another superb area. Access into the proximal parts of the reserves is easy from the D902, especially at the Col de l'Iseran, but considerable walking is needed to get to the farthest reaches. As with the previous site, the interest of the area by no means stops at the reserve boundaries.

Flowers include the rare Alpine Bells, species of *Astragalus (A. leontinus* and *A. sempervirens), Oxytropis lapponica,* Large-Flowered Bellflower, *Androsace helvetica,* Edelweiss, Spring Gentian, and many others.

Breeding birds include both species of chough, Ptarmigan, Wallcreeper, Alpine Accentor, Wheatear, Rock Partridge, Crag Martin, Snow Finch, and Golden Eagle in the general area. Butterflies include Apollo, Peak White, Mountain Clouded Yellow, Scarce Copper, Cynthia's Fritillary, and others, whilst Alpine mammals include Ibex, Chamois and Marmot.

Other areas of interest in and around the Vanoise include the Col du Mont Cenis, south of Lanslebourg; Mont Cenis itself, well known for its Alpine flowers; or the Col du Petit Mont Cenis, south-west of Lac du Mont Cenis.

*A Peak White butterfly (*Pontia callidice) *opening its wings to catch the sun.*

12. SOUTHERN FRENCH ALPS

INTRODUCTION

Whilst sharing much with the northern French Alps, the southern French Alps (as defined here) differ in that they become increasingly affected by the Mediterranean climate towards the south. The northernmost areas within the region share the somewhat unpredictable climate of the main bulk of the Alps, whereas the Queyras Regional Natural Park, and the Maritime Alps both have drier, more reliable summer weather. For the naturalist, this has the advantage of bringing in a range of different species that prefer these warmer drier conditions, in addition to retaining much of the general flora and fauna of the Alps. In other words, these southerly mountains are very rich in species.

In general, these southern areas are also less spoilt by skiing and general development, and they are superb areas to visit, with exceptional scenery, generally good weather, and a great range of species. There are four major protected zones within the region: The Vercors and Queyras Regional Natural Parks, and the Ecrins and Mercantour National Parks. Most of our selected sites fall within these zones, though there are enormous areas of great natural beauty and interest between them.

The Maritime Alps, and particularly the Mercantour National Park at its centre, have

A female Ptarmigan (Lagopus mutus) relying on her coloration for camouflage.

more endemics, or species that occur nowhere else in France, than anywhere else in the country. Butterflies like Larch Ringlet and Small Apollo; plants like The Ancient King *Saxifraga florulenta,* an extraordinary plant, that rarely flowers; and a particularly large number of bulbous plants like fritillaries, *Allium* species, tulips, and lilies, are all specialities of the area. If possible, a visit should be made a little earlier than for other parts of the Alps, since much flowers or flies here before June, when the hot sun tends to burn things up at lower altitudes or on southern slopes.

THE VERCORS REGIONAL NATURAL PARK

The Vercors is a superb sub-alpine region, lying south-west of Grenoble, little known outside France, but with striking scenery and rich wildlife. It consists primarily of hard limestone, with north–south oriented ridges of hills with plateaux in between. The highest point is the 2,341m peak of le Grand Veymont, and there are numerous striking peaks, gorges and cliffs in the area. It is also well known as an area seamed with caves and subterranean waterways.

The area occupies an intermediate position between the northern and southern hills, and to some extent between those of east France and the Massif Central. It, therefore, has a

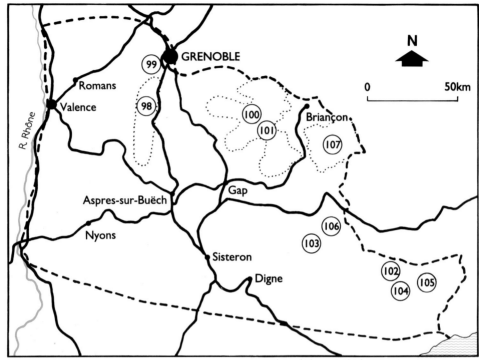

Map of the Southern Alps. Sites are numbered as in the text. Only main roads and the major rivers of the region are shown

flora and fauna that is a mixture of numerous types. It is noticeable that, for example, the southerly slopes have a predominantly Mediterranean type of vegetation, with species to match, whilst north-facing slopes are more forested with more northern or shade-loving species. Once, almost all the open land was grazed by vast flocks of sheep moved up from the coast in summer, but numbers have dropped considerably in recent years.

The whole area is of great interest, though the lower plateaux are more intensively

The beautiful Vercors mountains in late winter. Although best visited in spring and summer, the Vercours are magnificent at any time, and winter can be better for seeing some birds and mammals at close quarters.

FIFTY INTERESTING SPECIES TO LOOK FOR

Alpine Chough	Nutcracker	Ibex	Lizard Orchid
Bearded Vulture	Peregrine Falcon	Mouflon	Maritime Alps Crocus
Black Grouse	Pygmy Owl	Mountain Hare	Narcissus-Flowered
Black Kite	Ptarmigan	Red Deer	Anemone
Black Woodpecker	Red Kite	Red Squirrel	Orange Lily
Bonelli's Eagle	Ring Ouzel	Wild Boar	Snowbells
Buzzard	Rock Partridge	Alpine Clematis	Trumpet Gentian
Citril Finch	Short-Toed Eagle	Ancient King	Violet Limodore
Chough	Snow Finch	Bulbocodium	Vitaliana
Crossbill	Tengmalm's Owl	Dog's-Tooth Violet	Wild Tulip
Firecrest	Wallcreeper	Elder-Flowered Orchid	Ascalaphids
Golden Eagle	Alpine Marmot	Hepatica	Black-Veined White
Goshawk	Chamois	Late Spider Orchid	

farmed and settled. There is a major nature reserve, the largest in France, occupying much of the main range, though the site lacks adequate protection and it is misused badly in both summer and winter. Nevertheless, it is an area that demands more than a brief stop – the reserve alone covers 16,662 ha, and there is a huge amount to see.

98 THE HIGH PLATEAUX OF VERCORS NATURE RESERVE

Maps:	MA p. 131; IGN No. 52
Location:	The S part of the E side of the Vercours Park, from Villard de Lans S to near Châtillon
Access:	Open
Season:	Spring and summer for flowers and birds
Terrain:	Woodland; pastures; cliffs; screes – mainly very dry
Specialities:	Orchids; Golden Eagle, Peregrine Falcon, Nutcracker, Wallcreeper

The reserve comprises most of the high peaks and cliffs of the park, and, as such, has the most exciting scenery and wildest, least-spoilt country. Access has to be mainly on foot, though roads lead into the area from either side and there are tracks from the D518 and the D8A. Long-distance footpaths cross the area.

The bird life is very fine. Breeding species include Golden Eagle, Short-Toed Eagle, Bonelli's Eagle, Peregrine Falcon, Eagle Owl, Tengmalm's Owl, Pygmy Owl, Nutcracker, Wallcreeper, Crossbill, Black Grouse, Ptarmigan, and Red Kite, amongst others.

The flora is particularly rich in orchids, with most limestone species occurring in abundance. Other species of interest include various gentians, Rock-Jasmine, Mountain Avens, Dog's-Tooth Violet, *Allium narcissiflorum*, *Primula auricula*, Decumbent Treacle-Mustard, Large-Flowered Bellflower, and the composite *Berardia subacaulis*, amongst many more common species. The sub-alpine meadows are especially fine.

Mammals are scarce, with most Alpine specialities having become extinct. Unfortunately, neither Regional Natural Park nor nature reserve status necessarily precludes hunting in France, and most larger species have been steadily exterminated. Apparently there are plans to re-introduce Lynx here. To see a good range of species, head for either Grand Veymont or the lower slopes of the superb Mt Aiguille.

99 GORGE D'ENGINS	
Maps:	MA p. 131; IGN No. 52
Location:	Just SW of Grenoble
Season:	Spring and summer for flowers, insects, reptiles
Terrain:	Limestone gorge with cliffs
Specialities:	Spider orchids, Trumpet Gentian; Ascalaphids; Green Lizard

After leaving the N532 just west of Grenoble, the D531 climbs steadily towards the Vercors plateau through the Gorge d'Engins. This has a good representative sample of the more lowland element of the Vercors, with an attractive mixture of southern and northern species. Along the gorge, there are woods, pastures, meadows and cliffs – all worth a look.

Flowers include Bee, Fly, Early and Late Spider, Military, Monkey and Lizard Orchid, often in abundance; the blue flowers of the Mediterranan *Aphyllanthes monspeliensis*; Trumpet Gentian *Gentiana clusii*, *Alyssum montanum*, the blue-flowered lettuce (*Lactuca perennis*), Montpelier Maple, Blue Gromwell, and much else. Green Lizard are common in rocky areas, and easily approached, whilst Ascalaphids (*Libelloides longicornis*) fly rapidly around the meadows in the sun. Butterflies are abundant, and include numerous blues, fritillaries, skippers, Black-Veined White, and others.

There are various car-park areas along the road, and all will produce something of interest in spring and early summer.

*A Green Lizard (*Lacerta viridis*) emerging to sun itself on the limestone rocks of the Vercors.*

PARC NATIONAL DES ECRINS

The Parc National des Ecrins, though larger than the Vanoise, is much less well known than its more northerly neighbour. With an area of 1,080km², it is, in fact, the largest of the French national parks. The centre of the park is dominated by very high mountains, the highest part of the Dauphine Alps, culminating in the Barre des Ecrins at 4,102m. There is some superb Alpine scenery, with glaciers, cliffs, lakes and high peaks. The park area includes over one-third of French permanent glaciers, totalling 12,000ha, and there are seventy lakes, mostly of natural glacial origin.

Climatically, the park straddles the zone in which central European begins to give way to a more Mediterranean climate, and there is a noticeable change in the weather pattern from north to south. Geologically, the park is varied, and this mixture of terrain, geology and climate has given rise to an extremely rich flora.

100 NATURE RESERVES OF THE PARK DES ECRINS	
Maps:	MA pp. 132–3; IGN No. 54
Location:	Scattered around the edges of the park
Access:	Open; limited only by snow
Season:	Late spring and summer for flowers, birds, mammals, insects
Terrain:	Woodland; valleys; grassland; mountain habitats; snow lies very late in higher areas
Specialities:	Orange Lily, Lady's Slipper Orchid; Golden Eagle, Tengmalm's Owl; Mountain Hare

101 OTHER AREAS WITHIN THE NATIONAL PARK	
Maps:	MA pp. 132–3; IGN No. 54
Location:	The NE parts of the park
Season:	Late spring and summer for flowers, birds, insects
Terrain:	Generally mountainous; parts accessible direct from roads
Specialities:	Golden Eagle, Ptarmigan; Mountain Hare; Alpine flowers

There are six official nature reserves within the park. They are combined here as one site only, because they represent only a very small part of the interest and variety of the park, and some seem barely worthy of the status. Many other areas of the park are at least as worth exploring.

The Gorges du Béranger, running up to Valsenestre, are well wooded with a good flora in the Spruce forests and old meadows. The Combeynot area is the largest reserve, and it occupies the north-east corner of the park, running north to the Col du Lautaret. It includes some fine Alpine scenery, and a good flora, with King-of-the-Alps, *Primula hirsuta* and *P. latifolia*, saxifrages, Mountain Avens, Alpine Avens, and *Allium victorialis*. Birds include Rock Partridge, Snow Finch and Ptarmigan. The St Pierre Reserve and the Bérarde Reserves, a moraine and a valley respectively, are of relatively little interest.

The Col du Lautaret is a high pass at the north end of the park, on the N91 Briançon to Grenoble road. Access is open, but the pass is closed for much of the winter.

The pass itself is a well-known centre for Alpine flowers. Species include bulbs such as *Bulbocodium vernum, Lloydia serotina,* and *Crocus vernus*; various *Primula spp.*, Three-Veined Pink, King-of-the-Alps, the beautiful Vitaliana, Large-Flowered Bellflower, Elder-Flowered Orchid, and various rest-harrow ·species, amongst others. Birds include Snow Finch, Chough, and visiting eagles.

Close to the pass lies the famous Lautaret Alpine Garden, run by the University of Grenoble. The garden lies at 1,829m, covers about 2ha, and contains at least 3,500 species. Entry is free, and the garden is open daily from late June to September. It is well worth a visit.

The mountain of la Meije (3,983m), just south of the town of la Grave, is a superb area for flowers, birds and scenery. Mt Pelvoux (3,946m), accessible from the east side via the D994E, is another exceptional area, with a rich flora. Just north of the park, on the D902, lies the Col du Galibier (2,545m) an impressive place with good flowers.

A lovely clump of Vitaliana (Vitaliana primuliflora), a close relative of the primroses.

at least 200 are rare. Amongst the very rich insect flora, around 100 species are known to occur nowhere else. The region, and especially the National Park, is one of the best places in France to see large mammals, and one could expect to see some of the following: Chamois, Mouflon, Ibex, Alpine Marmot, Red Deer, Roe Deer and Wild Boar. Bird life is also very rich, with (for example) thirty-one pairs of Golden Eagles known to be breeding, and Bearded Vultures (Lammergeiers) just beginning to re-establish.

A Red Deer hind (Cervus elaphus), keeping a wary eye on the photographer.

THE MARITIME ALPS

The Maritime Alps are an area of exceptional natural interest and scenery. Although lacking the very high snowy peaks of Alpine areas farther north, they combine extensive high areas with a superb climate and an extremely rich natural life that includes many endemic or rare species. For example, over half of the total French flora of 4,200 species occur in the Maritime Alps (almost half, in the Mercantour National Park alone), and out of these some forty are endemic to the area and

Previous page: a view in spring looking east from Col de Restefond in the Maritime Alps.

The Mercantour National Park represents the best of the Maritime Alps. However, it has an exceptionally tightly drawn boundary due largely to local and commercial opposition to it, and there are numerous areas of interest outside the actual park area. However, the pressures are such that this interest will probably steadily diminish through activities such as skiing, all-terrain driving, forestry, and general development, all of which are permitted around the park.

In general, all of the higher areas of the Maritime Alps will be found to be interesting, and much depends on accessibility rather than other factors. The sites picked out do not, therefore, cover all of merit in the area. The National Park Service runs many guided nature walks in summer (*see* Useful Addresses, page 234).

102 LE BOREON AREA	
Maps:	MA p. 165; IGN No. 61
Location:	Due N of Nice, almost on the Italian border, nr St Martin-Vésubie
Access:	Difficult in spring and winter
Season:	Best from mid-May onwards for everything
Terrain:	High mountain country, with good paths; woods and pastures
Specialities:	Superb mountain mammals, birds, flowers and insects

The starting-point for this area is reached by following the D2565 northwards through St Martin-Vésubie, then the D89 north to le Boréon hamlet; from here one can drive on eastwards and upwards to the Vachérie du Boréon. The National Park organizes a shuttle service to Boréon during summer, and various organized activities operate from here.

Walking onwards up the valley from here towards the Refuge de la Cougourde takes you through Fir forest and then into more open woodland with Larches and other trees; higher up, flower-rich pastures predominate, and ultimately rocky areas with cliffs. This area covers the ground from which the National Park was extended – the old Mercantour National Park. It is of great importance for large mammals, with an estimated 1,500 Chamois, 300 Mouflons and good numbers of Ibex, all best seen (as with most mammals) in early morning or late evening. It is also a good area for flowers, mainly those of more acid ground, with *Crocus versicolor* (in spring), Trumpet Gentian, Alpenrose, Snowbell, various violets including *Viola valderia*, several *Primula* species and many others. Bird life includes Black Woodpecker, Crested Tit, Nutcracker, Firecrest, Alpine Chough, Ptarmigan and Golden Eagle. Insect life is rich, and butterflies are abundant around the forest–pasture boundaries.

Alternative possibilities include the walk north from le Boréon up to the Col de Cerise on the Italian border (famed for its flowers), or westwards towards the Refuge de Salse.

103 COL DE LA CAYOLLE/ CAYOLLE PASS	
Maps:	MA p. 147; IGN No. 61 (or IGN Tourist map 'Alpes-Maritimes')
Location:	About 16km (direct) SSW of Barcelonette
Access:	Not feasible until late spring
Season:	Best May–July for flowers, birds, insects
Terrain:	High mountain pastures; woodland; scree; care needed in higher zones
Specialities:	Flowers, birds, insects; Botanic Garden

The col lies on the D902 road from Barcelonette to Guillaumes and, ultimately, Nice. The highest point on the road lies at 2,327m, giving easy access to some good high country. Both sides of the pass are of interest, as well as the area above it; the north side is liable to be closed until late spring, and flowers and insects are later here than on the south side.

Bird life is very rich and includes Golden Eagle, Goshawk, Short-Toed Eagle, Alpine

Alpine Choughs (Pyrrhocorax graculus) are frequent, and often tame, residents of the high Alps.

104 LA MADONE DE FENESTRE VALLEY	
Maps:	MA p. 165; IGN No. 61
Location:	10km NE of St Martin-Vésubie
Season:	Late spring and through summer for all aspects
Terrain:	Pastures; woodlands; some high-mountain habitats within reach
Specialities:	The Ancient King (*Saxifraga florulenta*), *Primula* species; birds and insects

and Common Chough, Ptarmigan, Black Woodpecker, Alpine Swift, Alpine Accentor, Ring Ouzel, Rock Thrush, Crossbill, Snow Finch and Citril Finch, amongst many others. Alpine Marmots are common in places, and readily seen and heard, whilst Chamois can be seen around the edges of woods. The flora is very rich, reflecting the varied geology, and is at its best from late May onwards.

At Estenc, on the south side of the col, there is an Alpine garden (though it is not as extensive as the one on the Col de Lautaret), as well as a refuge and café.

To the west lies the Col d'Allos (2,240m), which also has superb scenery and natural history. From Allos, south of the col, the D226 leads eastwards up to le Lausson, from where it is a short walk to the remarkable large high-altitude lake of Allos.

St Martin-Vésubie is a significant town which can be reached easily by car, or bus (run regularly) from Nice. From here, the D94 runs eastwards up the valley to the Refuge of Madone de Fenestre at 1,900m.

The road itself is worth looking along. The Spruce forests, and riversides, have good middle-altitude birds, and pastures or rocks have good plants, including the red Viscid Primrose, and the bluish-pink *Primula marginata*.

The meadows around the church and refuge have a very rich flora, which includes several orchids, butterworts, White False Helleborine, gentians, pinks, houseleeks, speedwells, pansies, and the beautiful Alpine Clematis.

This is a good area for the superb Ancient King (The National Park emblem) and its symmetrical rosettes can be seen on rockfaces, though it rarely flowers.

There is easy access upwards from the church into the high country around the

Opposite: *the beautiful* Primula marginata *flowering in the Maritime Alps, soon after the snow melts.*

Cime du Gélas and Mt Neillier, where there are excellent high-altitude birds, flowers and insects, and easy views of Ibex and Chamois. Alternatively, there is an easy walk to the Lac de Fenestre, where there are Alpine dragonfly species.

105 THE GORDOLASQUE VALLEY AND THE MERVEILLES VALLEY	
Maps:	MA p. 165; IGN No. 61
Location:	NE of Roquebillière in the Vésubie valley
Access:	From late spring onwards; later for the high areas in some years
Season:	Best from June to August
Terrain:	Forests and grassland lower down; serious mountain walking higher up
Specialities:	Alpine mammals; excellent flowers; much of archaeological importance

Roquebillière is on a main bus route and an easy road from Nice. From there, take the D171 up the Gordolasque valley. Along the route there are valley meadows, coniferous woods, and pastures, all of interest, especially in June. From the end of the road, there are numerous walks into high country, and the Refuge de Nice or the Refuge de Merveilles make longer trips into the area a realistic possibility.

The flora is rich, with, amongst much else, *Hyacinthoides italica*, fritillaries (especially *Fritillaria tubiformis moggridgei*), Wild Tulip, numerous pinks, Thrift, pansies, gentians, *Allium spp.*, *Adenostyles leucophylla*, sheets of Rosebay Willow-Herb in its natural habitat,

Arnica, and various *Primula* species. Ponds have newts and Common Frog, and there are numerous Alpine grasshoppers in late summer. The butterfly fauna is very rich, especially in meadow areas. Birds include Raven, Chough, Golden Eagle and others.

It is possible to walk onwards into the Vallée des Merveilles from here. The valley can be approached on foot or by hired jeep from the Casterino valley, to the east. It is an extraordinary place, with approximately 100,000 open-air carvings dating from the Bronze Age, at an average altitude of 2,200m. It also has a good flora and fauna, and there are ample information boards along the GR52 footpath.

This whole area is superbly unspoilt and very rich.

106 THE CIME DE LA BONETTE AND COL DE RESTEFOND (RESTEFOND PASS)	
Maps:	MA p. 147; IGN map No. 61
Location:	About 15km (direct) SE of Barcelonette
Access:	Higher parts not accessible until mid- to late June; lower parts worth visiting earlier for flowers and birds
Terrain:	High-altitude pastures; mountain habitats; the highest road in France
Specialities:	The whole range of high-altitude birds, flowers, insects and mammals

The D64 passes over the cols *en route* from Jausiers (east of Barcelonnette) to St Sauveur. At 2,802m, the Col de la Bonette is the highest surfaced road in France, giving excellent access to some superb high Alpine country, as well as offering the chance to see a great deal of wildlife on the roads on either side.

Lower Larch forests give way to high sheep-grazed pastures, and the whole area is extremely rich in flowers. Species to be seen include *Bulbocodium vernum, Gagea fistulosa,* several high altitude buttercup species, Vita-liana, *Primula marginata, Anemone baldensis,* Stemless Cotton Thistle, Mountain Avens, Large-Flowered Bellflower, and Moss Campion, amongst many others.

A mass of Narcissus-Flowered Anemones (Ranunculus narcissiflorus) on the Col de Bonette.

Marmots are abundant here, especially on the north side, with many colonies near the road. It is well worth going up early in the morning, or staying towards evening for good views of these fascinating mammals. Other mammals in the area include Chamois, Ibex, Mountain Hare and Red Fox. Bird life includes Golden Eagle, Alpine Chough, Alpine Accentor, Citril Finch, Snow Finch and Ptarmigan.

From the cols, and adjacent high areas,

Alpine Marmot
Marmota marmota
L 50–58 (head and body)

Alpine marmots are delightful large rodents that occur frequently in the Alps and, more locally, in the Pyrenees, where they have been re-introduced. They are active in the day, retreating below ground if disturbed, and readily spotted by their loud piercing alarm whistles. They are easily distinguished from other rodents by their much larger size (head and body up to 60cm), furry tail, and high-mountain habitat. They are most likely to be found above the tree line and up to about 3,000m, hibernating from October onwards to avoid the long snowy winters, and reappearing in spring. They breed shortly after the end of the hibernation period.

there are superb views on a clear day, and this is probably the easiest place to experience real high-altitude mountain country in this region.

The Col de Larche, lying north-east of here, and best reached via Jausiers and the D900, is another good starting-point for walks, and the route southwards (along GR55-56) to Lac du Lauzanier is well worth while. All of this area is very rich in flowers, insects and birds, and views of large mammals are always possible.

107 THE REGIONAL NATURAL PARK OF QUEYRAS	
Maps:	MA p. 133; IGN No. 54
Location:	S of Brianon, running up to the Italian border
Access:	Open, but limited through till spring by snow
Season:	Best from late May to August for most groups
Terrain:	All types from woodland to high mountains
Specialities:	Very rich alpine flora and fauna

The Queyras Park is a superb and relatively little-known part of the French Alps, half-surrounded by Italy. Access is best from Briançon, south-eastwards along the D902 to the Col d'Izoard, which, at 2,360m, gives good access to some fine country. South of here, the D947 leads eastwards up the Guil valley into the heart of the park. The weather in the area is excellent in late spring and summer, and visitors are not too numerous, though ski developments are increasing ominously (not excluded from Regional Natural Parks). Resident humans are few in number.

Botanically, the mountains are exceptionally rich, with around 2,000 species recorded – a mixture of mediterranean, Alpine and widespread species. Habitats include high pasture, meadow, larch and other woodlands, and various high-altitude areas – screes, cliffs, flushes and rocky grazing areas. Collectively, there are so many plants that it is unnecessary to pick out individual species. However, features of interest include various orchids on the predominantly limestone lower regions, *Gentiana cruciata*, several *Dianthus spp.*, various *Primula spp*, Pyrenean Whitlow Grass, fritillaries, snowbells, saxifrages, wintergreens, Jovesbeard, and Globe-flowers.

Bird life is similar to adjacent areas, with Ptarmigan, Common and Green Sandpipers, Alpine Accentor, Snow Finch, Citril Finch, Raven, Chough and Golden Eagle. Mammals include Alpine Marmot, Chamois, and Mountain Hare.

All of the park is of interest to the naturalist, but useful areas to start with include the Col d'Izoard; the walk to the Col d'Urine from beyond the hamlet of le Roux; and the area around the Belvédère de Viso, close to the Italian border.

13. PYRENEES

INTRODUCTION

Although small when compared with the Himalayas, Rockies or Andes, the Pyrenees hold great importance as a mountain range in Europe. They stretch as an unbroken chain from the Atlantic to the Mediterranean Sea, cutting off the Iberian Peninsula from the rest of Europe like a vast wall nearly 450km long and tens of kilometres wide.

They have served as a physical barrier to the spread of plants and animals (humans included), and exert a considerable influence on the climate of areas on either side. From north to south the change is dramatic, with the French slopes receiving considerable rainfall from the north-west Atlantic whilst the southern slopes count amongst some of the driest places

A single flower of the beautiful Pyrenean Turks Cap (Lilium pyrenaicum), common throughout most of the Pyrenees.

in Europe. As a consequence, the French Pyrenees look much greener than their Spanish counterparts.

In total, the area generally known as the Pyrenees covers some 40,000km², as measured on the map, rather than the ground, where the area would be much greater. On the French side the edges of the Pyrenees are relatively clear-cut as the ground rises steeply from the lowlands to the high plateaux. The southern side of the ridge is much more complex as the Pyrenees merge southwards into a chain of sierras stretching away into Spain.

Over the earth's surface, mountain 'building' takes place because of the almost imperceptible movement of the 'plates' on which continents and oceans sit. The Pyrenees were formed in two main stages when the Iberian and European plates were in collision. The last major period of building took place during the Alpine orogeny, when the Alps were being formed, some 30 million years ago. Over countless millennia, erosion has shaped the mountains and created the jagged peaks we see today.

A considerable area (some 457km²) of the Pyrenees has been designated as National Park. This includes the Nature Reserves of Néouvielle, Mont Vallier and the Carlit Massif. Impressive as this seems, a vast area is still without any protection at all.

The barrier effect of the Pyrenean chain, together with the isolation of valleys, has enabled plants and, to a lesser extent, animals, to evolve separately, creating a considerable number of endemic species. The fact that so many plants carry the word *pyrenaica* as a part of their scientific names is not an absolute guarantee that they are restricted the Pyrenees, although many of the more attractive species are: Pyrenean Turk's Cap, Columbine, Fritillary and Gentian. Other endemics include Yellow, Pyrenean, Hairless Mossy, Geranium-Like and Neglected Saxifrages, and three of the rock

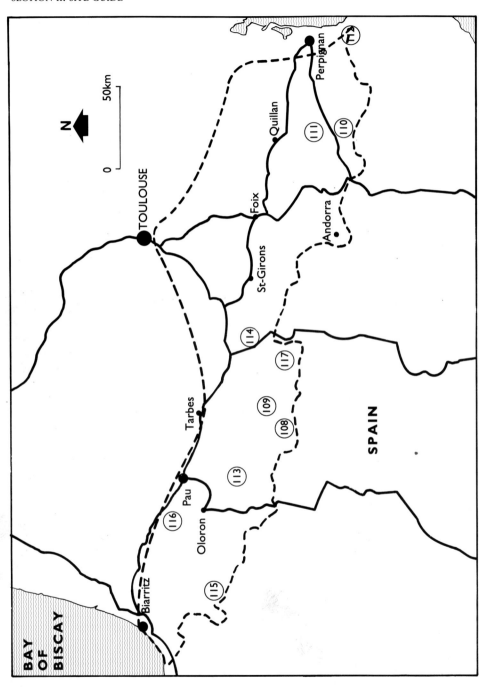

jasmines: Cylindrical, Ciliate and Hairy. But best known of all the endemic plants is an inhabitant of shady rock crevices – the purple-flowered Ramonda, a distant relative of gloxinias and African violets.

There are endemic races of several butter-flies (Apollo, blues and browns), of reptiles, such as the Pyrenean Viper, and also of amphibia. There are even endemic species of mammals like the Isard and the curious Pyrenean Desman.

Bird life is varied, with many of the larger raptors such as eagles, harriers and vultures able to breed relatively undisturbed because of the isolation of much of the land. The varied terrain with once-extensive forests has enabled Genet, Wild Cat, Wild Boar, marten, Fox and Badger to survive the seemingly determined efforts of France's vast army of hunters to wipe them out.

Opposite: map of the Pyrenees. The sites are numbered as in the text. Only main roads of the region are shown.

108 CIRQUES – GAVARNIE AND TROUMOUSE	
Maps:	MA p. 168; IGN No. 70
Location:	S of Lourdes
Access:	Skiing in winter; some passes closed until July
Season:	All year
Terrain:	Cliffs; rock outcrops; Alpine meadows
Specialities:	Pyrenean endemics (saxifrages, Columbine, rock jasmines); mountain birds: Citril and Snow Finches, Wallcreeper, Chough, Alpine Chough

Gavarnie can be reached via the N21 south of Lourdes and then the N921 via Gèdre. This cirque tends to suffer from its proximity to Lourdes and the fact that a detour there seems to be *de rigeur* for pilgrims. In spite of that, a walk during the early morning or late evening can provide one of the most dramatic scenic spectacles available in the mountains of Europe.

A footpath from the Cirque leads up to the Brèche de Roland, where the high alpines that grow in this staggering panorama include rock jasmine (*Androsaces*). Another

FIFTY INTERESTING SPECIES TO LOOK FOR

Alpine Accentor	Night Heron	Lynx	Lefebres Ringlet
Alpine Chough	Ptarmigan	Pine Marten	Map Butterfly
Bearded Vulture	Short-Toed	Wild Cat	English Iris
Black Redstart	Treecreeper	Midwife Toad	Garland Flower
Black Woodpecker	Snowfinch	Pyrenean Salamander	Large-Flowered
Capercaillie	Wallcreeper	Pyrenean Viper	Butterwort
Chough	Dartford Warbler	Blind Scorpion	Merendera
Citril Finch	Orphean Warbler	Crayfish	Pyrenean Alyssum
Dipper	Sub-Alpine Warbler	Apollo	Pyrenean Columbine
Golden Eagle	Pyrenean Desman	Cleopatra	Pyrenean Gentian
Goshawk	Dormouse	Clouded Apollo	Pyrenean Lily
Griffon Vulture	Glis Glis	Gavarnie Blue	Pyrenean Ramonda
Little Egret	Isard	Gavarnie Ringlet	Pyrenean Saxifrage

endemics, and Ramonda. In autumn the turf is studded with magenta flowers of Merendera.

It is possible to reach the Vallée d'Ossoue via the D128 which leads through a botanically rich landscape to the glaciers of Vignemale (3,298m); *en route* there are drifts of the yellow narcissi *Narcissus juncifolius*.

The Cirque de Troumouse lies near Gèdre and, although less dramatic than Gavarnie, is certainly a sight not to be missed. It lies at the head of the Val d'Héas which happens to be a flower-filled valley with a correspondingly rich butterfly fauna (Apollo, Clouded Apollo, Gavarnie Blue, and Mountain Clouded Yellow). To the east from Gèdre a path climbs up to the Cambieil Plateau through Beech woods, some 1,000m above, which is another haven for butterflies and sub-alpine flowers (Spring Squill, Oxlip, narcissi, Garland Flower and endemic Pyrenean Hyacinth, fritillaries, Honeysuckle and violets).

A group of English Irises (Iris xiphoides), with the spectacular Cirque de Gavarnie beyond.

path follows the ancient pilgrim's trail up to the Port de Gavarnie with lots of endemic plants *en route*, including plumes of Pyrenean Saxifrage, Pyrenean Teucrium, Tufted Soapwort and masses of blue English Iris. If you start early, the ascent of the Pic entre les Ports (2,476m) can be attempted. If any bonus is needed, on a clear day it is possible to see Golden Eagle, Bearded Vulture and Griffon Vulture, Citril Finch, Chough and Alpine Chough, Snow Finch and Wallcreeper.

The return to Gavarnie via the south bank of the Gaves des Tourettes passes through wild, boulder-strewn country with gentians, saxifrages, rock jasmines, Pyrenean

109 NEOUVIELLE	
Maps:	MA p. 168; IGN No. 70
Location:	S of Lannemezan
Access:	Extensive system of paths within the reserve
Terrain:	Very varied; slopes (grassy and stony); lakes; woods; peaks
Specialities:	Endemic Pyrenean plants; mountain birds; reptiles and amphibia; mammals

The name Néouvielle comes from '*vielle neige*', meaning persistant snow, appropriate for the permanently snow-capped peaks of a region that has had National Park status since 1936. The terrain within the park includes an extraordinary range of habitats from rocky, boulder-strewn slopes, through Alpine grasslands, to lakes, torrents and forests of broad-leaved and coniferous trees. It is hardly surprising that this diversity produces a range of plant and animal species to match, especially since the line of jagged peaks that borders the reserve to the north-west permits a comparatively mild climate for a mountain area. Pines still grow up as high as 2,500m, which is well above the usual tree line.

Many of the Pyrenean flowering plants (over 1,200 species) mentioned in other sites in this section occur in Néouvielle but extensive study has shown that there is tremendous richness in other plant groups – twenty-two species of *Sphagnum* moss, for example.

Butterflies are often abundant in the flower meadows and there are over 250 species of beetle known to occur. The list of amphibia is quite remarkable and includes the Midwife Toad, Common Frog, Palmate Newt and the curious rare Pyrenean Salamander; amongst the reptiles are Green Lizard and Pyrenean Viper.

Although Brown Bears have not been seen in the reserve for two decades at least, there

A strikingly coloured form of the Common Frog (Rana temporaria) in high pastures on the Col du Pourtalet.

are other mammals, including Isard, Fox, Hare, Otter and the Pyrenean Desman. Birds are typical of the high-mountain and forest regions of the Pyrenees – Ptarmigan, Capercaillie, Black Woodpecker, Wallcreeper, Rock Pipit, Black Redstart, Ring Ouzel, Alpine Accentor, Dipper, Short-Toed Treecreeper and Snow Finch.

There are several ways to gain access to the region covered by the park and one of them involves travelling from Lannemezan to Arreau (or from Bagnères de Luchon via the Col de Péyresourde to Arreau). From Arreau take the D929 to Fabian where the road turns north and climbs up towards the Lac de Cap de Long with the Lac d'Orédon down below. Laid out before you is a staggering panorama of jagged peaks in the very centre of the Massif de Néouvielle.

110 MASSIF DE LA CARENCA	
Maps:	MA p. 176; IGN No. 72
Location:	SE of Font Romeu
Access:	Unrestricted on foot
Terrain:	Woodland; moorland; rocky slopes; cliffs
Specialities:	Pyrenean plants, butterflies; Isard, Wild Boar, Genet, Wildcat

The reserve is really a group of three adjoining territories: Mantet (3,028ha), Prats de Mollo (2,185ha), and Py (3,930ha), which together embrace an area of 9,143ha bordered to the east by the Massif du Canigou, to the west by the Carença valley and varying in altitude from 1,000–2,700m.

Although much of the terrain includes metamorphic rocks such as gneiss and granite, there are some limestone deposits (the lower part of the Py is white marble) and the contrast between the flora of the two is quite remarkable. The reserve area can be reached by turning off the main N116 south-west of Prades and taking the D6 to Sahore. Then, carry on along he D6 until you reach Py or Mantet.

The lower ground within the reserve is largely forested with Beech; Sessile Oak and chestnut predominate in the damper places. Higher up, these are replaced by Mountain Pine with a few Silver Fir and Scots Pine; there are Hazel, Red-Berried Elder and Alpine Rose in the under-storey. On open ground, Pyrenean Broom and Alpenrose can cover extensive areas. Geranium-like Saxifrage and Pyrenean Gentian are common, with Large-Flowered Butterwort in seepages. Pyrenean Turk's Cap grows in the woodlands. Butterflies occurring within the reserve include the local race of the Apollo butterfly, Gavarnie Ringlet, and Lefèbre's Ringlet.

The list of birds in the reserve includes some uncommon and interesting species. Conifer forests provide a home for the Capercaillie which feed throughout the winter on bark and pine needles. Ptarmigan are resident on the open ground. Golden Eagle soar over the open moorland in search of prey and Goshawk occupy the same ecological niche within the woodlands. On rocky slopes and cliffs, Wallcreepers are not infrequent, searching the narrow cracks for suitable food.

The endemic Pyrenean Desman is found more or less throughout the reserve wherever a suitable habitat exists – streams and torrents are the best places to begin searching and watching. The larger mammals are particularly interesting with populations of the Isard and Wild Boar in and around the forest areas. Rarely seen but detected from tracks and droppings are two carnivores, the Wild Cat and the Genet.

III MASSIF DU MADRES AND MT CORONAT	
Maps:	MA p. 176; IGN No. 72
Location:	NE of Font Romeau
Access:	Free, snow permitting
Terrain:	Mountain woods; grasslands; rocky areas
Specialities:	Endemic plants; Crayfish; Golden Eagle; Genet, Wild Cat

Like the Massif de la Carença natural reserve, the Massif du Madrès and Mt Coronat really embrace three distinct areas (Nohèdes, Conat and Jujols) to give a total area of 3,160ha. An altitude range of 800–2,400m exists within the reserve, the highest points being reached on le Roc Nègre (2,469m) in the Massif du Madrès and Mt Coronat (2,120m). There is considerable variation in the rock types within the reserve. For example, around the village of Nohèdes there is Devonian limestone, in Conat you can come across a reddish limestone rich in fossil shells, whilst elsewhere there are granites shaped by past glacial action and lakes established in the same period (le Gourg Blau and le Gourg Estelat). As usually happens in these mountains, the woods of the lower slopes are mainly broad-leaved with Beech, Sessile and Downy Oaks. On the banks of a river in the reserve, 'l'Homme Mort', the woodland tends to be Ash and Alder.

Warm air from the Mediterranean, rising up via the Tet valley, creates a microclimate in places which allows some of the more tender plants to survive – Prickly Juniper, Thyme and Lavender. Plants such as Etruscan Honeysuckle, Sun-Rose and Trailing Rock-Rose are clear markers for the presence of calcareous soils. In stony places or rocky crevices there are several saxifrages (*Saxifraga aizoon, S. media, S. pentadactylis*), Mountain Aven, Alpine Toadflax, Asthionema, Aragon Rest-Harrow, Pyrenean Ramonda, and a rarity, Pyrenean Alyssum.

Wherever there is such a diversity of plants, there will be an insect flora to. match. The butterfly list includes Marbled Skipper and Small Mountain White together with three burnet moths (*Zygaena carniolica, Z. romeo* and *Z. viciae*). 'Oddities' known to occur are the Blind Scorpion (*Belisarius xambui*) and an increasingly rare animal, the Crayfish.

A pair of Golden Eagle breeds regularly in the reserve and, with the warmer weather there are sufficient reptiles to justify the appearance of feeding Short-Toed Eagle. Other nesting birds include Eagle Owl, Dipper, Crag Martin and Chough.

Both the Genet and Wild Cat survive in small numbers in the wooded parts of the reserve whilst Red Deer, Isard and Wild Boar would be more numerous if it were not for the effects of hunting. Perhaps the most exiting creature in the reserve is the Lynx and the

number of local placenames with 'Os' or 'Ours' (Bear) suggests that in days gone by Brown Bear was well known to the inhabitants of the region.

112 FORET DE LA MASSANE	
Maps:	MA p. 177; IGN No. 72
Location:	W of Argelès-sur-Mer
Access:	Restricted to paths
Terrain:	Woodland
Specialities:	Insects (particularly beetles); small mammals

The forest, also known as the Forêt de Couloumates, consists of 336ha, owned by the Commune d'Argelès-sur-Mer and is situated at the eastern end of the Massif d'Albères. To get there, you need to walk from Argelès-sur-Mer. A path leading eventually to the Tour de la Massane begins at the intersection of the

Tour Madeloc above the Forêt de la Massane, with the Mediterranean beyond.

D114, through the town centre, and the N114 which by-passes it. From the Tour, a path descends towards the river and follows the valley where the reserve is situated. Alternatively, take the D2, which follows the River Massane, via the Gorge de Lavall and walk from Lavall along the valley bottom.

The reserve, which lies at an altitude varying between 600 and 1,150m, is crossed by the River Massane and has an origin dating back somewhere before the glacial epochs. Lying partly on schist and partly on granite, the woodland is mainly Beech (plus Downy Oak, Field and Montpellier Maple) and has attracted the attention of botanists for centuries because of its unspoiled nature. By virtue of its position, (it is, in effect, isolated from the rest of the Pyrenees by the Col du Perthus at 290m) and, freed from the influences of the rest of the *massif* and from human activity, it can claim several endemic insect species. The climate is essentially Mediterranean with infrequent but heavy showers, though these are not sufficient to disturb the rich humus layers. This encourages a diverse insect population. Beetles are especially numerous with some 1,250 species recorded in this limited area (compared with 3,000 for the whole of Fontainebleau which occupies 170km²). Two particularly attractive species are *Hoplia coerula*, which is a brilliant turquoise blue, and *Chrysocarabus rutilans* with patches of shining red and gold on a green background.

In sunny rides, butterflies flourish and the larger fritillaries (High Brown, Silver-Washed and Cardinal) are in evidence. White Admirals are common and can be distinguished from the similar-looking Great Banded Grayling (also with white-banded wings) by a much stronger flight. Smaller butterflies are represented by Purple and White-Letter Hairstreaks.

Ascalaphids

A striking feature of the insect-life of southern France, especially in flowery pastures in hilly and mountain areas, is the presence of the dragonfly-like ascalaphids. There are several species, all belonging to the genus *Libelloides*, related to the ant-lions and lacewings. The adults are large, day-flying, with a fast flight about a metre off the ground, from which they will settle, motionless, on vegetation for a while. They have four transparent net-veined wings, and long clubbed antennae.

They extend northwards to central France, and are most common from May to July in warm, sunny, flowery grasslands in the Alps, Pyrenees, Vercors, and parts of the Massif Central.

Although there are no really rare mammals in the area, such a rich insect population supports large numbers of smaller insectivorous mammals, such as Pipistrelle and Noctule Bats, Glis Glis, Dormouse, Water Shrew and numerous woodmice belonging to a number of closely related species. Birds include Orphean, Dartford and Subalpine Warblers. In the autumn in particular, the variety of fungi is quite astonishing.

113 VALLEE D' OSSAU	
Maps:	MA pp. 167-8; IGN No. 70
Location:	Running S of Pau along the D934
Access:	Restricted to reserve; elsewhere free
Terrain:	Limestone cliffs; valley
Specialities:	Birds of Prey, nesting Griffon Vulture

The Ossau valley has to be one of the finest in the Pyrenees, not only because of its scenery, but also because of the number and variety of large raptors that patrol its length and soar high into the mountains on either side. Goshawk, Red and Black Kites, Short-Toed and Golden Eagles, Peregrine and vultures (Griffon and Egyptian) are frequently seen, but it is the vulture that the valley is best known for.

Since 1974, a region of limestone cliffs covering some 82ha in two parts has been set aside for a breeding colony of Griffon Vulture. The reserve is situated roughly half-way between Arudy and Laruns and occupies cliffs near Asté-Béon. During the breeding season, access to the reserve is prohibited (this period extends from 10th January until 15th August and has to encompass some fifty days between laying and hatching and a subsequent 120 days until the young are fully fledged). For anyone intent on seeing the vultures, this is no hardship since they are clearly visible as they soar locally on thermals. Sadly, there have been problems with egg collectors and those photographers more intent on a saleable picture than on the welfare of the subjects.

To encourage the Griffon Vultures to stay in this colony, feeding places have been established where carcasses of sheep and other animals are left. The fact that around fifty breeding pairs nest here out of about 100 in the French Pyrenees bears testament to the success of the project.

The Benou plateau which lies above the village of Bielles is a very good place to see many or all or the raptors mentioned in connection with this region as well as Raven and an occasional Eagle Owl.

114 VAL D'ARAN	
Maps:	MA p. 169; IGN No. 70
Location:	N of Bagnères de Luchon
Access:	Free all year
Terrain:	River-bank
Specialities:	Butterflies

One of the routes through the Pyrenees into Spain follows the N125 roughly south of St Gaudens to the border at Pont du Roi. From Valabrère to Chaum there is a choice of routes via the west or eastern side of the River Garonne. The advantage of taking the latter is that it hugs the bank for much of its length and Buddleia has become established at numerous places along the river course. In gardens, the nectar-rich flowers act as a magnet for a variety of butterflies and other insects. Here, the variety is astonishing and, in terms of species, can vary dramatically from the beginning of a fortnight's holiday to its end.

Both Common and Scarce Swallowtails are frequent, as are both the Brimstone and the Cleopatra (the bright-orange patches on the wings of the males of the latter making recognition easy). The larger fritillaries are well represented by Dark-Green, High-Brown, Silver-Washed and Cardinal . Other showy butterflies include Peacock, Small Tortoiseshell, Red and White Admirals, Painted Lady and, in July, the summer race of the Map Butterfly looking like a tiny White

*A female Cleopatra butterfly (*Gonepteryx cleopatra*).*

Admiral. Bath, Large, Small and Green-Veined Whites, Clouded Yellow, Pale Clouded Yellow, blues, browns, skippers and day-flying hawkmoths (Broad and Narrow-Bordered Bee Hawks, and Hummingbird Hawk) complete the picture.

The clearing of roadside verges on the French side makes a sad contrast with the Spanish side and, if one is in the area it would be shame not to cross the border. Rubbish-tips nearby have both Red and Black Kites as regular scavengers and small roads climbing above tributaries of the Garonne (Salardu to Bagerque and Pla de Beret) have flowers cascading over the roadside where butterflies rise up in clouds as you pass.

115 COL D'ORGAMBIDE	
Maps:	MA p. 166; IGN No. 69
Location:	SW of Oloron-Ste Marie
Season:	Best for autumn migration from August to November
Terrain:	Hill-top
Specialities:	Vantage-point for migrant watching

To get to the col means approaching from Larrau south-east of Oloron-Ste Marie on the D19 towards St Jean-de-Pied-de-Port, the col lies roughly south of St Jean close to the border with Spain. An alternative route involves leaving St Jean on the D301 which follows the River Nive. At Beherobie the road turns westwards and rises via a tortuous series of bends to the col.

Although not the most convenient of places to get to, it is justifiably famous as one of the best places in France to watch migrating raptors in the autumn. September is probably the best month in which to see a wide range of species including Honey Buzzard, Hobby, Marsh Harrier, Osprey and Black Stork. Later, in October, there are Buzzard, Sparrowhawk, Red Kite, and innumerable smaller birds. Around the end of October and the beginning of November there are Crane and the last of the migrant Red Kite.

116 LAC D'ARTIX	
Maps:	MA p. 149; IGN No. 69
Location:	On the Pau, SE of Orthez
Access:	Not permitted to reserve and lake; best observation points along the dykes enclosing the lake
Terrain:	Wooded marshland; open water
Specialities:	Water birds nesting and migrants

The lake itself is a reservoir for a Geothermal Power Station and is fed by the waters of the River Pau. It can be reached by taking the N117 from Orthez and then at Artix the D281 towards Mourenx.

The wet woodlands are, to a large extent, almost impenetrable and so the site is a refuge for water birds of all sorts. However,

A resplendent male Pintail duck (Anas acuta), with a female beyond.

the dykes enclosing the lake afford excellent observation points for the visitor with binoculars or telescope.

In spring-time there are colonies of nesting Night Heron and Little Egret as well as Gadwall and Black-Headed Gull. Regular passage migrants include Hobby, Marsh Harrier and Buzzard, as well as numerous small birds. In autumn the lake becomes an important stop-over for numbers of herons, waders and Spoonbill as well as numbers of raptors; in some years it lies on the migratory path of Crane and White Stork. Winter visitors are numerous – in number and in terms of species – especially ducks. Mallard, Shoveler, Pintail, Wigeon, Teal, Tufted Duck and Pochard are all present. Other birds include Lapwing, Snipe and Little Egret.

Lac D'Oredon.

117 BAGNERES DE LUCHON	
Maps:	MA p. 169; IGN No. 70
Location:	S of St Gaudens
Access:	Valley all year, ski lifts to slopes; heights accessible in summer
Terrain:	Grass and rocky slopes
Specialities:	Sub-alpine and Alpine plants; butterflies; mountain birds; dramatic scenery

Bagnères de Luchon lies in valley headed by an imposing snow-capped ridge and it offers a very good centre for walks in search of flowers and birds. The local tourist office has details of guided walks which are a very good way of safely getting to some of the higher places.

Superbagnères (1,804m), as its name suggests, lies above the valley and is reached by a winding road. In early summer the turf around is studded with gentians, Pink Rock Jasmine and a host of colourful Alpine plants. The other attraction is a chair lift, open in summer, which climbs to 2,450m in a landscape faced by a gigantic wall of peaks of around 3,000m altitude. It is an exellent region for Alpine plants and for birds such as Rock Bunting, Citril Finch, Chough and Alpine Chough.

From Luchon, a road leads via the Col de Peyresourde (D618) to Arreau. A turning south on the D76 follows the Oo valley where, from its end, one can climb the well-trodden path up to the Lac d'Oo (1,504m) with its waterfall at the far end, finding Ramonda *en route* and yellow heads of Pyrenean Lily around the lake.

The path climbs higher to Lac d'Espingo (1,967m) and finally to the Lac du Portillon in a wonderful setting below the three peaks, Crabioules (3,116m), Perdiguère (3,222m) and Gourgs Blancs (3,129m). Similarly, one can approach the wall of peaks by travelling to the Hospice de France, south of Luchon, where there are meadows rich in plants and butterflies. The D618 south of Luchon leads, via the Col du Portillon, into Spain and the Val d'Aran.

The violet-blue trumpets of Pyrenean Gentian (Gentiana pyrenaica) are a frequent sight in the eastern Pyrenees growing in damp areas and boggy places. The Pyrenean Trumpet Gentian (G. occidentalis) has larger, deep-blue trumpets and occurs in the west.

14. MEDITERRANEAN FRANCE

INTRODUCTION

Mediterranean France, as we define it here, is the ultimate goal of vast numbers of tourists and naturalists from more northern areas, including much of the rest of France. Its familiar attractions are sun, sea and good food and wine. However, it also possesses a superb range of natural habitats and an enormous variety of species from all groups.

We have defined this area as a relatively narrow band stretching along the coast from Perpignan to Nice, but the hilly nature of much of the region ensures that it is by no means wholly coastal in character. Large areas of the coast are devoted almost exclusively to the tourist industry, and much of the remaining flat land is devoted to intensive agriculture. Yet, somehow, it manages to retain an aura of unspoilt wildness, and there is a genuine *embarras de richesses* for the naturalist with time to spend.

Geologically, it is highly complex, with everything from large recent alluvial plains to small volcanic outcrops. Inland, the predominant feature of the hilly areas tends to be limestone, whilst much of the coast, especially to the west of Marseille, is alluvial and low-lying. The predominant natural habitats are those typical of Mediterranean Europe, i.e. garrigue and maquis, two names referring

*Black-Winged Stilt (*Himantopus himantopus*) in the marshy lagoons of the Camargue.*

to the opposite ends of a spectrum of open bushy stony habitats that occur throughout the area. Although natural in appearance, these are actually man-induced habitats, replacing the ancient forests of the area after early clearances. Despite their semi-artificial origins, they are frequently very rich in species. Limestone areas are especially rich in orchids, but all areas are likely to hold something of interest, and they are excellent habitats for reptiles, insects, and a range of birds, in addition to the many plants.

In some areas, old forests, or recolonized approximations of them, occur. Port-Cros island still holds much natural evergreen forest, as does the St Tropez peninsula. Other areas, such as the Massif des Maures, have some fine Chestnut forest, whilst the Massif des St Baumes has areas of ancient Beech forest on its northern slopes.

The coast is highly developed for the tourist industry, though there are a number of large brackish lakes in the western area that are still of interest, and small patches of sand-dunes here and there that have escaped development. The Camargue, on the Rhône delta, still forms a huge complex of coastal and wetland habitats, including an enormous stretch of dunes, despite the many pressures on it.

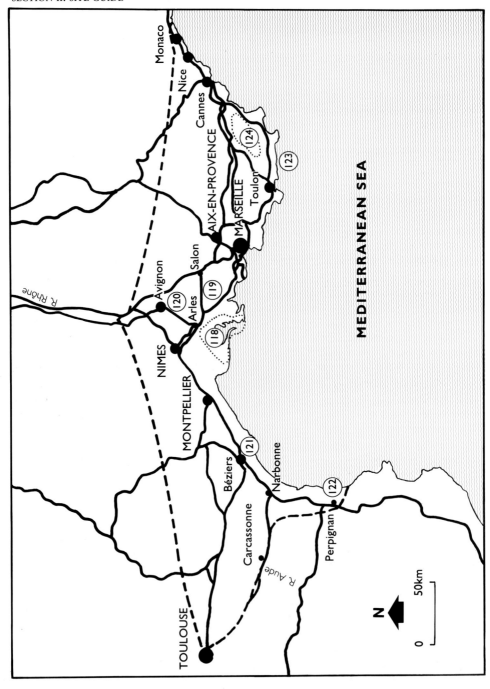

Opposite: *map of Mediterranean France. The sites are numbered as in the text. Only main roads and the major rivers are shown.*

Climatically, the area is typically Mediterranean, that is, having mild wet winters and hot dry summers, and the area around Perpignan is the sunniest and driest in France. This means that flowering is concentrated into a period between March and early May in the coastal areas, though hilly areas retain botanical interest through the summer, and a few species, such as Sea Daffodil, flower in midsummer. Birds begin to breed early, and a visit for these should not be left too late. Reptiles and insects, however, flourish virtually throughout the summer, especially in hillier areas, and there is always something to be seen.

In general, visitors with a strong interest in natural history would be advised to visit the region in the period April to June, thereby avoiding the crowds as well as the time of greatest heat. This will also coincide with seeing the flowers and any breeding birds at their peak.

118 THE CAMARGUE	
Maps:	MA pp. 157–8; IGN No. 66
Location:	S of Arles, between Marseilles and Montpellier
Access:	Open in places; limited in main reserve and much of any private land
Season:	Good at all times, especially spring–summer for birds, flowers, amphibians, invertebrates; good winter birds
Terrain:	Marshes; open water; sand-dunes; mudflats; mosquitoes a problem in summer
Specialities:	One of the great wildlife sites of Europe

The Camargue is probably the best-known single wildlife site in France, with a well-deserved reputation. We cannot give adequate details of such a rich and complex area

FIFTY INTERESTING SPECIES TO LOOK FOR

Alpine Swift	Gull-Billed Tern	Cytinus Parasite	Viperine Snake
Avocet	Hobby	Early Spider Orchid	Western Spadefoot
Bee-Eater	Hoopoe	Giant Orchid	Toad
Bittern	Little Tern	Provence Orchid	Black-Veined White
Black Kite	Mediterranean Gull	Red Helleborine	*Crocothemis erythraea*
Black-Winged Stilt	Purple Heron	Sea-Ball Grass	(dragonfly).
Blue Rock Thrush	Red-Crested Pochard	Sea Daffodil	Humming-Bird Hawk-
Bonelli's Eagle	Scop's Owl	Strawberry Tree	Moth
Dartford Warbler	Stone Curlew	Violet Limodore	Norfolk Hawker
Eagle Owl	Subalpine Warbler	Hermann's Tortoise	Oleander Hawk Moth
Egyptian Vulture	Wallcreeper	Montpellier Snake	Two-Tailed Pasha
Golden Oriole	Woodchat Shrike	Moorish Gecko	
Greater Flamingo	Brown Bee Orchid	Ocellated Lizard	
Great Spotted Cuckoo	Cottonweed	Stripeless Tree-Frog	

here, but there is plenty of information and there are good books (some in English) at the Park Information Centres and local bookshops in places like Arles and Stes-Mairies. The IGN 1:50,000 No. 33 map is ideal as an aid to searching the area.

The Camargue is essentially the delta of the River Rhône, built up naturally over a very long period, but now more or less stabilized by sea-walls and drainage channels. The predominant habitat is water, with a wonderful mixture of situations from tidal inlets, through sheltered lagoons, to freshwater, with ditches and canals everywhere. Associated with the open water are a huge number of wetland habitats – reed-beds, marsh, salt-marsh, and damp grassland. There is also a very extensive area of sand-dunes and sandy beach, good for flowers and birds. Other key factors in the importance of the site include its vast size, (the park covers 850km²), its warm climate (allowing a wide range of species to winter or breed), and its position on main migration routes.

Sand dunes and saltmarshes in the southern part of the Camargue.

The Camargue is best known for its bird-life. Breeding birds include Purple, Squacco and Night Herons, Bittern and Little Bittern, Greater Flamingo, Red-Crested Pochard, Bonelli's Eagle, Black Kite, Marsh and Montagu's Harriers, Spotted Crake, Kentish Plover, Avocet, Black-Winged Stilt, Collared Pratincole, Gull-Billed Tern, Little Tern, Whiskered Tern, Bee-Eater, Golden Oriole, Roller, Hoopoe, numerous warblers, and many others. In winter, there are large numbers of wildfowl and waders.

Reptiles and amphibians are of interest, and include Stripeless Tree Frog, Viperine Snake, Montpellier Snake, various frogs and toads, European Pond Terrapin and abundant lizards. Mammals of interest include Coypu, Wild Boar (especially in winter), Beaver and many common species.

Although the Camargue is not famous for its flowers, these are of considerable interest. It lacks many of the special plants of the dry rocky hillsides, found elsewhere in Provence, but it does have a wide range of marsh plants and the best dunes on the French Mediterranean coast. Plants on the dunes include Sea

Greater Flamingos (Phoenicopterus ruber), one of the specialities of the Camargue region.

Daffodil, Sea Dock, Sea Kale, Sea Stock, Cottonweed, numerous broomrapes, *Dorycnium suffruticosum*, Sand Crocus and many others, varying according to the degree of stability. Giant Orchid is frequent on some roadsides in early spring.

The area is generally rich in Mediterranean invertebrates, and particularly good for some groups. Aestivating snails, clustered together on vegetation, are a notable sight in summer. Dragonflies and other forms of aquatic life are varied and numerous, and include, amongst many others, Norfolk Hawker, *Erythromma viridulum*, *Anax parthenope*, the striking red-pink *Crocothemis erythraea*, *Orthetrum brunneum*, and *Sympetrum meridionale*.

All parts of the Camargue are of interest, especially to those not familiar with the nature of the area. A visit to one of the various information centres (marked on most maps) is recommended. Good areas and roads to try include:

1. The shore and étangs around Stes-Mairies.
2. The area around Cacharel, on the west side of the Réserve des Impériaux.
3. Mas Neuf du Vaccares and Mas d'Agon, just north of the étang de Vaccarès for heron roosts, Bee-Eaters, etc.
4. The D36b takes you through an excellent selection of sites down the east of Vaccarès.

Aestivating snails (Theba pisara), a common sight on vegetation in summer.

5. The Digue à la mer, between Stes-Maries and the lighthouse Phare de la Gocholle, runs for 15 kms or so between the sea and the main étangs. Lots of birds, and some easy diversions to look at the dunes. Foot or bicycle only.

The Petite Camargue lies to the west of Stes Maries-de-la-Mer, towards Aigues-Mortes, and partly inside the Regional Park. It is a rather inaccessible area, but full of interest for bird-watchers, and there are dunes along the foreshore.

119 THE PLAINE DE LA CRAU	
Maps:	MA p.158; IGN No. 66
Location:	SE of Arles, towards Marseilles
Season:	Late spring–summer for birds and flowers
Terrain:	A dry stony plain
Specialities:	Little Bustard, Pin-tailed Sandgrouse, Calandra Lark, Stone Curlew, Roller

Access into this area is straightforward by the busy N568 south east of Arles, though some walking is necessary to get right into the area. The plain of Crau is an extraordinary place, unique in France. It has the characteristics of a stony desert, not so much for climatic reasons, but more because it is a huge flat stony area that has been virtually impossible to cultivate. Once, it covered about 600km², but now there are barely 100 left, split up into blocks. It is grazed by huge flocks of wandering sheep.

La Crau is best known for birds, and is usually on the itinerary for anyone visiting the nearby Camargue. Birds are much less in evidence here, but those that do occur are specialists, in some cases to be found nowhere else in France. The main species are Pin-Tailed Sandgrouse (the only breeding area in France), Little Bustard, Lesser Grey Shrike (about one-third of the French population), Calandra Lark, Roller, and Stone Curlews – a mixture of species found nowhere else in the country.

The flowers are also of interest, though not spectacular, and there is a good range of lizards and larger insects here.

Generally, the area is similar in species content wherever the unimproved stony plains still exist; the rubbish-dump at Entressen has a reputation for kites and vultures, though the numbers have declined in recent years.

One of the vast wandering sheep flocks that roam the stony plain of la Crau.

120 CHAINE DES ALPILLES	
Maps	MA p. 158; IGN No. 66
Location:	NE of Arles
Access:	Open
Season:	Best in spring–summer for birds, spring for flowers
Terrain:	Rocky hillsides; dry woodlands
Specialities:	Egyptian Vulture, Eagle Owl, Alpine Swift, Blue Rock Thrush, Bonelli's Eagle; orchids

The Chane des Alpilles is a striking, though not specially high, ridge of limestone hills just north-east of Arles. Road access is easy from Arles, St Rémy-de-Provence, or other directions. The striking citadel village of les Baux brings large numbers of tourists, and it is worth a visit for the views. Regular buses run to the village.

Although by no means the only such place in the south of France, les Alpilles are well known for their birds, especially raptors. The FIR maintains a summer information centre on la Caume, and key nest-sites are watched. Likely species include Peregrine, Egyptian Vulture, Eagle Owl, and Bonelli's and Short-Toed Eagles. Other birds are good: Alpine Swift, Wallcreeper, Subalpine Warbler, Blue Rock Thrush and Alpine Accentor.

Above: Giant Orchids (Barlia robertiana) are frequent in much of southern France, flowering very early in the year.
Left: Val d' Enfer in les Alpilles.

Flowers are good here, especially in April–May, and include many typical of the area such as the attractive blue *Aphyllanthes monspeliensis*. Orchids are quite frequent, and they include *Ophrys bertolonii*, various sub-species of *O. sphegodes*, together with *O. arachnitiformis*, *O. fusca* and *O. fuciflora*. Violet Limodore occurs under pines, and *Orchis provincialis*, here and there. Giant Orchid is widespread. Insect-life is typical, and includes many butterflies such as fritillaries and blues.

The best areas are les Baux, Val d'Enfer, la Caume, and the open pine forests to the east of les Baux. The long-distance footpath, GR6, runs all along the chain, and passes some lovely places *en route*.

121 LA DOMAINE DE ROQUEHAUTE	
Maps:	MA p. 173; IGN No. 65
Location:	c. 15km SE of Béziers
Access:	Open
Season:	Best in spring and summer for flowers, insects and birds
Terrain:	Garrigue; scrub woodland; temporary lakes
Specialities:	Garrigue flowers; flowers of temporary lakes; Hoopoe, Scop's Owl

This is a relatively small site, easily accessible from Béziers via the N112 and the D37, running southwards from there, passing directly through it. It represents an island of unspoilt land in an increasingly built-up and intensively-farmed area. The hill of Roquehaute is the last southerly outpost of the chain of ancient volcanoes that forms the Auvergne (*see* page 99).

The primary significance of the site is botanical. The flowers of the garrigue and woodland are attractive, though generally of widespread species. The acid soil precludes many of the orchids from occurring here, for instance. More unusual is the presence of a number of special plants of temporary pools such as the annuals, *Ranunculus lateriflorus*, *Lythrum tribracteatum*, and various non-flowering plants such as two quillworts *Isoetes durieuei* and *I. setacea*, the Least Pillwort, and *Marsilia pubescens*. The attractive *Narcissus tazetta* occurs in the marshy fields to the south. Although not studied, the temporary pools may have an interesting invertebrate fauna as they do elsewhere. Amphibians, especially Edible Frog, are abundant.

Breeding birds amongst the scrub include numerous Nightingales, together with Hoopoe, Scop's Owl, Great Spotted Cuckoo, Nightjar, and other garrigue species.

Turn left (if travelling east) off the D37 about 2km east of Portiragnes and head north; stop near the top of the hill, or at the farm, and walk on either side of the road – if you reach the N112, you have gone too far.

122 MAS LARRIEU	
Maps:	MA p. 177; IGN No. 72
Location:	On the coast, 15km SE of Perpignan
Access:	Nominally limited to footpaths
Season:	Best in spring–summer
Terrain:	Dunes; woodland; marsh
Specialities:	Penduline Tit, Melodious Warbler, Woodchat Shrike; Western Spadefoot Toad

Access to this site is straightforward from the D81 north of Argelès-Plage, around where the road crosses the River Tech. There is a parking area south of the river. Although not the richest of sites in this book, Mas Larrieu is important and interesting as one of the last refuges of semi-natural coastal habitat in this highly developed part of the Mediterranean. Unfortunately, its protection and management are not strong enough to guarantee its survival.

The reserve consists of sand-dunes, river-valley forest and marshes. There are good breeding birds, with Penduline Tit (now very rare in France), Melodious Warbler, various wetland warblers, Woodchat Shrike, Golden Oriole, and others. The Western Spadefoot Toad occurs, and an uncommon lizard is the Spanish Psammodromus.

The riverine forest includes some good examples of Black Poplar, in a typical natural situation, and other plants of interest include Globe Thistle, Sea Holly, various broom-rapes, *Paronychia argentea*, the pink-flowered *Convolvulus althaeoides*, and impressive stands of giant reed.

The marsh lies south of the parking area; the dunes are the best area for flowers; the river-valley forest is best for birds, with careful looking.

123 PORT-CROS ISLAND NATIONAL PARK	
Maps:	MA p. 161; IGN No. 68
Location:	Offshore island, S of le Lavandou, E of Toulon
Access:	By boat from le Lavandou
Season:	Best in spring and early summer for flowers, insects, birds, reptiles, amphibians
Terrain:	Mainly dry, rocky garrigue; maquis and forest
Specialities:	Precious remnant of evergreen Mediterranean forest; marine-life

The National Park of Port-Cros is the smallest in France, and the only island park. It was established to protect a remnant of semi-natural Mediterranean forest from exploitation and development, and covers a total of about 1,800ha, well over half of which is below the sea in a band around the island. There is a very small village at the north-west corner of the island, with a good information centre, cafés,

A view of the main village and harbour on the island National Park of Port-Cros. This bay has superb clear water, and there are extensive beds of Sea-Ball Grass (Posidonia oceanica) here, with rich marine life. A glass-bottomed boat makes regular trips to view the marine life.

Clathrus ruber 5–10 (diameter)

This extraordinary fungus has no ordinary English name. It appears in spring, normally, in open woodland, scrub, and even gardens in warmer areas, and it is mainly southern and western in distribution within France. It is sporadic in appearance, and may disappear as suddenly as it appeared in any one site. This specimen was photographed in May on Port-Cros island, in open evergreen forest.

and a hotel. Boat trips run regularly to here from le Lavandou or Port d'Hyères. Foot access is permitted over virtually the whole of the island, and an early boat is recommended as there is a lot to be seen.

The woodlands of Holm Oak, Strawberry Tree, Phoenician Juniper, Cork Oak, Myrtle and Aleppo Pine are impressive. The flora is rich, though not with spectacular species generally, and orchids, for example, are more limited than in many mainland areas. The fungal flora is very rich, with hundreds of species in spring and autumn, including the impressive and extraordinary *Clathrus ruber*. On and around the shores there are impressive amounts of Sea-Ball Grass.

Breeding birds include Peregrine and Eleonora's Falcon, Cory's Shearwater, and the eastern race of Manx Shearwater. The poorly translated English information leaflet from the park lists 'Ashy-Grey Puffin, or Yelkouan Puffin' and 'Tufted Sea-Raven from Corsica' as breeding, but we have no further information on these! There is a good range of birds at passage periods.

Reptiles and amphibians are of special interest, with the Tyrrhenian Painted Frog at its only French site (other than Corsica), two species of gecko, and Ladder and Montpellier Snakes.

Invertebrates are very rich and varied, though not easy to see. The figure of 220 butterflies given by the park information actually includes many larger moths, so this is a very low total, suggesting under-recording; however, the list does include the remarkable Two-Tailed Pasha butterfly and the Oleander Hawk-Moth.

The marine-life is very rich and can be viewed by snorkelling, diving, or from a glass-bottomed viewing boat, which is expensive.

The nearby island of Porquerolles is inhabited, but part of it is run by the National Park, and it has much of interest. Access is from Hyères or Giens.

124 MASSIF DES MAURES	
Maps:	MA p. 161; IGN No. 68
Location:	Between Toulon and Cannes
Access:	Generally open
Season:	Best in spring and early summer
Terrain:	Mainly dry, rocky; wooded or scrubby
Specialities:	Hermann's Tortoise; Tongue Orchid, Violet Limodore; Woodchat Shrike; garrigue flowers

Access into the hills is very easy by road from the coastal towns of St Tropez, le Lavandou and Toulon. La Garde-Freinet is an excellent centre.

This is an area of wooded hills on ancient schistose rock, unlike much of Provence. The hills are beautifully unspoilt with extensive areas of garrigue, woodland and maquis, and marvellous spring flowers including several *Cistus* species with their parasites *Cytinus spp.*, French Lavender, Large Spurge, Cineraria, Violet Limodore, Tongue Orchid and many more. Strawberry Trees are abundant. *Anemone hortensis* is frequent in early spring through much of the area.

A special feature of this area is the presence of a good population of Hermann's Tortoise, now virtually absent from the rest of France. There is a re-habilitation and re-introduction centre, open to the public, just east of the village of Gonfaron. The best way to find the tortoises in the wild is to sit quietly and listen, as they are very noisy moving through undergrowth. Early morning is the best time. Other reptiles present are also of great interest, with Ladder Snake, Ocellated Lizard, and Pond Terrapin, amongst numerous others.

Insect life is rich, with many butterflies (over sixty species recorded), including cicada, grasshoppers and crickets from spring onwards, and the bird-life includes a wide range of Provence specialities such as Roller, Woodchat Shrike, Bee-Eater, Golden Oriole, Hoopoe, Hobby, and many others.

To the north, between the Massif and the A8 motorway, from les Mayons towards le Cannet-des-Maures, lies a flatter rather heathy area, with interesting plants and birds. Heart-Flowered Serapias is abundant, for example. Reptiles are also rich and varied in this area. It is unusual to find this sort of habitat on level ground in Provence.

Hermann's Tortoise *Testudo hermanni* L 25

Most people do not think of France as having wild tortoises. In fact, they were once relatively common in Mediterranean France, but are now virtually confined to the Massif des Maures, and possibly the Esterel. Tortoises are herbivorous egg-laying reptiles that hibernate through the winter and are active through the summer. They move around in maquis or scrub, looking for food, making a noise that can be heard from some distance away. If you hear a persistent rustling in the undergrowth somewhere in the Massif des Maures, it is always worth moving quietly towards the noise to see if it is a tortoise. It will stop if it sees you, and probably withdraw into its shell, but will soon re-emerge if all seems safe. The easiest place to see tortoises in France, in near-natural conditions, is at the Tortoise Village in the Massif des Maures near Gonfaron.

OTHER SITES

The Forest of Conques-sur-Orbeil
About 6km north of Carcassone, on the D118, there is an area of scrub, woodland and open stony grassland over limestone, known as the Forêt Domaniale de

Conques-sur-Orbeil. It has many similarities with the southern Causses country, with a few added Mediterranean ingredients. The flora is good, with many orchids amongst a scrub of Juniper, Kermes Oak, Box and species of *Cistus*. Reptiles include Mont pellier Snake, Green Lizard and others. The plant Hutchinsia is common on roadsides.

The Lubéron Regional Natural Park

This regional park lies to the north of Aix-en-Provence, between Cavaillon and Manosque. It consists mainly of the superb Lubéron mountains, divided into two by the Combe de Lourmarin, an impressive rocky gorge. Although the park has numerous villages, it retains a wild feeling, and there are vast areas of rocky hill or mountain country, partly forested. The Forêt des Cèdres is a large ancient (but planted) Cedar forest in the Petit Luberon, worth a visit. Orchids are frequent on the limestone soils, especially those with a slightly more northerly distribution, such as Monkey, Military, Lizard, Lady and Red Helleborine. In all, over 1,000 species of flowering plant have been recorded. About 130 breeding birds occur, and it is a good area for raptors.

A typical farm in the Lubéron mountains in Provence.

Massif de la Sainte Baume

Between Marseille and Toulon, a few kilometres inland, lies the superb and dramatic range of mountains known as Massif de la Sainte Baume. They are composed mainly of Jurassic and Cretaceous rocks, with several peaks reaching well over 1,000m. Access is easy from the N560 or from Gémenos on the N396.

They contain the usual range of Provence vegetation-types with typical species, and there is also an area of ancient Beechwood (unusual for this part of the country) on the north-facing slopes of St Pilon.

The St Tropez Peninsula

Although so much of the coast of this region of France is highly developed, parts of this beautiful peninsula have escaped and are protected as reserves. It is reminiscent of Port-Cros island, with its semi-natural forest on acid soils. The extreme coastal area between Gigaro and Cap Camarat is best, and a footpath runs right round the coast, though road access is (fortunately) difficult. It is an excellent area for frost-sensitive plants such as Tree Spurge, and butterflies are similar to those of Port-Cros, with Two-Tailed Pasha also occurring here (on Strawberry Tree).

The Haut Languedoc Regional Natural Park

This large Regional Natural Park lies to the east of Castres and Mazamet, running as far east as Bédarieux. It is very different from most of Mediterranean France, with the combination of acidic ancient rocks, a relatively high rainfall, and high rounded hills being more reminiscent of the Vosges or other northern areas. The flora is not exceptional, but it is a pleasant area in which to escape the summer heat and traffic of the coast, and breeding birds, including kites, Buzzard and Short-Toed Eagle, are frequent.

15. CORSICA

INTRODUCTION

Although definitely part of France, the island of Corsica is very different to mainland France in many ways. It lies 160km south of the Provence coast, yet is only 12km from Sardinia and 80km from mainland Italy, so it is hardly surprising that it is influenced by factors other than those of mainland France.

Corsica is a large and exceedingly mountainous island, over 160km long and with an area of nearly 9,000km². It is also the least populated of the larger Mediterranean islands. This combination of rugged topography with low population means that a large proportion of the island's vegetation is semi-natural in character, and its relative isolation from mainland Europe has allowed a fascinating mixture of widespread and endemic species to flourish. For various reasons, Corsica also has a less-developed tourist industry than equivalent Mediterranean islands, so far less coastal and mountain habitat has been lost, though, of course, the pressure is growing.

The rare and beautiful Corsican Storksbill (Erodium corsicus), a Corsican endemic.

Geologically, the island is dominated by granites of varying character, which make up most of the main mountain areas. The northeastern quarter of the island, including the 'finger', is made up mainly of hard schists. Here and there a few outcrops of limestone occur, of which the most notable is that around Bonifacio. This produces some superb scenery, and also allows a different, and very rich, flora to develop in this warm southern part of the island.

A large part of the island is designated as a Regional Natural Park. Although this does include many of the more interesting sites, in practice there is little difference in management or vegetation inside or outside the boundary, so we have not treated it as a specific site here. Information about the park area can be obtained locally from the various sub-offices in the park, or from the main office in Ajaccio.

Climatically, Corsica is essentially Mediterranean, though it tends to be rather milder and damper than adjacent Continental areas. Rain is more likely to fall in summer, especially up until June, and the mountains generate some of their own weather. Thus, although spring starts early, as in other Mediterranean zones, there is more to be seen through the summer, especially in the mountains.

The natural history is very rich, and no naturalist is likely to be disappointed by Corsica. Large mammals are somewhat limited, thanks largely to hunting pressure, but bird life is extremely rich, and includes the endemic Corican Nuthatch as well as many uncommon, but more widespread, species such as Bearded Vulture (Lammergeier), Golden Eagle, or Osprey. The plants are superb, with a very wide range of Mediterranean species, mountain species and Corsican specialities

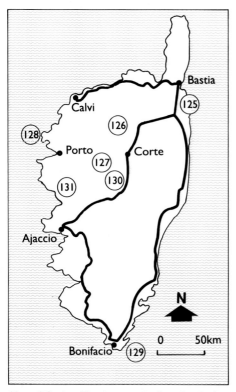

Map of Corsica. The sites are numbered as in the text. Only main roads of the region are shown.

(though actually most of the endemics are Tyrrhenian, i.e. shared with Sardinia). In general, the mountains are not quite as flower-rich as adjacent mainland mountains, partly through isolation preventing colonization, but also because of the wholly acid rock and, perhaps, through lack of extensive meadows and pastures created elsewhere.

Altogether, it is a superb place, with dramatic scenery, generally good weather, and an enormous amount to be seen by the naturalist. The best times to go are between April and the end of June, though high summer still holds plenty of interest, and late winter can reveal a few flowers and some wintering birds.

125 LAKE BIGUGLIA	
Maps:	MA pp. 179; IGN No. 73
Location:	S of Bastia, on the NE coast
Access:	Easy at all times
Season:	Spring and early summer
Terrain:	Large shallow lake with muddy, partly reed-fringed shores
Specialities:	Breeding wetland birds

FIFTY INTERESTING SPECIES TO LOOK FOR

Alpine Accentor	Kingfisher	Corsican Hellebore	Yellow Bee Orchid
Alpine Chough	Marmora's Warbler	Corsican Pine	Bedriaga's Rock Lizard
Bearded Vulture	Marsh Harrier	*Cyclamen repandum*	Corsican Brook
Bee-Eater	Osprey	Hepatica	Salamander
Buzzard	Pallid Swift	*Leucojum longifolium*	Gecko (3 species)
Citril Finch	Peregrine Falcon	Mirror Orchid	Tyrrhenian Painted
Corsican Nuthatch	Raven	*Morisia monanthos*	Frog
Cory's Shearwater	Redstart	Pink Butterfly Orchid	Tyrrhenian Rock
Crossbill	Red-Crested Pochard	Provence Orchid	Lizard
Dipper	Red Kite	Sand-Crocus	Cleopatra
Golden Eagle	Sardinian Warbler	Sawfly Orchid	Clouded Yellow
Goshawk	Wallcreeper	Tazetta Narcissus	
Great Reed Warbler	Mouflon	Tongue Orchid	
Hoopoe	Corsican Crocus	Tree Spurge	

Etang de Biguglia, a large lagoon just outside Bastia.

Lake Biguglia (Etang de Biguglia) is easily the largest lake in Corsica, at 1,450ha surface area, which is roughly half of the island's open water. It is easily reached by taking the N193 from Bastia, then following the unclassified road (signed as circuit d'Etang) which runs all along the east side of the lake. To reach the southern part, take the D207 towards the lake.

The lake is fed by fresh water, but connects with the sea via a narrow channel at the

*A Bee-Eater (*Merops apiaster*) close to its nesting hole in a low sand cliff.*

north end. It is, therefore, partly saline, varying according to tidal influences and the amount of fresh water flowing in. Overall, the southern section is freshest, and this part is best for birds. The northern section has interesting salt marsh and salt-tolerant plants, but is generally rather messy. The eastern side of the lake suffers from the adjacent holiday developments to some extent.

Breeding birds around the lake include Marsh Harrier, Hobby, Bee-Eater, Hoopoe, Kingfisher, Cetti's and Fan-Tailed Warbler and many other warblers, as well as Red-Crested Pochard, Purple Heron, and Water Rail. Huge numbers of Coot are usually present, and in winter there are good, though not enormous, numbers of duck. Considering the rich fish fauna that exists, the number of fishing birds is relatively low here (and generally in Corsica), though Ospreys regularly pass through. Passage times are excellent, with a wide variety of species calling in here *en route* for elsewhere.

The lake is not a noted botanical or entomological site, though there is a good range of marsh and salt-marsh plants, and reasonable, though not marvellous, dragonflies. There is also a good range of southern European amphibia, though these are not well recorded.

The north end has the easiest access and best views of the lake surface, but the southern reed-fringed end is much better for breeding birds. To the south, the Etang de Diane and the Etang de Sale, either side of the village of Aléria, are similar, much smaller, sites worth a visit.

Moorish Gecko
Tarentola mauritanica L 12–16

The geckoes are an extraordinary group of lizards, mainly found in tropical parts of the world, but with three species occuring in Mediterranean France. The most common two species are the Moorish Gecko (illustrated above) and the Spanish Gecko, which occur widely along the coastal areas, while the European Leaf-Toed Gecko is much more local. They are primarily nocturnal animals, hunting largely by sight, and they therefore have unusually large eyes (with a vertical pupil, unlike other European lizards). They are most frequently found on the walls of buildings, and will readily come to areas that are lit at night, because this attracts so many insects. They can climb superbly, thanks to their wide-spreading feet with adhesive pads, and are often to be seen upside-down on ceilings.

126 THE ASCO VALLEY	
Maps:	MA pp. 178–9; IGN No. 73
Location:	Between Corte and Calvi
Access:	Open; snow may block higher reaches at times
Season:	Best April until July for all groups
Terrain:	Cliffs; forest; high-mountain country
Specialities:	Corsican Nuthatch, Wallcreeper, Bearded Vulture, Golden Eagle; Corsican Crocus

From Corte, take the N193 northwards, bear left onto the N197 at Ponte Leccia, and then turn left on the D47. This is a spectacular and varied site, with stony plains and foothills with maquis lower down, a superb gorge, extensive coniferous forests above this, and easy access to high mountain slopes at the top. The whole valley from here to Haut Asco is of interest.

Birds include Golden Eagle, Bearded Vulture and smaller birds of prey, especially around the dramatic gorge areas. The Corsican Pine forests are best for Corsican Nuthatch, as well as Crossbill and Citril Finch. Beyond the dense forests, there are superb ancient Corsican Pines, and from here upwards is good for Raven, Alpine Chough, and Alpine Accentor.

Plant-life is rich, and includes *Crocus minima* lower down, and masses of *C. corsicus* higher up, as well as Sand Crocuses (*Romulea spp.*) here and there. *Cyclamen repandum* and Corsican Hellebore are both common, as are several orchid species, Yellow Star-of-Bethlehem, *Leucojum longiflorum*, and others.

This is a good place for lizards on rocks by the roadsides; Bedriaga's Rock Lizard is common, with Tyrrhenian Rock Lizard at lower altitudes. Butterflies are plentiful, and insects

like tiger beetles are common right up to the snow line.

A wide range of species and habitats can be seen simply by following the road up the valley. It is worth continuing on to Haut Asco, and walking beyond if time permits. The views are spectacular, with Monte Cinto (the highest peak on the island) very close.

127 THE SPELUNCA GORGES AND FOREST OF AITONE	
Maps:	MA p. 178; IGN No. 73
Location:	Due E of Porto on the road to Corte
Access:	Open
Season:	Best from April to July
Terrain:	Rocky and steep in places; dense forest; open high-altitude scrub and pasture
Specialities:	Corsican Nuthatch, Red Kite, Citril Finch; *Leucojum longifolium*

This dramatic area lies either side of the D84 on its course from the coast near Porto to the

Corsican Pines (Pinus nigra var laricio) on the slopes of Monte Cinto, in the upper Asco valley.

Col de Vergio at an altitude of 1,477m. The lower area, between Ota and Evisa, is the dramatic rocky Spelunca gorge, whilst the upper area, between Evisa and the col, is the Forest of Aitone. At the highest levels, from just below the col upwards, there is a sizeable area of high-altitude scrub, moorland and pasture with cliffs and rocks, and superb views. The whole area is of great interest.

Breeding birds include Red Kite, Goshawk, Corsican Nuthatch, a local subspecies of Treecreeper, Crossbill, Citril Finch, Golden Eagle (in the general area), Buzzard and Raven. The rubbish-tip below Evisa is particularly good for Ravens.

The flora is rich and varied. The gorge area has a good range of maquis plants, together with specialities, such as the early-flowering *Leucojum longifolium, Cyclamen repandum,* and the two local *Crocus* species. Corsican Hellebore is locally common. Other species of interest include *Gagea nevadensis* and the Butterfly Orchid. Butterflies include the striking Cleopatra.

Corsican Crocus *Crocus corsicus* H 10

The beautiful Corsican Crocus is a true endemic, confined wholly to the island of Corsica, and nowhere else in the world (unlike many other Corsican specialities, which also occur in nearby Sardinia). In fact, the differences between this species and some other crocuses is relatively small, but, coupled with the geographical isolation, they are just enough to make it different.

In Corsica, the crocus is common in the mountains, especially at higher levels, occuring from the wooded areas up into the high pastures. Many visitors miss it altogether, as it starts flowering in the lowlands in February and then flowers up the mountains in a band following the melting snow.

The whole area is not well known away from the road, and exploration would undoubtedly be rewarding in this wild and unspoilt mountain area.

To the west, bordering the coast along the D81, lies the Forest of Piana, noted for its dramatic rock scenery, and good orchids, especially Provence Orchid. To the north lies the Fangu Forest along the River Fangu, reached by taking the D81 from Porto towards Galeria, then turning east up the valley

on the D351. Rough tracks lead high into impressive Corsican Pine and Holm Oak forest with good flowers and birds.

128 THE SCANDOLA NATURE RESERVE	
Maps:	MA p. 178; IGN No. 73
Location:	On the NW coast, between Calvi and Porto
Access:	Limited; normally by boat only
Season:	May onwards through summer
Terrain:	Coastal cliffs and headlands
Specialities:	Osprey, Peregrine Falcon, Pallid Swift, Blue Rock Thrush; endemic flowers

A superb, isolated coastal site protected by nature reserve status. It consists of extensive impressive and varied coastal cliffs with offshore islands and rocks, togther with a large area of inland maquis, devoid of habitation. The nearest village is the small fishing settlement of Girolata, but even this is only accessible by a long footpath route from the land side. The only practical access is by boat; one can be hired from Calvi or Porto (Porto is closer, but boats are less frequent), from May onwards only. Landing is restricted, except at Girolata, which is outside the reserve.

The cliffs support good numbers of many birds, including Osprey (absent from the remainder of France), Cormorant, gull, Rock Dove, Alpine and Pallid Swifts, Crag Martin, Peregrine Falcon, and others. Flowers include the endemic Corsican Storksbill, the thrift, *Armeria soleirolii*, the ragwort, *Senecio leucanthemifolius*, *Lotus cytisoides*, and various other more widespread species.

The inland maquis has Blue Rock Thrush, Marmora's, Sardinian and Dartford

Warblers, and others. The reptiles and amphibia include most Corsican species, such as Tyrrhenian Wall Lizard, three out of the four European species of gecko, Tyrrhenian Painted Frog, Corsican Brook Salamander, and the Corsican form of Tree Frog.

The marine-life is exceptionally rich offshore, with numerous fish species and varied invertebrates. Monk Seal used to breed here, but have not since 1950. Altogether, this is an exceptional site, without close parallel.

129 BONIFACIO	
Maps:	MA p. 181; IGN No. 74
Location:	The southernmost tip of Corsica (see map)
Access:	Open at all times
Season:	Best from March to July for flowers, birds, insects
Terrain:	Maquis; grassland; cliffs; shore habitats
Specialities:	Numerous orchids; endemic flowers; Cory's Shearwater

Access to this site is straightforward, via the N196 or N198, from either side of the island. However, accommodation in the area is very limited. The Bonifacio area is very different from the rest of Corsica, partly because it forms the extreme southern tip of land, and partly because it is formed of limestone, unlike the rest of the island. It is, to an extent, isolated from the bulk of Corsica by the Trinity range of granite mountains.

Plant-life is very rich, with numerous endemics as well as more widespread Mediterranean species. Orchids are particularly good, as one might expect on limestone; Sawfly, Long-Spurred, Butterfly, Early Spider (in several forms), *Ophrys bombyliflora, O. speculum, O. fusca, O. lutea, O. bertolonii*, and *O. holoserica*, amongst others. Other flowers include the attractive crucifer, *Morisia monanthos*, with piles of large yellow flowers on miniature rosettes; the endemic *Silene* species; the curious endemic composite *Evax rotundata*; several species of sand crocus (*Romulea spp.*), and many more. This is an important botanical site.

Birds are less exceptional, but include breeding Cory's Shearwater, Rock Sparrow, Spanish Sparrow, Cirl Bunting, Spotless Starling and other southern species. Butterflies include Clouded Yellow, and several

The extraordinary limestone cliffs at Bonifacio, with Tree-Mallow (Lavatera arborea) in the foreground. The flowers along the top of these cliffs, southwards from the town, are of tremendous interest. Flowering begins here in late winter.

species are present all the year round. The intertidal and marine-life is very rich on the calcareous rocks.

Good areas include the cliffs around the citadel of Bonifacio (with exceptional views), and shearwaters can be heard opposite the large rock known as the Grain de Sable. For flowers, follow the D260 and its minor branches south-east, looking mainly at grassy maquis and rocky outcrops. Most of the area is of interest, though a few areas are spoilt.

The Iles Lavezzi, just offshore, form a nature reserve, accessible by boat from Bonifacio during summer. They have breeding sea-birds, good flowers (granite species, not those of limestone), rare reptiles, and lovely views towards Sardinia.

Above: *Beechwoods and a stream in the upper parts of the Vizzavona forest.*

Below: *a Dipper* (Cinclus cinclus) *pausing in mid-stream.*

130 VIZZAVONA FOREST AND MONTE D'ORO	
Maps:	MA p. 179; IGN No. 74
Location:	On the N193 roughly midway between Corte and Ajaccio
Access:	Open on foot at any time
Season:	Best in spring and summer for flowers and birds
Terrain:	Mixed woodland rising up to steep mountain country; mainly easy walking
Specialities:	Corsican Nuthatch, Citril Finch, Red Kite

A superb area of managed medium – to high-altitude forest on the slopes of Monte d' Oro (2,389m), one of the highest mountains on the island. Unusually, there is an extensive area of ancient Beech woodland, and this contains plant species which generally have a more northerly distribution. The N193 passes through the forest and allows easy

access. A good starting-point is opposite the Forest Office (marked as Maison Forestiale), just south of Vizzavona village; the track marked as running up through the forest to the west is not open to cars, but makes easy walking, initially along the GR20 footpath.

The bird life includes a good population of the Corsican Nuthatch, recognizable by its white eyestripe, which occurs mainly in the coniferous forest above the Beech. Also present are Citril Finch, Red Kite, Goshawk, Dipper, Common Redstart, and Crossbills. Flowers include species such as Hepatica, Ramsons and Stinking Hellebore, as well as the more typically Corsican species like *Cyclamen repandum*, *Crocus corsicus* and Corsican Hellebore.

By following the GR20 footpath westwards, it is possible to ascend the slopes of Mt d'Oro, with a different range of species, and good views of raptors such as Golden Eagle.

To the north, about 24km south of Corte by road, the D273 runs westwards into the Forest of Venaco and the Valley of Verghello. The lower part is a beautiful gorge, with lizards, raptors and orchids to be seen, grading

Pastures full of Narcissus tazetta *near Sartène in south-west* Corsica.

upwards into predominantly coniferous forest. Bearded Vulture occur in the area.

131 THE LIAMONE RIVER MOUTH	
Maps:	MA pp. 178 & 10; IGN No. 74
Location:	On the W coast, 15km due N of Ajaccio
Access:	Open west of the D81; more limited inland
Season:	Best in spring, summer and autumn for birds, late spring for flowers
Terrain:	Sandy beach; dunes; reed-bed; wetlands
Specialities:	Water Rail, Great Reed Warbler, Kingfisher; endemic dune flowers

An interesting and varied coastal area, easily reached by the D81 which runs close to the sea where it crosses the river. Notable for the variety of habitats which, though well visited in summer, have not suffered from development. Habitats include extensive sand (partially built up into dunes), reed-beds, carr woodland, rocky shore and riverside.

The dune flowers are somewhat damaged by vehicles, but include the endemic *Silene* species (*S. sericea* and *S. succulenta ssp. corsica*), Sea Bindweed, Cottonweed, Sea Daffodil, Sea Spurge, Sea Medick, Sea Rocket (as *var. aegyptica*), *Hypecoum procumbens*, and various others. Tongue Orchids occur in more stable areas.

Breeding birds include Little Ringed Plover, Tawny Pipit and Short-Toed Lark in the open areas; the wetlands support Reed and Great Reed Warbler, Water Rail, Kingfisher, and others. Woodchat Shrike,

Red-Backed Shrike and Bee-Eaters all breed in the area, and are readily seen.

The insect fauna on the dunes is less damaged than that of most west-coast sites, and includes beetles such as the tiger beetle (*Cicindela trisignata*), and *Ateuchus sacer*.

The best sandy areas lie mainly south of the river, whilst the best reed-bed and carr lies to the north.

OTHER SITES

Gorges de la Restonica
This area is located immediately south-west of Corte, and is reached via the D623 which runs well into the mountains. The area includes fine mixed forest (with some old planted Chestnut here), and a good range of endemic or local flowers such as *Cyclamen repandum, Leucojum longiflorum* and Corsican Hellebore. It is also a good area for woodland birds and raptors.

Cap Corse
The northern extremity of Cap Corse, especially between Barcaggio and the Pointe d'Agnello, is a well known site for the observation of birds on spring passage. There is a good range of habitats here, and a very wide variety of resident and visiting birds can be seen between March and June. Autumn passage is less good.

Désert des Agriates
The Agriates desert is an extraordinary place, almost totally devoid of human habitation or cultivation, though not a desert in the true sense. It lies on the north coast between l'Ile Rousse and St Florent, marked on most maps. The great bulk of the area consists of dry rocky maquis or garrigue, with typical birds, insects, and flowers. On the coast

around Loto and Punta Mortella, there is a superb complex of undisturbed coastal habitats, protected as a reserve. Access is not easy, and four-wheel-drive would be helpful for the rough tracks that lead into the area.

Golfe de Rondinara
This is an attractive circular bay on the south-east coast between Porto-Vecchio and Bonifacio, reached by a branch of the D158. The bay is virtually undeveloped, and has a good sand-dune flora, with sheets of Sand Crocus in spring. There are two lagoons with amphibia breeding, and various rocky areas. Extensive *Posidonia* (Sea-Ball) beds lie just offshore, and marine and intertidal life is rich. There are good passage birds in the scrub.

The Col de Bavella
The Col and the Aiguilles de Bavella lie in the south-eastern mountains of the island. The D268 from Zonza to Solenzara passes over the col, at 1,218m. Besides the usual range of mountain flora and fauna, this area is of great value as a Mouflon reserve, and it is the best place for observing these superb mammals. Generally, Mouflon are shot mercilessly, even in the Regional Natural Park, but here they have survived reasonably well. The GR20 and a variant of it run through the area, west of the road.

Opposite: *masses of foliage and compacted 'sea-balls', washed up from underwater beds of the grass,* Posidonia oceanica, *in south-east Corsica.*

SECTION III
FIELD GUIDE TO COMMONER
ANIMALS AND PLANTS

France is a large country with varied topography, great difference in climate between north and south, lowlands and high ground, and, to match this diversity, there is a very rich wildlife. Selecting the species to include on colour plates is never easy and the choice has to be personal. We have resisted the temptation to illustrate the rarer animals and flowers in favour of those species you often seem to find but to which you cannot put a name. We are well aware that are choice might not be everyone else's. Inevitable space restrictions in a book designed to be portable mean that descriptions are brief to the point of terseness. However, similar and closely related species are mentioned, together with any critical features to enable accurate identification, and in this way the number of species covered has been increased dramatically.

The plates cover birds, mammals, reptiles and amphibia, butterflies, trees, and flowers; other insects have been left out here but are mentioned in the main text wherever appropriate. The plates have been designed to make identification as easy as possible. With birds, sex and seasonal differences are shown; details of flowers are given where critical.

Where a measurement is given in the descriptions it is always metric (in centimetres):

Birds – Beak-tip to tail-tip.
Mammals – Head and body excluding tail (this is given separately in some cases).

Opposite: Oleander Hawk Moth, Daphnis nerii.

Reptiles and amphibians – Total length, head to tail.
Butterflies – From tip to tip of the forewings (wingspan, WS) measured across the body.
Plants – Ground to top of the spike where appropriate (this is often so dependent upon where a particular plant species is growing that a general small/medium/large is used).

Common names are those that are the most widely accepted. We object to the practice of coining names for the sake of it where no English name exists. It is well worth getting used to Latin names, because they are universal and cross the boundaries of language in a way that local names never can. Although they can seem formidable at first one soon gets used to them. Many of the French names in current use are very similar to the Latin names and, on numerous occasions, we have had valuable help from local naturalists simply by asking about what (to us) sounds like the French version of a Latin name. Where French names in wide use are known to us they have been included.

Identification in the field is always a problem. Unless one travels in a minibus with a mobile library (and there are those who do), it is wise to take a notebook. Many keen naturalists, when not using their own transport, pack any available space in cases with fieldguides, with a careful eye on weight. We are no exception and even when travelling through France in cars, we tend to have a box of books, cases of cameras, and functional, easily washable, durable lightweight clothes.

Grey Heron *Ardea cinerea* **L90**
Héron cendre
Common, colonial nester usually in trees. Grey plumage, white head and neck, black crest; immature birds with grey crest. Slow flight, majestic, outer-wing halves black. At nest, calls raucous; otherwise harsh *kraank*. Purple Heron is a summer visitor in south and south-west.

Tufted Duck *Aythea fuligula* **L43**
Fuligule morillon
Widespread winter visitor, occasional breeder, on still or slow-moving freshwater sites (rarely on salt water) with marginal vegetation. Drake with drooping black tuft and contrasting black and white plumage: duck has short crest, brown plumage and yellow eye. Blue-grey bill and white wing bar in flight shown by both sexes.

Great Crested Grebe *Podiceps cristatus* **L48**
Grèbe huppé
Widespread resident on freshwater pools, lakes, rivers. Breeding adults with double-horned dark crest prominent in courtship ritual involving displays of neck movements. White 'cheeks' conspicuous in winter. Call: honk or harsh song a crooning note; shrill piping in juvenile. Black-Necked Grebe has breeding plumage with black neck and light chestnut ear tufts.

Mallard *Anas platyrhynchos* **L58**
Canard colvert
Most common, widespread dabbling duck. Nests in reed-beds, occasionally in low trees. Familiar *quack* uttered by duck; drake, softer *queek*. Drake unmistakeable with irridescent green head (purple tinged near moult); duck, brown with distinctive blue speculum. Visits estuaries and coasts in winter.

Pintail *Anas acuta* **L66 (drake) ; L56 (drake)**
Canard pilet
Widespread winter visitor on fresh water, brackish pools, marshes, and estuaries, breeding in some sites. Drake with elongated tail feathers (10cm), dark head and throat, white breast; duck with shorter pointed tail, brown belly and bronzed speculum. Flight fast. Drake produces low *gsee*; duck a hoarse *quack*.

Sparrowhawk *Accipiter nisus* **L28–38**
Epervier d'Europe
Frequent in woodland areas. Dashing flight along hedgerows or glide interspersed by several wing flaps on open ground. Chattering call *kek* or *kew*. Has blunt, shorter, broader wings than the smaller falcons. Male, grey-backed, rufous under, wings more pointed than female; female, brown with grey-brown barring on underparts. Preys on small birds.

Kestrel *Falco tinnunculus* **L34**
Faucon crécerelle
Common over open country, towns, sea-cliffs, motorway verges. Constant hovering flight. Male with blue-grey head and tail, chestnut mantle; female, brown, lacks grey head but pointed wings and flight pattern distinguish it from Sparrowhawk. Barred tail with terminal bar in both sexes. Lesser Kestrel, summer visitor in south; gregarious, colonial nester on ruined buildings and cliffs; tail translucent against sky. Hobby, over open country following prey (swallows and swifts) like small Peregrine. Outline, large swift.

Buzzard *Buteo buteo* **L51–56**
Buse variable
Common over forest and scattered woodland. Variable plumage according to season/maturity from pale to dark. Tail with dark band at tip, barred (often faintly); large pale patch common on underwing. Call high pitched *mew*, gull-like. Honey Buzzard, dark, broad double bars near base of tail; more slender with longer neck, narrower wings. Call shriller – male *puihu*; female *piah*.

Black Kite *Milvus migrans* **L56**
Milan noir
Summer breeder (uncommon), light woodlands, and open country near water. Tail only slightly forked. Like dark Buzzard in appearance but wings held slightly crooked, and flight more flapping, much tail-twisting; glides with wings level (Marsh Harrier, wings canted upwards). High-pitched squealing cry. Red Kite is slightly larger, tail deeply forked, rufous plumage, pale head. Inhabits deciduous woodland and open areas with scattered tree cover. Call, shrill mew (Buzzard-like); flight soaring, buoyant with angled wings.

Marsh Harrier *Circus aeruginosus* **L48–56**
Busard des roseaux
Frequent over extensive reed-beds, marshes, swamps, fens. Low glide, wings slightly canted upwards. Broader winged than other harriers (Buzzard-like, but flight different). Male, largely brown, grey on wings and tail; female and immature adult, with pale head (Osprey with white underparts). Shrill female alarm call *chinka chinka*; male *chukara chukara*. Both usually silent out of breeding season.

Grey Heron

Tufted Duck
male
female

Great Crested Grebe
winter
summer

Mallard
female
male

Sparrowhawk
female
male
male in flight

Pintail
female
male

Kestrel
male
female
Kestrel hovering

Black Kite

Buzzard

Marsh Harrier
female
male

Moorhen *Gallinula chloropus* **L33**
Poule d'eau
Common freshwater resident wherever marginal growth thick. Distinguished by red forehead and bill, flick of white under-tail coverts and jerking head movement when swimming. Laboured take-off from water with legs trailing; flight weak. Juveniles show white under tail; less white on throat than Coots. Young all dark. Call loud, abrupt *kittik* or *curruk.*

Coot *Fulicula atra* **L38**
Foulque macroule
Common resident on fresh water. Conspicuous white forehead and bill with all-black plumage. Young with rufous head and neck. Call distinctive, loud *kowk*. Gregarious but quarrelsome. Flight laboured like Moorhen.

Oystercatcher *Haematopus ostralegus* **L43**
Huîtrier pie
Common resident, frequent in coastal and estuarine regions, occasionally river valleys. Long orange bill and longish pink legs distinguish it from other pied shore birds (Avocet, Black-Winged Stilt). Throat white in winter, black in summer. Rapid flight, low over water often accompanied by shrill *kleep kleep*. Nest often no more than scrape in shingle.

Little-Ringed Plover *Charadrius dubius* **L15**
Petit gravelot
Local, summer resident nesting on sand or shingle beside fresh water (larger Ringed Plover usually found on sandy or shingly sea shores). Distinguished in flight from Ringed Plover by the absence of a pale wing bar: also has white line above black forehead. Call *pee-oo, pip pip*. Ringed Plover produces sounds *too-i* and *queep*.

Snipe *Gallinago gallinago* **L27**
Becassine des marais
Local, resident on wet moors, heaths, damp meadows, bogs and marshes; summer visitor in extreme south. Bill proportionately longer than other medium brown waders. Zig-zag flight. Harsh call when disturbed (*creech*), dives at angle of 45°, 'drumming' display flight. Jack Snipe, winter visitor. Smaller with shorter bill; hovers and bobs in display flight.

Mediterranean Gull *Larus melanocephalus* **L39**
Mouette mélanocéphale
Frequent on coastal waters, marshes and flats. Has red legs and bill with black head in summer (Black-Headed Gull, dark-brown head). Outline closer to

Common Gull, build stockier, white-tipped wings and longer legs. Flight jerky with shallower wing beats than Common Gull. Winter and immature birds have dark region around eye; second-year birds have dark wing-tips. Calls higher in pitch than Common but deeper than Black-Headed.

Black-Headed Gull *Larus ridibundus* **L35–38**
Mouette rieuse
Common resident breeding in reedy areas of bogs and marshes, also islands in lakes, dunes and shingle. Common inland in winter. Bill and legs red but head dark brown in summer, not extending to nape (black in Mediterranean Gull and Little Gull, and extending to nape) turning white with dark 'smudges' in winter. Forewings conspicuous white in winter (black only at tip). Flight strong over distance, otherwise wavering.

Lesser Black-Backed Gull *Larus fuscus* **L53–56**
Goéland brun
Winter visitor in many coastal areas. Breeds in Brittany on cliffs and islands. Variability of Herring Gull makes confusion easy. Herring Gull generally larger with stouter beak; mantle varies from silver to slate grey. Lesser Black-Backed, mantle dark grey to black. Lesser considerably smaller, with yellow legs, than Great Black-Backed, with pink legs.

Common Tern *Sterna hirundo* **L35**
Sterne pieregarin
Widespread summer resident nesting close to fresh or salt water; noisy colonies on sand or shingle. Graceful flight, hovering before plunging into water after small fish. Tail deeply forked, wings and overall build more slender than gulls. Bill vermillion with black tip in breeding season, head and nape black. In winter forehead turns white.

Black Tern *Chlidonias niger* **L24**
Guifette noir
Summer resident in much of France, passage migrant elsewhere. Breeds by fresh and brackish waters with nest in shallow water floating on vegetation. Flight graceful, stooping to water surface to catch insects, not usually plunging below surface. Distinguished by being black or very dark grey. Bill black; legs red, under tail coverts white. Female has greyer throat and underparts. In winter: pale grey above, white below, but bill more slender and tail less forked than Common and other sea terns.

Moorhen

Mediterranean Gull
1st winter
adult summer

Coot

Black-headed Gull
adult summer
1st winter

Oystercatcher

Lesser Black-backed Gull
adult
1st winter

Little Ringed Plover
juvenile
male

Common Tern
adult summer
adult winter

Snipe
'drumming'

Black Tern
adult summer
adult winter

Pheasant *Phasinus colchicus* **L66–89**
Faisan de chasse
Common, introduced game-bird in open country,
scattered woodland, copses. Whirring flight. Call of
cock a harsh *kor kok*. Juveniles lack long tail but distinguished from Grey Partridge by grey breast-colour
of latter.

Grey Partridge *Perdix perdix* **L30**
Perdix gris
Widespread over open country: moors, downs,
heaths and dunes. Unspotted grey breast. Call high-
pitched *keev*. Red-Legged Partridge has black spotting on upper breast and call a loud *chuka chuka*.
Much smaller Quail distinguished from young partridge by buff head-streaks, no chestnut in tail and
dark throat markings in male.

Woodpigeon *Columba palumbus* **L41**
Pigeon ramier
Common in wooded country and in town parks.
Prominent white patches on neck and wings dis-
tinguish it from Rock Dove and Feral Pigeon. Flight
fast, direct. Call a repetitive soft *coo coo coo*. Stock
Dove, smaller with shorter tail, no white patches and
black wing-tips. Call a double *coo coo.*

Collared Dove *Streptopelia decaocto* **L32**
Tourterelle turque
Recent colonist, common in towns and villages. Dull
brown plumage, blackish wing tips; underside of tail
white with black base, black part-collar on nape.
Song: *coo cooo cuh*. Turtle Dove, widespread summer
resident, darker with chestnut uppers and black and
white patch on neck. Tails separate Collared and
Turtle Doves in flight. Latter, black with white edging. Call soft *turr turr.*

Cuckoo *Cuculus canorus* **L33**
Coucou gris
Common summer resident in wide range of habitats,
wintering in Africa. Call of male familiar *Cooc oo*; female call, a bubbling trill. Bird large compared with
size of egg (laid in nests of warblers, Dunnock, wag-
tails). Outline like Sparrowhawk but bill straight and
wings pointed.

Barn Owl *Tyto alba* **L34**
Chouette effraie
Widespread, nocturnal, local in farmland and open
country, nesting in barns, churches, ruins. Decreasing due to habitat-loss, poisoning, etc. White,
ghost-like appearance in silent flight at dusk. Face
and underparts white. Call a lengthy strangled *screech*
with hisses. Snores near nest.

Little Owl *Athene noctua* **L22**
Chouette cherêche
Widespread, partly diurnal with loud Curlew-like
call *kiew, kiew*. Found in farmland, open country
with scattered trees, orchards. Has short tail with
bounding flight, often at night. Can hover for insects. Scop's Owl, summer visitor in south, smaller
with less bounding flight. Heard rather than seen
with monotonous, repetitive, sharp *piu*. Nocturnal,
feeding on insects often close to habitation.

Tawny Owl *Strix aluco* **L38**
Chouette hulotte
Frequent in open deciduous woodland, nocturnal,
mobbed during day. Dark-brown face and underparts distinguish it from Barn Owl; absence of ear
tufts and possession of black eyes, from Short- and
Long-Eared Owls. Call sharp *ke wick*. Nests in tree
holes. Feeds on small birds, rodents, larger beetles.
Short-Eared Owl, often day flying on moors, dunes,
downs. Flight-call harsh bark, also deep booming
hoot in display. Long-Eared Owl, slimmer, more
elongated face, conspicuous ear tufts. Moaning *hoot*.
Eagle Owl, in Massif Central, prominent ear tufts,
size of small eagle usually seen hunting at dusk. Prey:
larger mammals and birds.

Nightjar *Caprimulgus europaeus* **L27**
Engoulevaut d'Europe
Summer resident, local on open heaths and moors.
Hawk-like appearance, long wings and tail, but
straight bill. Swift flight, usually nocturnal. Feeds on
moths, beetles, etc. Calls at dusk or night a distinctive *churr*. During day, only seen in flight when
flushed from ground. Eggs laid on bare ground.

Swift *Apus apus* **L16.5**
Martinet noir
Common summer visitor in open country and urban
areas. Cry a harsh scream. Scythe-shaped silhouette.
Short tail, dark plumage and long curved wings distinguish it from Swallows and martins. Pallid Swift,
in far south, similar but has distinctly paler plumage,
more obvious white throat patch. Alpine Swift, in
high mountains and gorges, larger with pale-brown
plumage, white underparts and brown breast-band.

Pheasant
male
female

Barn Owl

Grey Partridge
male
female

Little Owl

Wood Pigeon

Tawny Owl

Collared Dove

male

male

Nightjar

male

female

Cuckoo

Swift

Kingfisher *Alcedo atthis* **L16.5**
Martin-pêcheur d'Europe
Local throughout much of France beside lowland fresh water. Brilliant plumage: irridescent blue-green above, chestnut below. Nests in holes in banks beside fresh water; visits coasts in winter. Feeds by hovering or perching before diving to catch fish.

Hoopoe *Upupa epops* **L28**
Huppé fasciée
Frequently heard in south and Massif Central where it is a summer breeding bird. In flight resembles enormous black-and-white moth. Unmistakeable with black-and-white crest, barred wings, long, dark curved bill and pinkish plumage. Occurs in parks, gardens, woodlands, farmland and orchards, nesting in holes and feeding chiefly on insect larvae, small lizards, spiders and centipedes. Repeated far-carrying call *hoopoopoop*.

Green Woodpecker *Picus viridis* **L32**
Pic vert
Widespread in broad-leaved and mixed woodland, gardens and parks. Both sexes: green plumage with yellow-green rump, easily visible in characteristic dipping flight; scarlet head and black moustache (scarlet extends to moustachial stripe in male). Feeds on ground (ants) as well as on insects in trees. Grey-Headed Woodpecker, male red on forehead only, moustache streaks reduced; head and underparts mostly grey. Mixed woodlands; range increasing.

Great Spotted Woodpecker
Dendrocopos major **L23**
Pic épeiche
Widespread and frequent in coniferous, broad-leaved and mixed forest. Black crown and red nape in male (juvenile with crown and nape red); female lacks red nape. Both sexes with white patch on each wing and red undertail coverts. Drums in short bursts (c. 1 sec) in spring, flight bounding. Middle Spotted Woodpecker, white patch on wings, crown of head red (not black): not in pure conifer woods. Lesser Spotted Woodpecker, much smaller (sparrow-sized); inconspicuous; no red undertail coverts. Female has no red on head; drumming bursts longer than Great Spotted.

Crested Lark *Galerida cristata* **L17**
Cochevis huppé
Widepread resident on stony and sandy soils throughout France with song thinner but more plaintive than Skylark. Longer, erect crest, orange buff patch visible on underwing in flight and buff rather than white feathers providing tail border serve to distinguish from Skylark.

Skylark *Alauda arvensis* **L18**
Alouette des champs
Common in open country, farmland, heaths, moors, grassland and dunes. Soaring, extended song delivered in the air (not usual with Crested lark). Plumage plain brown; crest inconspicuous; fairly long tail bordered with white feathers. Juvenile lacks crest. Woodlark, crest not always visible, tail shorter than Skylark; buff eyestripes extending to neck. Tail with white tip not border. Mellow song. Flight path curved, whereas Skylark rises almost vertically.

Swallow *Hirundo rustica* **L19**
Hirondelle de cheminée
Common summer visitor, breeding in buildings. Adults with long tail streamers; juveniles shorter forks. Chestnut throats and foreheads. Twittering call a repetitive *tswit*. Red-Rumped Swallow, in limestone regions of the extreme south. Has clearly visible reddish rump and nape.

House Martin *Delichon urbica* **L12.5**
Hirondelle de fenêtre
Common summer visitor breeding under eaves, on cliffs, and under bridges. Underparts pure white, rump white, tail short with indented 'V'. Sand Martin has brown breast-band across otherwise white underparts. Nests colonially in holes in sand, gravel-banks, or sandy soils of cliffs. Crag Martin, cliff breeding. Brownish underparts with speckled throat; no breast-band.

Yellow Wagtail *Motacilla flava* **L16.5**
Bergeronnette priutanière
Widespread over damp grasslands, salt-marshes, and often around herds of cattle. Numerous races distinguished only by details of head patterns. Flight bounding, gait jerky, wagging tail. Distinctive flight note *tsweep*. Grey Wagtail, longer tail than Yellow; blue-grey above, yellow beneath, distinctive black throat. Breeds by fast-moving streams, and weirs.

White Wagtail *Motacilla alba*
Bergeronnette gris
Widespread, often near human habitation. Nests near fresh water in walls, under bridges etc. Distinguished from other black-and-white birds of similar size by long tail, distinctive jerking gait, and wagging tail. Numerous races known.

Kingfisher

crest
raised

Hoopoe

Skylark

Swallow

male

male

House Martin

Green Woodpecker

Great Spotted
Woodpecker

female

male

Yellow Wagtail

Crested Lark

female

male

White Wagtail

Wren *Troglodytes troglodytes* **L9.5**
Troglodyte miguou
Widespread throughout France. Brown barred plumage and prominent cocked tail. Call surprisingly loud warbling song. On ground almost mouse-like in movements and appearance.

Dunnock *Prunella modularis* **L14.5**
Acceuteur mouchet
Common in parks and gardens as well as woodlands. Grey head and underparts. Thinner bill and streaked plumage distinguish it from female House Sparrow. Call high-pitched *tseep*.

Robin *Erithacus rubecula* **L14**
Rougegorge familier
Common in parks, gardens, open country and woodlands. Unmistakeable red face and breast. Juvenile speckled until moult. Melodious warbling song; call an indignant *tic tic*.

Nightingale *Luscinia megarhynchos* **L16.5**
Rossiguole philomêle
Widespread summer resident in town or country; particularly frequent in Massif Central, and Cévennes. Complicated melodious song evident by day or night. Like larger, slimmer, all-brown Robin in appearance, can be skulking in habit or, in south, delivering song confidently from high perch.

Black Redstart *Phoenicurus ochruros* **L14**
Rougequeue noir
Widespread resident and summer visitor in hill and mountain regions. Robin-like outline. Male, distinctive black; female, lighter. Chestnut-red rump obvious as bird flits around on stones, walls, etc. Song clipped warble with call *tsip*. Common Redstart, breeding male with black throat, white forehead and red breast; female, brownish with light throat and underparts. Both have chestnut-red rump.

Wheatear *Oenanthe oenanthe* **L15**
Traquet motteux
Common in hill and mountain regions on moors, and grassy downs. Grey crown, black cheeks, white eyestripes. Song a rather squeaky warble.

Blackbird *Turdus merula* **L25**
Merle noir
Common in urban and rural habitats (trapped, with other thrushes, in large numbers in some regions as constituent of traditional pâté). Male is all black with yellow bill; female, brown. Song fluty, mellow; alarm call chattering 'scream'. Ring Ouzel, in mountain regions. White throat.

Fieldfare *Turdus pilaris* **L25**
Grive literne
Winter visitor, often in flocks in open coniferous and deciduous woodland. Blue-grey head and rump, with chestnut back separate it from other thrushes. In flight resembles Mistle Thrush with white underwing flashes. Redwing, smallest of winter-visiting thrushes. Obvious chestnut underwing and flanks. Garden visitor in severe winters.

Song Thrush *Turdus philomelos* **L23**
Grive musicienne
Common in woods, scrub, parks and gardens. Distinct dark spotting on breast serves to distinguish it from hen and young Blackbirds. Song loud and clear. Warmer brown uppers, lack of white in tail and more direct flight than Mistle Thrush.

Mistle Thrush *Turdus viscivorus* **L27**
Grive draine
Widespread in coniferous and broad-leaved forests, parks and gardens. Flight distinct from Song Thrush as wings closed periodically; undulation slight. Larger than Song Thrush with larger breast-spots. Underwings whitish in flight. Loud reverberating song without repetitive element of Song Thrush.

Wren

Wheatear
female
male

Dunnock

Blackbird
female
male

Robin
juvenile
adult

Fieldfare

Nightingale

Song Thrush

Black Redstart
female
male

Mistle Thrush

Whitethroat *Sylvia communis* **L14**
Fauvette grisette
Summer resident. Widespread in tangled vegetation, and scrub. Male with grey head, white throat, rufous wings; female, rufous-winged. Both sexes with white feathers in tail. Staccatto song *whit*. Lesser White throat, greyer, more skulking; not rufous. Dark patch on ear coverts. Main song a rattle, subsong warbling. Garden Warbler, roundish head, short bill and uniform plumage (no eyestripes or white throat).

Cetti's Warbler *Cettia cetti* **L14**
Bousecarle de Cettio
Frequent resident in south and west. Likes bushy vegetation near fresh water, and marshes. Inconspicuous. Tail rounded, cocked: upperparts dark rufous-brown. Heard rather than seen. Song loud distinctive burst *chewee chewee cheweeweewee*.

Sedge Warbler *Acrocephalus schoenobaenus* **L13**
Phragmite des joucs
Summer visitor. Widespread, except in extreme south, in bushes, hedgerows, and coarse vegetation near water. Dark streaks on upperparts, broad whitish eyestripe. Song sweet, jumbled harsh and sweet notes. Moustached Warbler, in extreme south. Darker crown; white square-ended eyestripe; whiter throat and cheeks.

Reed Warbler *Acrocephalus scirpaceus* **L12.5**
Rouserolle effarvette
Widespread summer resident in reed-beds. Rufous-tinged brown above, pale below. Marsh Warbler, distinguished only by song: much louder, jerkier, more musical with mimicry than Reed or Sedge Warblers. Great Reed Warbler, widespread, much larger version of Reed Warbler. Stouter bill; more pronounced eyestripe; loud song; croaking.

Blackcap *Sylvia atricapilla* **L14**
Fauvette à tête noire
Widespread. Resident in south and west in gardens, open scrub, and woodland. Distinctive crown not extending to cheeks: black in male, blackish-brown in immature adult; brown in female. Song high-pitched, sustained. Orphean Warbler, summer resident in south, in scrub, and open woods. Larger, jet-black cheeks and crown; white eye; white throat. Female browner. Sardinian Warbler, southern resident, like Blackcap but with conspicuous red eye.

Chiffchaff *Phylloscopus collybita* **L11**
Pouillot véloce
Widespread. Resident in south and west in tall bushes and small trees. Call a monotonous repetitive *chiff-chaff* interspersed with *chirr chirr*. Willow Warbler, song of descending notes. Wistful; greener than Chiffchaff. Wood Warbler, larger with white underparts, yellowish breast and yellow eyestripe.

Goldcrest *Regulus regulus* **L9**
Roiteolt huppé
Widespread. Resident in woods and gardens, especially near conifers. Black-bordered cap: orange in male; yellow in female. Very high-pitched call *tzi tzi tzi*. Can be confused with tits or Treecreeper. Song *zeda zeda zeda zeda sissu-peee*. Firecrest, has black-and-white eyestripes, bronze patch on side of neck and call *peeep*; in broad-leaved or conifer woodland.

Nuthatch *Sitta europaea* **L14**
Sitelle torchepot
Widespread but inconspicuous resident. Juvenile lacks chestnut but has white in tail. Creeping movement over trees. Colour and longish straight beak distinguish it from Treecreeper or Lesser Spotted Woodpecker. Corsican Nuthatch, smaller with black crown (grey in hen); underparts pale. Conspicuous white stripe above black eyestripe. Pine forests in Corsica.

Blue Tit *Parus caeruleus* **L11.5**
Mésauge bleue
Common in broad-leaved woodland and open country with scattered trees. Coal Tit, with black cap and white nape patch. Marsh Tit, black crown, nape and chin, but cheeks and underparts pale. Crested Tit, distinctive crest; no wing bar; white cheeks. Call *tsi tsi tsi tsi* frequent in mountain conifer woodland.

Great Tit *Parus major* **L14**
Mésauge charbonnière
Common in town and country in woodland or where there are scattered trees. Larger size and black-and-white head distinguish it from Blue Tit. Song *teecher teecher*.

male

female

Whitethroat

Chiffchaff

Goldcrest

Cetti's Warbler

Nuthatch

Sedge Warbler

Reed Warbler

Blue Tit

female   male

Blackcap

Great Tit

Jay *Garrulus glandarius* **L34**
Geai des chênes
Common over woodlands, parks and large gardens. Conspicous white rump as it flies away. Call scolding screech *skaak skaak*. Flight undulating. Collects and buries acorns in autumn.

Magpie *Pica pica* **L46**
Pie bavarde
Common in town and country. Large nest with roof of twigs familiar sight in trees and thorny bushes. Long tail and black-and-white plumage make bird unmistakeable at rest or in flight. Call a loud harsh chattering or 'yacking'.

Jackdaw *Corvus monendula* **L33**
Choucas des tours
Common over open and cultivated country, old buildings, ruins and sea-cliffs. Call repeated *chacks* or *kyow*. Flight more agile than larger crows (Rook and Carrion Crow). Grey nape on black body distinguishing feature. Chough, rare except near coast in Brittany. Larger, longish curved red bill and red legs; no grey on nape. Flight aerobatic. Frequents grassy areas on cliffs searching for ants. Call *kyow*. Alpine Chough, high-mountain regions. Yellow curved bill and red legs. Flight similar to Chough. Call metallic *chirrish*.

Chaffinch *Fringilla coelebs* **L15**
Pinson des arbres
Common over town and country: woodland, parks and gardens. Distinguished by white shoulder patch and wing-bar plus white in tail. Song variable with region. Familiar call *pink pink*, similar to Great Tit. In winter seen with other finches in open country. Bullfinch, unmistakeable with bright reddish-pink underparts, black cap; female, pinker, more subdued. Frequent in orchards feeding on unopened buds in spring.

Greenfinch *Carduelis chloris* **L14.5**
Verdier d'Europe
Widespread in gardens, open country, woodlands and forest edges. Large size with bright-yellow wing patches and rump. Siskin, winter visitor but resident in some mountain areas. Smaller, dark-streaked plumage, black chin and crown; yellow patches at base of tail. Serin, resident in south; summer resident elsewhere. Small, yellowish-green, streaked. Shorter bill. More obvious yellow rump than Siskin; also no yellow at sides of tail.

Goldfinch *Carduelis carduelis* **L12**
Chardonneret élégaut
Common, especially in orchards and where there are seeding thistles in autumn. Distinctive appearance, dancing flight. Collects in small groups ('charms'). Juvenile streaked, lacks red. Unlike young Greenfinch, has no yellow in tail. Song *tswitt-witt-witt*.

Linnet *Acanthis cannabina* **L13.5**
Linotte mélodieuse
Common in open areas: heaths, maquis and vineyards. Song a twittering melody. White wing-patch prominent at rest and in flight. Hen and juvenile lack red. Redpoll, winter visitor distinguished from Linnet by red forehead in both sexes, and black chin.

Yellowhammer *Emberiza citrinella* **L16.5**
Bruant jaune
Common bird of farmland, scrub, clearings and hedgerows. Song 'little bit o' bread and no cheese'. Call *twit-up*. Cirl Bunting, resident; much rarer, decreasing. Grey crown, black throat and greyish-green band across yellow breast. Call higher-pitched *tzit*. Ortolan Bunting, summer resident, rather dull pinkish-brown with grey-green head; yellow throat; white eye-ring.

Reed Bunting *Emberiza schoeniculus* **L15**
Bruant des roseaux
Frequent in fens, reed-beds and marshy places of all sorts. Squeeky song *tweek tweek tweek tititick*. Flicks tail continually. Male distinctive with black head and white moustache.

Corn Bunting *Emberiza calandra* **L18**
Bruant proyer
Widespread resident, decreasing in most areas. Frequent in Massif Central. High-pitched song like jangling keys. Larger size and overall streaked brown appearance distinguish it from other buntings. Rock Bunting, head pattern grey with three black stripes; grey throat. Resident, inhabits rocky and stony hillsides in southern France.

Jay

Goldfinch

Magpie

female

male

Linnet

Jackdaw

male

female

Yellowhammer

female

male

Reed Bunting

male

female

Chaffinch

male

female

Greenfinch

Corn Bunting

Hedgehog *Erinaceus europaeus* **L22.5–27.5**
Hérisson
Common in the country, parks and larger gardens. Underside ranges from dark-brown to almost white, uniform. Very narrow spine-free parting on crown. Algerian Hedgehog, very limited distribution in west and south, probably introduced. Very pale underside; obscure face pattern. Wider spine-free parting on crown. Food: insects, worms, and slugs.

Mole *Talpa europea* **L12–15**
Taupe
Common on agricultural land, and parks; evidenced by 'molehills'. Comparatively large eyes can be opened, enlarged front feet. Blind Mole, in extreme south; smaller (head and body 100–130mm). Food: worms, slugs, and insect larvae.

Common Shrew *Sorex araneus* **L6–8**
Muse araigne
Restricted distribution: central and deep south. Coat, three-coloured: dark-brown back, pale belly and band of intermediate colour on flanks. Active by day in places with necessary ground-cover. Millet's Shrew, far more widespread in France, slightly smaller but very similar; skull and chromosome measurements needed for positive identification! Food: insects, spiders, woodlice, and snails. Pyrenean Desman, endemic; very long muzzle; front feet not enlarged; tail long. Inhabits rivers, streams and canals. Food: aquatic invertebrates.

Noctule Bat *Nyctalus noctula* **L (forearm) 4.6–5.5**
Noctule
Widespread, mainly in woodland, roosting in trees. Coat golden-brown all over with hair colour extending to roots, wings narrow. On warm summer days tree roosts can be located by the squeaking that comes from them. Great Noctule, distribution restricted to widely scattered colonies in south-west, centre and south of France. Similar colouring, but much larger (forearm 6.2–6.9cm). Food: moths and other winged insects.

Brown Hare *Lepus capensis* **L50–65**
Lièvre
Widespread in open country and farmland. Longer ears than rabbit (black-tipped); coat yellowish-brown throughout year; tail black and white; legs longer, body larger. Young (leverets) produced above ground. Chases and 'boxing' matches part of spring mating ritual. Mountain Hare, Alps; shorter ears; white tail; coat greyish brown in summer, white in winter. Food: grass, and sedges.

Rabbit *Oryctolagus cuniculus* **L35–45**
Lapin
Common on grassland: downs, dunes and cliff-tops; potential agricultural pest. Colonial in burrows. Shorter legs and ears without black tips distinguish from Hare. Food: grass, bulbs, crops, and young trees.

Red Squirrel *Sciurus vulgaris* **L18–25**
Ecureuil
Widespread, especially in coniferous forests (also in Beech woodland). Variable coat: red and dark greyish forms existing together (more greyish appearance in winter). Ear tufts prominent. Grey Squirrel absent from France, thus no problem in identification. Especially active just after dawn and just before dusk. Food: tree seeds (cones, beech-mast), tubers and fungi.

Bank Vole *Clethrionomys glareolus* **L8–11**
Campagnol glaréole
Common wherever shrubbery is dense. Active day and night. Animals use 'runways' through vegetation and tunnels below ground so seldom seen. Coat with russet back, tail moderately long but ears and eyes larger than other voles. Food: insects, buds, seeds, and fruit.

Muskrat *Ondatra zibethicus* **L30–40**
Rat musqué
Widespread by fresh water: rivers, lakes, ponds and marshes. Originally from North America, established after escapes from fur farms. Larger than Water Voles; smaller than Beaver and Coypu. Coat soft and dense. Hind feet (not webbed) and tail used when swimming: animals can dive and swim long distances under water. Extensive burrows made in banks. Especially active in early morning. Food: water plants.

Brown Rat
Rattus norvegicus **L20–26 (tail 17–23)**
Rat
Common in most man-made habitats especially farms, cellars, sewers, rubbish-dumps and also riverbanks. Coat usually brown, occasionally black. Tail virtually naked (length of tail and large ears distinguish it from Water Voles). Rats make extensive burrows, primarily nocturnal. Good climbers. Food: grain and seeds when available, otherwise eggs, worms, buds and fruit.

Hedgehog

Common Shrew

Mole

in flight

Noctule Bat

Brown Hare

Rabbit

Bank Vole

Red Squirrel

Muskrat

Common (Brown) Rat

Red Fox *Vulpes vulpes* **L75 (tail 45)**
Renard commun
Common and widespread in countryside and, increasingly, as an urban animal visiting gardens. Coat usually reddish-brown, ears large and pointed, muzzle narrow. Tail very bushy with white tip. Mainly nocturnal, spending the day in a shallow burrow or 'earth'. Food: mainly rodents, but fruit, carrion and refuse taken.

Stoat *Mustela erminea* **L20–30 (tail 6–12)**
Hermine
Widespread. Found where necessary cover is available. Variable in size. Even when size of large Weasel, distinct black tip to tail is distinguishing feature. Inquisitive by nature, often hunting by day. Food: birds, mice, voles, rabbits and hares, killed with a bite on the neck.

Weasel *Mustela nivalis* **L13–23 (tail 3–6)**
Belette
Widespread. Size variable, males much larger than females. Tail relatively short never with black tip. Agile climbers, active day and night. Food: eggs, nestlings, small birds, voles, mice, rats, and small rabbits.

Western Polecat
Mustela putorius **L32–4 (tail 13–18)**
Putois
Solitary, nocturnal animals. Widespread but nowhere common. Living in woodland in lowland country, river-banks, and marshes. Coat dark-brown all over except for white snout-tip and on face between eye and ear. The pale yellowish underfur shows through, making coat appear lighter in patches. Mink has very dark, uniform coat with white fur only on lower jaw but Feral Ferret very similar to Polecat. Pine Marten, larger than Mink and Polecat; ears more prominent; throat-patch pale-yellow to dull-orange; longer legs; longer bushier tail. Local, solitary, living in coniferous and mixed forest. Beech Marten, like Pine Marten, but throat-patch pure white. Very local in deciduous woodland. Food: mainly rodents.

Badger *Meles meles* **L67–80**
Blaireau
Widespread in woodland and on agricultural land. Sets in woodland recognized by bare ground around and extensive 'earthworks'. Thick-set appearance; striped face pattern, grey back and short tail unique. Social in habit; nocturnal but not hibernating. Food: omnivorous – voles, moles, rabbits, frogs, grubs, carrion, berries, roots, nuts, and bulbs.

Wild Boar *Sus scrofa* **L up to 180**
Sanglier
Frequent in regions with extensive deciduous forests. Like domestic pig (of which it is the ancestor) in appearance, but with coat of dense bristly hair. Male with protruding tusks; young, striped, making camouflage effective. Animals solitary or in small groups. Nocturnal, spending day in thick undergrowth. Males separate except during rutting season. Food: mainly vegetables – bulbs, roots and fruit.

Red Deer *Cervus elaphus* **L up to 260**
Cerf commun
Mainly in north. Large animals. Coat reddish-brown in summer; greyish brown in winter with pale patch on rump in both sexes at all ages (never white). Mature stags have two forward branches close to base; young males, only one. Sika Deer also only one. Antlers only carried by males and grow from spring to early autumn when they are covered with 'velvet'. Food: grass and meadow plants, bark, heather and conifers in winter.

Roe Deer *Capreolus capreolus* **L up to 120**
Chevreuil
One of the smallest of the cervids, the Roe Deer occurs in both coniferous and broad-leaved woods as well as in forest margins and fields. Males grow up to 75cm tall at the shoulders with antlers up to 30cm long. Coat sandy to reddish in summer, greyish to dark brown or black with pale underparts in winter. Diet mainly leaves, grasses and herbs; animals both browsers and grazers.

Red Fox

Stoat

Weasel

Western Polecat

Badger

Red Deer

male

female

Wild Boar

young

Roe Deer

male

Fire Salamander *Salamandra salamander* **L20–28**
Salamaudre tachetée
Restricted to high-mountain regions. During day
hidden under stones, leaves, and bark; emerging in
rainy weather, evening or night. Hibernates until
March or April. Larva with gills borne live in water,
metamorphosing after two to three months. Skin se-
cretion venomous.

Common Tree Frog *Hyla arborea* **L5**
Rainette
Widespread in south and west; in spring on reeds
close to water, summer on shrubs and trees. Colour
and small size make it difficult to see. Croak surprisingly loud and far-carrying. Eggs laid in clusters in
spring (metamorphosis in August/September).
Food: small insects and spiders. Stripeless Tree Frog
lacks dark side-stripe.

Natterjack Toad *Bufo calamita* **L7–8**
Crapand des roseaux
Local with preference for sunny damp places on sandy
soil, e.g. heaths and dune-slacks. Short-limbed; crawl-
ing rather than jumping; emerging in twilight to feed
on insects, slugs and worms. Distinguished from
Common Toad by light band of wartless skin running
down middle of olive back.

Common Toad
Bufo bufo **L 8 (male); 13 (female)**
Crapaud commun
Common in fields, gardens and parks; in lowlands
and mountains. Adults powerfully built, warty.
Copper colored eyes. Active by day or night. Feeds
on slugs, earthworms, arthropods. Eggs laid in
March, in strings 3–5m long, coiled around water
plants. Metamorphosis June and July.

Edible Frog
Rana esculenta **L 7–8 (male); 9–12 (female)**
Widespread and abundant, particularly in coastal
marshes. Grass-green or olive-back with dark spots,
often with yellowish dorsal band. Rests on banks of
ponds, streams, etc. 'Plops' into water at hint of danger. Hibernates from October to April in bottom
mud. Eggs laid in small clusters in shallow water.
Feeds on insects, worms, slugs, small fishes, tadpoles
and smaller frogs.

Common Frog *Rana temporaria* **L8–10**
Grenouille
Common in woods, fields, meadows, peat-bogs: in
north in lowlands; in south in foothill and mountain
regions. Brown back, dark-spotted; underbelly dirty

white with greyish-brown spots, often with light
streak along centre of back and dark blotch behind
eyes. Hibernates in large numbers in bottom mud.
Eggs laid in early spring in large floating clusters –
'frogspawn'. Metamorphosis two to three months.

Green Lizard *Lacerta viridis* **L30–50**
Lézard vert
Frequent in south in lowland and mountain areas and
in dry places overgrown with shrubs. Tail twice the
length of rest of body. Male grassy green with numer-
ous small black spots; female, brown-green above.
Male throat bright-blue in breeding season. Mates
after hibernation (April). Six to twenty eggs laid late
May July. Young (4cm) hatch after six to eight weeks.
Food: insects, small lizards and rodents.

Sand Lizard *Lacerta agilis* **L16–20**
Widely distributed in lowlands and hilly regions.
Preference for sunny, sheltered places: slopes covered
with grass, dune-land, heaths, wasteland, old quar-
ries. Winters below ground. Five to fifteen longish
eggs laid. Young (3–4cm) hatch in six to eight weeks.
Colouring highly variable: male with sides grass-
green in spring/early summer: female brownish.
Both with dark circular patches with whitish centres.
Food: grasshoppers, locusts, beetles, flies, spiders and
other arthropods.

Common Lizard *Lacerta vivipara* **L15–16**
Widespread. Common from lowlands up to mountains. Movements less agile than Sand Lizard. Hibernates in deep burrows. Back varies in colour from
dark-brown to grey-brown, darker streak along
spine. Sides flanked by dark, discontinuous stripe;
belly yellowish or grey in female; yolk yellow (orange
in male). Mating May/June. Three to ten young
(3cm) born live about three months.

Montpellier Snake
Malpolon monpessulanus **L180 200**
Couleuvre do Montpellier
Frequent in sunny, overgrown places, field-edges,
scrub. In the south (as with all snakes), numbers have
suffered because of human ignorance. Stout bodied,
dorsal and lateral with numerous black speckles partly edged yellow, sometimes joining in rows. Belly
uniform yellow-grey (sometimes spotted). Skull de-
pressed between eyes. Venom fatal to small prey
(lizards, birds, small mammals, snakes). Bite painful;
wound takes a long time to heal. Venom of large
adult may cause illness in humans.

212

Fire Salamander

Common Tree Frog

Natterjack Toad

Common Toad

Edible Frog

breeding male

Common Frog

male

Green Lizard

breeding male

Sand Lizard

male

Montpellier Snake

Common (Viviparous) Lizard

Common Swallowtail
Papilio machaon **WS 6.4–10.0**
Widely distributed. Fast agile flyer. Caterpillar striking: green striped black, dotted red – on Fennel, Milk Parsley, and Wild Carrot. Little sexual difference. Deeper colour in first generation. Corsican Swallowtail, endemic in the mountains of Corsica and Sardinia, similar but with wavy sub-marginal band on underside of forewing. Tail less pronounced; foodplant: Giant Fennel. Southern Swallowtail rare in Alps. Resembles Common Swallowtail in ground colour, but smaller red 'eye-spots'. Markings more restricted with yellow, rather than black basal area; four transverse stripes. Foodplant: Mountain Seseli and other Umbilliferae.

Scarce Swallowtail
Iphiclides podalirius **WS 6.5–9.0**
Frequent in Dordogne (more so than common Swallowtail). Swift, strong flight. Appears much paler than Common on wing. Forewing, six transverse stripes. In spring-time seen up to 1,600m, but in summer prefers moister lowlands, meadows, orchards, light woodlands. Foodplant: Sloe, Cherry, Hawthorn.

Black-Veined White *Aporia crataegi* **WS 5.6–6.8**
Local, but numbers can fluctuate dramatically. Often found in some numbers in small colonies. Seen flying over orchards, clover fields with 'laboured' flight. Female larger with more transparent wings. Larva colonial in early stages in silken 'hibernaculum'. Black veining and abscence of wing blotches distinguish it from other Whites. Clouded Apollo over mountain regions, has flapping flight and black veining but with faint blotching on wings.

Large White *Pieris brassicae* **WS 5.7–6.6**
Common, serious garden pest on brassicas. Summer generation larger, with more black on wing-tips than spring and autumn broods. Male forewing white with black apex (two spots on underside); female with two black spots, black bar at apex on white forewing (underwing pale-yellow with single spot).

Green-Veined White *Artogeia napi* **WS 3.6–5.0**
Common. Widespread with preference for damp meadows up to 1,500m. Numerous races, some much yellower than others, all have prominent green veining evident on underwing when butterfly is at rest. Summer race larger with paler veins. In flight, when veins not apparent, resembles Small White which is a pest. Foodplant: various crucifers such as Hedge Mustard.

Clouded Yellow *Colias crocea* **WS 4.6–5.4**
Widespread. Migratory numbers vary dramatically each year. Restless, strong flier. Upper wings bright orange-yellow with broad black margins. Underside yellow with green tinge. Male with wider margins enclosing yellow spots of uneven size: hindwing dusky with orange spot(s). F. *helice*, widespread female form with pale green-white uppers and grey suffusion over hindwings. Pale Clouded Yellow, migrant from south, with preference for Lucerne. Male uppers pale-yellow (female paler, greenish), forewing border grey-black with pale-yellow spots.

Brimstone *Gonepteryx rhamni* **WS 5.2–6.0**
Common. Widespread. Hibernates as adult. Familiar as early-spring butterfly with powerful flight. Characteristic 'gothic' wing shape: male bright sulphur yellow; female paler, greener; both with single orange spot on each wing. Foodplants: Buckthorn and Alder Buckthorn. Cleopatra common in centre and south, bright-orange patch on male forewing.

Wood White *Leptidea sinapis* **WS 3.6–4.8**
Widespread but local in forest clearings.Fragile butterfly with weak, fluttering flight close to ground. Delicate appearance, flight and rounded wings separate from other whites. Male has more prominent grey apical spots on forewings. Second generation whiter with smaller, darker spots. Foodplants: Everlasting Pea, Birdsfoot Trefoil.

Common Blue *Polyomamatus icarus* **WS 2.8–3.6**
Widespread. Common. One of large number of species of blues in France. For many, underwing detail needed for positive identification. Females often brown above. Met with frequently: Common Blue (male uppers violet blue with black marginal line), Adonis Blue (male uppers shining bright-blue, fine black marginal line), Chalkhill Blue (male uppers silvery blue, wide brown margin on forewings, marginal black spots on hind wing), and Holly Blue (pale lilac-blue upperwings edged with fine black line, underwings light-blue with fine black spots).

White Admiral *Ladoga camilla* **WS 5.2–6.0**
Widespread. Locally common in woodland glades feeding freely on nectar from blackberry flowers. Flight slow, steady, gliding. Female slightly larger and paler than male. Foodplant: honeysuckle. Southern White Admiral frequent from the Dordogne, south. Slightly smaller; upper wings very dark with bluish tint, central white spot on forewing. Underside darker with distinct single row of black sub-marginal spots. Foodplant: honeysuckle species.

Swallowtail

Scarce Swallowtail

Black-veined White

Large White

Green-veined White

Clouded Yellow

Brimstone

male

female

Wood White

Common Blue

male

female

White Admiral

Camberwell Beauty *Nymphalis antiopa* **WS 6.0–6.5**
Widespread but nowhere common. Migrant with strong, powerful flight. Adults feed on tree sap. Basks in sun with wings outspread and hibernates as adult. At rest with wings open or closed the creamy white border makes recognition easy. Foodplant: willow.

Red Admiral *Vanessa atalanta* **WS 5.6–6.3**
Widespread. Common. Strong flier, migrant, visitor to gardens for nectar plants and orchards (feeds on over-ripe fruit). Adults territorial, survive winter in south but not north. Foodplant: nettle.

Painted Lady *Cynthia cardui* **WS 5.4–5.8**
Widespread. Very common in some years. Strong, rapid flier, migrant. Appears and breeds anywhere (more common in south). Foodplant: thistles.

Small Tortoiseshell *Aglais urticae* **WS 4.4–5.0**
Very common, easily recognized. Adults common in gardens. Comes into houses to hibernate. Foodplant: nettle. Large Tortoiseshell is much scarcer, frequenting trees (foodplants: elm, poplar, willow); wings squarer, larger (WS 5.0–6.3cm), colouring much less bright, basal area brown with long hairs (black in Small Tortoiseshell).

Map Butterfly *Araschnia levana* **WS 3.2–3.8**
Widespread in south, mainly in, and at edges of, light woodland. Very distinct difference in first (May–June) and second (August–September) generations. First with yellow-brown uppers and confused, marbled brown markings; second like miniature White Admiral with dark-brown uppers. Foodplant: nettle.

Silver-Washed Fritillary *Argynis paphia*
WS 5.4–7.0
Widespread in woods and forests. Strong flier, descending from trees on sunny days to feed on bramble and other blossom. Female larger than male; forewings more rounded. Two female forms: light orange-brown and dark silvery olive-brown (F. *valesina*). Underside hindwing in both sexes greenish with silvery bands. Foodplant: violet spp. Cardinal

occurs with Silver-Washed in south, larger (WS 6.4–8cm). Male and female with rounder forewings; most obvious difference in underwings. Hindwing greenish with lightly marked silver stripes; forewing with distinctive rosy-red patch. High-Brown Fritillary, smaller, silver blotches on hind underwing. Similar woodland habitat.

Marbled White *Melanargia galathea* **WS 4.6–5.6**
Variable. Widespread but occurring in well-defined colonies on chalk and limestone. Slow flight. Female larger than male. Foodplants: grasses. Western Marbled White in south, has brown veins on underside hindwing.

Grayling *Hipparchia semele* **WS 4.2–5.0**
Widespread. Frequent on dry ground and slopes. Settles, closes wings and becomes difficult to see because of marbled pattern of greys on hind underwing. On wing May to August. Foodplants: grasses (*Festuca spp.*). Corsican Grayling, restricted to Corsica, Elba, and Sardinia. Mainly on dry mountain slopes. Uppers dark-brown with wide orange-yellow bands.

Meadow Brown *Maniola jurtina* **WS 4.0–5.8**
Common. Widespread in range of habitats from lowlands to mountains. Female distinguished from male by amount of orange on forewings. Both sexes with single spot on forewings. Several ringlets occur in France with orange on wings but all have several spots on hind- and forewings, e.g. Piedmont Ringlet, Bright-eyed Ringlet, Dewy Ringlet and False Dewy Ringlet.

Gatekeeper *Pyronia tithonus* **WS 3.4–3.8**
Locally common and widespread, especially where brambles bloom. Both sexes with bright-orange areas on wings but larger and brighter in female. Foodplant: grasses (*Poa, Milium*). Southern Gatekeeper, in southern France, similar but no spots on underside hindwing. Sex brand (on male forewing) rectangular but crossed by orange veins. Hot scrubby areas.

Camberwell Beauty

Red Admiral

Painted Lady

Small Tortoiseshell

male 1st generation

male 2nd generation

Map Butterfly

Silver-washed Fritillary

Marbled White

Grayling

Meadow Brown

Gatekeeper

Juniper *Juniperus communis*
Genévrier
Widespread. Common on moors, heaths, mountains. Evergreen shrub, small tree, bushy, up to 6m tall. Leaves spine-tipped, whorls of three, grey-green (one whitish stripe per needle). Male and female flowers on separate plants in May/June. Fruit berry-like, green becoming blue-black in second year. Subspecies *nana*: prostrate form, high mountains and at coast. Similar species: Prickly Juniper (*J. oxycedrus*) Mediterranean maquis, shrub or small tree, leaves needle-like with two whitish stripes, cones red-brown, berry like. Phoenician Juniper (*J. phoenicea*) coastal maquis, leaves scale-like with membraneous margin: cones berry like, dark brown-red when mature.

Maritime Pine *Pinus pinaster*
Widespread. Extensive forests near coasts. Up to 40m tall. Deeply fissured red-brown bark. Leaves long needles (to 25cm), buds not sticky. Cones broad, large (up to 22cm long), arranged in clusters; scales with sharp ridge and pronounced boss. Yields oil of turpentine. Similar species: Black Pine (*P. nigra*) up to 50m, in mountains of Cévennes and Pyrenees. Bark dark-grey, deeply fissured. Cones ovoid-conical, shining light brown, needles in pairs.

Lombardy Poplar *Populus nigra cv 'Italica'*
Peuplier noir
Common. Widely planted at field boundaries, forming avenues on roads. Up to 30m tall. Dull dark-grey bark shallowly ridged. True form male only. Catkins expanding in early April.

Alder *Alnus glutinosa*
Aune
Widespread. Common, often forming wet woodland 'carr'. Spreading tree up to 20m. Dark-brown rugged bark. Leaves and twigs almost hairless. Male catkins yellowish-brown, female egg-shaped, reddish-purple. Fruits like small cones, persisting on trees.

Sweet Chestnut *Castanea sativa*
Châtaigne
Widespread. Often planted, sometimes forming extensive forests as in Cévennes. Spreading tree up to 30m tall, grey-brown rugged bark. Fruit: brown, edible nut enclosed in a spiny cup.

Wild Cherry *Prunus avium*
Merise
Widespread. Woods and hedges. Deciduous tree to 20m. Leaves often reddish, downy beneath. Flowers white; few in short-stalked clusters, appear with leaves (April/May). Fruit: bright red, bitter cherry.

Bird Cherry *Prunus padus*
Cerisier à grappes
Upland woods, often by streams in limestone areas. Tree up to 15m. Bark smooth, dark grey-brown. Flowers white, densely crowded on long spikes with leaves near base (late May). Fruit: globular, black.

Field Maple *Acer campestre*
Erable champêtre
Widespread, in woods and hedges. Small tree or shrub up to 20m, roughish grey bark. Leaves bluntly five-lobed (much smaller than pointed leaves of Sycamore). Fruit winged, in pairs, diverging more or less horizontally, red-tinged. Similar species: Montpellier Maple (*A. monspessulanum*) frequent in south. Bark dark-grey, cracked. Leaves with three blunt lobes.

Box *Buxus sempervirens*
Buis
Widespread. Forms extensive areas of low growth on dry hillsides on chalk and limestone, e.g. Massif Central. Small tree or evergreen shrub up to 5m. Twigs green, leaves oval, shiny leathery. Flowers small, yellow. Fruit: three-horned capsule.

Large-Leaved Lime *Tilia platyphyllos*
Tilleul à graudes feuilles
Common. Often planted as a street tree. Up to 30m. Bark dark-grey, finely fissured, sometimes ribbed (no trunk bosses); crown tall, narrow dome. Leaves with all veins prominent, uniformly downy grey below. First lime in flower, flowers hanging, three to four. Similar species: Small-Leaved Lime (*T. cordata*), spreading tree to 30m. Smooth, dark-brown bark; large bosses on trunk. Leaves smaller, heart-shaped, greyish beneath. Flowers yellowish in small clusters, half-joined by short stalk to oblong bract.

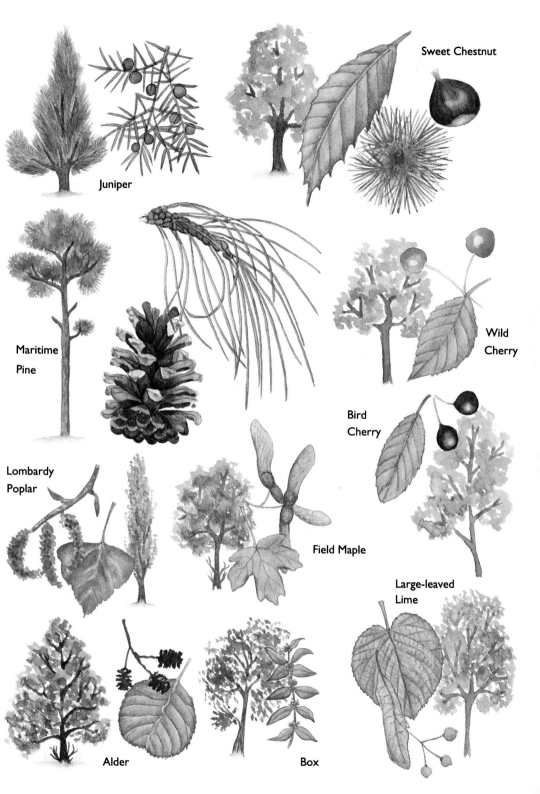

Juniper

Sweet Chestnut

Maritime Pine

Wild Cherry

Bird Cherry

Lombardy Poplar

Field Maple

Large-leaved Lime

Alder

Box

Wall Pellitory *Parietaria officinalis*
Parié Faire
Widespread in open places and common on walls, and banks. Medium, scarcely branched perennial. Stems reddish, leaves untoothed (leaves at least four times the length of stalks. Flowers June to October. Similar species: (*P. judaica*), shorter, much branched. Leaves up to three times length of stalks.

Mistletoe *Viscum album*
Gui
Widespread particularly on fruit trees and poplars. Woody parasite. Elliptical paired leaves. Flowers green, inconspicuous. Fruit: sticky white berry.

Birthwort *Aristolochia clematitis*
Aristoloche
Widespread. Particularly frequent on cultivated ground in the Massif Central. Hairless; perennial, medium/tall, leaves heart-shaped; flowers in clusters at base of upper leaves. Flowers yellowish, tubular, swollen at base, flattened at tip, foetid (June to September). Similar species: *A. pistolochia* frequent in waste places, in south. Leaves glaucous, rough below, finely toothed margins. Flowers brownish (2–5cm); dark-purple upper lip. Mediterranean France: Round-Leaved Birthwort (*A. rotunda*), leaves almost stalkless; rounded lobes encircle stem; flowers with yellowish tube, dark-brown strap-shaped lip. *A. longa*, leaves triangular oval; heart-shaped base; flowers with narrow brownish or yellow-green tube 3–6cm, lip shorter, brown-purple (April to June).

Bistort *Polygonum bistortum*
Bistorte
Common in meadows and woods, often near water, away from lime. Medium hairless perennial; patch-forming. Leaves triangular, narrow with stalks winged in upper part. Flowers in dense pink spike (June to October).

Greater Stitchwort *Stellaria holostea*
Stellaire holostée
Common in woods and hedges on heavier soils, rarely lime. Square-stemmed, short straggly perennial. Leaves are narrow and unstalked. Flowers 20–30mm in diameter, with petals white, split to half-way (April to June). Similar species: Lesser Stitchwort (*S. graminea*) flowers 12–18mm in diameter, petals equal to sepals (May to August).

Corncockle *Agrostemma githago*
Nielle des champs
Uncommon, local, decreasing. Tall hairy perennial. Leaves narrow, sepals project beyond five deep-pink petals. Formerly weed of cultivation, still in the Massif Central where agriculture 'basic' (May to August).

Soapwort *Saponaria officinalis*
Saponaire
Locally common. Medium tall, hairless, rather straggling perennial with runners. Flowers soft-pink, petals not notched. Campions and catchflys have notched petals (June to September). Rock Soapwort (*S. ocymoides*) mat and clump-forming, pink flowers familiar in gorges, e.g. the rocks of the Massif Central (May to September).

Maiden Pink *Dianthus deltoides*
Oeillet
Widespread on dry grassy soils, short to medium, flower stems roughly hairy. Flowers pink, spotted 15–20mm in diameter (June to September). Similar species: Cheddar Pink (*D. gratianoploitanus*) short, hairless, flowers 20–30mm in diameter. On limestone (May to July).

White Water Lily *Nymphaea alba*
Nénuphar blanc
Widespread on still shallow water. All leaves floating, almost circular. Flowers white, fragrant (50–200mm). Fruits carafe-shaped (June to September). Similar species: *N. candida* scattered distribution, flowers smaller, stamens deeper yellow, leaves with basal lobes overlapping.

Yellow Water Lily *Nuphar lutea*
Nénuphar jaime
Widespread on still or slow-flowing water. Leaves large oval, some submerged. Flowers, yellow, up to 60mm in diameter held above water on stalks. Fruits roundish, warty (June to September).

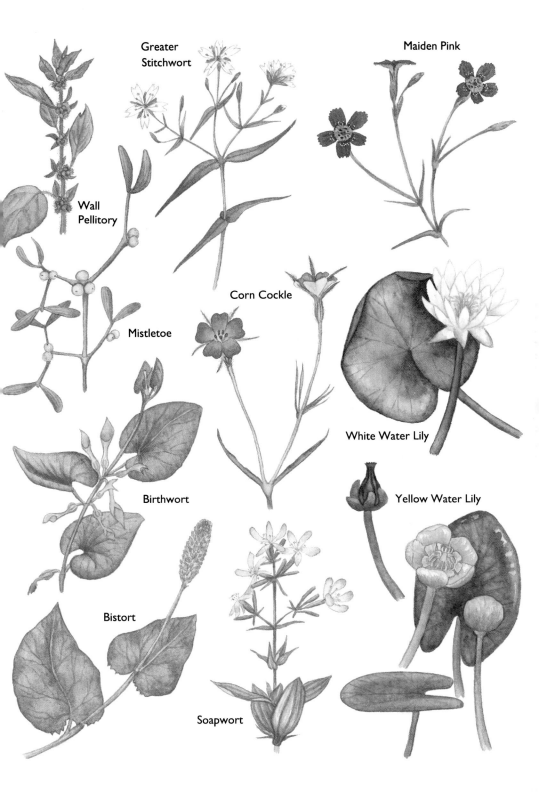

Greater
Stitchwort

Maiden Pink

Wall
Pellitory

Mistletoe

Corn Cockle

White Water Lily

Birthwort

Yellow Water Lily

Bistort

Soapwort

Globeflower *Trollius europaeus*
Mountain regions. Frequent in damp, grassy places. Medium hairless perennial, leaves palmate, deeply cut. Flowers large yellow almost spherical, formed from ten yellow sepals, no petals (May to August).

Marsh Marigold *Caltha palustris*
Populage des marais
Common in wet, boggy areas. Short stout-stemmed hairless perennial, stems reddish, leaves large, kidney-shaped, toothed, dark-green. Flowers (10–50mm) with five yellow sepals, no petals, fruit clustered, pod-like (March to May).

Hepatica *Hepatica nobilis*
Hepatique à troi lobes
Widespread in mountain regions, in woods and scrub on limestone. Short perennial, leaves with three rounded lobes, evergreen, purplish below. Flowers (15–25mm) solitary, blue-purple (occasionally white or pink), six to nine sepals with three bracts below.

Traveller's Joy *Clematis vitalba*
Vigne-blanche
Common on limestone, tall straggling woody-stemmed perennial often covering hedgerows with feathered fruits in autumn. Flowers with conspicuous stamens, four white petals, fragrant (July to September). Similar species: Alpine Clematis (*C. alpina*) occurs in Alpine regions in rocky woods, low-growing with large violet bell-shaped flowers (May to July).

Lesser Celandine *Ranunculus ficaria*
Ficaire
Common in woods, hedge and stream-banks on damp open ground. Short/low hairless perennial with rather fleshy, heart-shaped, dark-green leaves. Petals shining yellow, with eight to twelve sepals (March to May).

Common Poppy *Papaver rhoeas*
Coquelicot
Common on arable land and disturbed ground. Medium annual, roughly hairy. Flowers (70–100mm) deep-scarlet often with dark centre. Pod almost round, hairless (June to October). Similar species: Long-Headed Poppy (*P. dubium*), hairs closely pressed to stem, flowers paler (30–70mm) without dark centres. Pod longer than wide, hairless.

Cuckoo Flower *Cardamine pratense*
Cardamine des pris
Common in damp places. Medium hairless perennial. Flowers lilac or white (12–20mm) with yellow anthers. Pods about 40mm (April to June).

White Stonecrop *Sedum album*
Orpin à fleurs blanches
Common on rocks and walls, particularly in the south, mat-forming. Leaves (6–12mm) fleshy, bright-green, often red-tinged. Flowers white (6–9mm) dense flat-topped head, much-branched. Similar species: English Stonecrop (*S. anglicum*), greyish, soon reddening, low mat-forming evergreen, flowers (12mm) white, pink below.

Meadow Saxifrage *Saxifraga granulata*
Saxîfrage granulée
Widespread in grassy lowland areas. Short/medium with bulbils at leaf bases. Leaves mainly at base, kidney-shaped with shallow lobes. Flowers (20–30mm) in clusters; white, not spotted.

Dropwort *Filipendula vulgaris*
Filipendule
Widespread in dry grassland on limestone. Short to medium with sparsely leafy stem. Shorter leaves with up to twenty leaflets (each less than 20mm). Flower head flattened, petals 5–9mm. Similar species: Meadowsweet (*F. ulmaria*) common on swamps, fens, marshes, wet meadows. Leafy stemmed, leaves long with two to five pairs of leaflets, toothed (each more than 20mm). Flowers creamy, fragrant, in dense clusters (June to September).

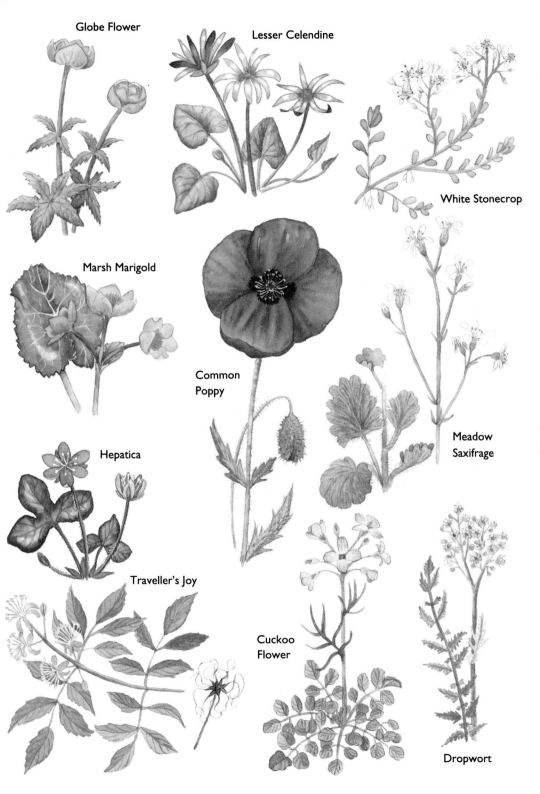

Globe Flower

Lesser Celendine

White Stonecrop

Marsh Marigold

Common Poppy

Meadow Saxifrage

Hepatica

Traveller's Joy

Cuckoo Flower

Dropwort

False Acacia *Robinia pseudacacia*
Acacia Robinier
Widely planted, originally from North America, deciduous tree (up to 25m) bark grey-brown, furrowed deeply, thorny shoots. Recognized by drooping spikes of white flowers in late May to June.

Meadow Vetchling *Lathyrea pratense*
Gesse des prés
Common in grassy places. Clambering perennial, height variable, hairy or downy, stems angled, paired leaflets. Flowers yellow (four to twelve in head), pods black (May to August).

Crown Vetch *Coronilla varia*
Common in grassy places. Straggling hairless perennial, medium to tall. Leaves pinnate with single terminal leaflet. Flowers in rounded heads, keel tipped purple, other parts pink/lilac (June to August).

Pitch Trefoil *Psoralea bituminosa*
Herbe au bitume
Widespread on waysides and waste ground in Mediterranean area. Stems up to 1m, leaves long-stalked with three leaflets. Stems and leaves smell strongly of tar. Flower-heads on long stalk up to 30cm long, seven to thirty dingy lilac flowers. Fruit with sword-shaped beak, 6–10mm long (April to August).

Perennial Flax *Linum perenne* agg.
Widespread on dry grassland, particularly limestone. Short to medium perennial, hairless. Leaves linear with one vein. Flowers pale- to bright-blue (25mm) in cluster or on short stalks. Similar species: *L. bienne*, leaves one to three veins, flowers pale bluish-lilac, dropping early. Common in Causse region. *L. campanulatum*, large yellow flowers. *L. suffruticosum*, large white flowers, yellow, pink or violet centres (May to August).

Meadow Cranesbill *Geranium pratense*
Géranium des prés
Frequent on grassy places, especially roadsides on limestone. Medium to tall perennial with leaves deeply cut. Flowers (25–30mm) blue with mauve tinge towards centre, petals not notched, anthers black (June to September).

Cypress Spurge *Euphorbia cyparrisias*
Hait des couleuvre
Widespread, often local on dry calcareous soils: scrub, paths, slopes. Plant (15–35cm) with narrow, alternate leaves. Non-flowering shoots densely leafy like small fir twig. Bracts on flower-heads start pale-yellow become red; leaves become red. Often attacked by rust fungus.

Musk Mallow *Malva moschata*
Mauve musquée
Widespread. Common in grassy places and scrub. Medium to tall perennial, leaves deeply, narrowly cut; stem hairs purple-based. Flowers (40–60mm) rose-pink, solitary on unbranched stalks. Outer sepal ring hairless (July to August). Similar species: *M. alcea*, larger; flower stalks with branched hairs, outer calyx downy.

Common Rock Rose *Helianthemum nummularium*
Héliauthème
Widespread. Common in rocky limestone areas. Variable, prostrate with leaves lanceolate-roundish, one-veined. Flowers yellow (white, cream orange or pink rare) 20–25mm in diameter (May to September). Similar species: White Rock Rose (*H. appeninum*), narrow leaves, in-rolled margins, white flowers with yellow centres. Hoary Rock Rose (*H. canum*), smaller, narrower leaves; flowers 10–15mm. Spotted Rock Rose (*Tuberaria guttata*), leaves elliptical, hairy, three-veined, petals with reddish-purple spot near base.

Purple Loosestrife *Lythrum salicaria*
Lythrum salicaire
Common in large numbers in damp places, stream and river-banks. Tall perennial, stems with four raised lines. Flowers (10–15mm) in whorled spikes, six-petalled, bright red-purple (June to August).

False Acacia

Perennial Flax

Musk Mallow

Meadow Vetchling

Meadow Cranesbill

Common Rock Rose

Crown Vetch

Cypress Spurge

Purple Loosestrife

Pitch Trefoil

Rosebay Willowherb *Epilobium angustifolium*
Osier fleuri
Common, forming extensive patches in woodland rides, on heaths, mountains, waste ground. Tall (50–150cm), stem bluntly angled, leaves long, narrow, alternate, stems reddish. Flowers (20–30mm), petals slightly unequal, bright pink-purple.

Field Eryngo *Eryngium campestre*
Erynge des prés
Widespread in bare dry places. Short to medium perennial, hairless, much branched. Leaves leathery, spiny grey-green with bluish tinge. Flower-head with numerous white/bluish green flowers. Similar species: Sea Holly (*E. maritimum*), leaves larger, rounded, spiny with white veins; flower head powder-blue. Sand and shingle beside sea (June to September).

Hemlock Water Dropwort *Oenanthe crocata*
Widespread in damp grassy places, boggy places, beds of streams. Tall (around 1.5m) with grooved stem and leaves pinnate with wedge-shaped, toothed leaflets, parsley scented. Flowers white. Plant highly poisonous (June to August).

Common Wintergreen *Pyrola minor*
Pyrole à fleurs petites
Local, woods, moors and dunes. Short perennial with rounded, toothed leaves in a rosette. Flowers (6mm) white or pale-pink, globular, in stalked spike with style straight, shorter than stamens (June to August). Similar species: Round-Leaved Wintergreen (*P. rotundifolia*), leaves more rounded, flowers pure white, larger (12mm) more open, style much longer, 'S'-shaped. Woods, dune-slacks. Intermediate Wintergreen (*P. media*), longer spikes, flowers (10mm) style slightly curved, protruding from flower. Yellow Wintergreen (*P. chlorantha*), flowers greenish/yellowish white with style protruding.

Bell Heather *Erica cinerea*
Cloche des bruyère
Common on drier heaths and moors, bogs, open woods, fixed dunes. Undershrub, short and hairless, leaves whorled in threes, dark-green with brownish tint. Flowers reddish-purple in stalked spikes (May to September). Similar species: Ling (*Calluna vulgaris*), leaves in opposite rows, linear, flowers pale-purple in leafy stalked spikes, covering large areas of heath and moorland or as understorey in woods.

Cowslip *Primula veris*
Primevère officinale
Locally common on grassy banks, scrub, woods, sea-cliffs, dunes, mountains. Short hairy perennial (10–20cm), leaves narrowed abruptly at base; flowers 1–25 in nodding one-sided cluster, deep-yellow with orange spot in centre, 10–15mm, fragrant (April to May). Similar species: Oxlip (*Primula elatior*) flowers pale-yellow (15–20mm) not fragrant, often in large numbers. Can be confused with natural hybrid Primrose x Cowslip; grows singly near one or other of the parents.

Sea Lavender *Limonium vulgare*
Statice
Common in coastal salt-marshes. Low perennial with rounded stems forming carpets, leaves long-stalked, elliptical. Flowers lilac/lavender at ends of stalks. Tightly packed in flat-topped clusters. Stalks branch from well above the middle of the stem (July to September). Similar species: Matted Sea Lavender (*L. bellidifolium*) stems branched almost from base forming numerous zig-zag branches, leaves oblong. Flowers pinkish-lavender with white bracts only on upper branches. Rock Sea Lavender (*L. binervosum*) stems branched from near base, leaves oval with three-winged stalk, flowers lilac on all but lowest branches. Coastal cliffs and rocks.

Fringed Water Lily *Nymphoides peltata*
Faux nénuphar
Locally abundant on still and slow-moving fresh water. Leaves floating, purple beneath, rounded with shallow teeth. Flowers yellow, much smaller than other water lilies and with five fringed petal-lobes. Fruit egg-shaped (June to September).

Vincetoxicum *Vincetoxicum hirundinaria*
Widespread on rocks, bare ground and woods on limestone. Plants slightly hairy (30–120cm), stem hollow; perennial, leaves heart-shaped, sharply pointed. Flowers with five jointed petals, greenish or yellowish-white, growing at base of upper leaves in clusters, poisonous (June to September).

Crosswort *Cruciata laevipes*
Common in wet woods, hedges, pastures, roadsides. Plant (10–50cm long) softly hairy: leaves in whorls of four, yellowish-green, elliptical. Flowers scented, pale-yellow in whorls at base of leaves (April to June).

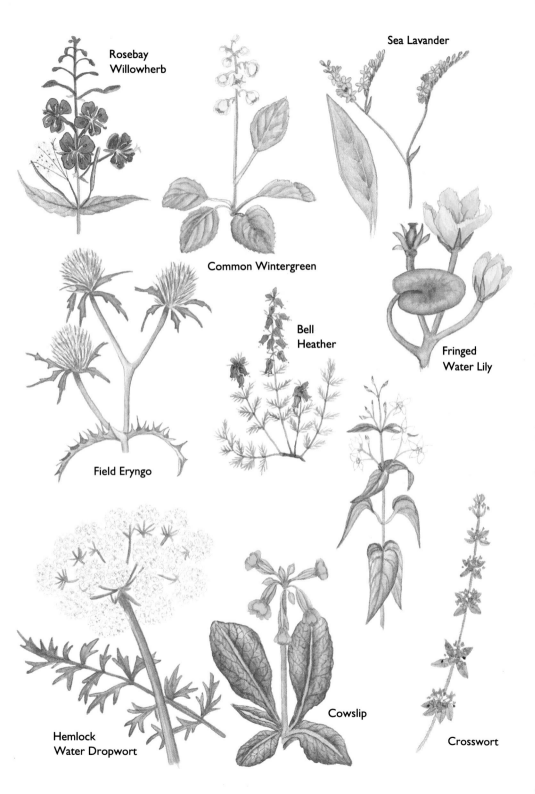

Rosebay
Willowherb

Sea Lavander

Common Wintergreen

Fringed
Water Lily

Field Eryngo

Bell
Heather

Hemlock
Water Dropwort

Cowslip

Crosswort

Viper's Bugloss *Echium vulgare*
Locally common in dry, bare waste places, dunes. Roughly hairy, medium perennial with lanceolate leaves. Flowers in branched spike, initially pink becoming bright-blue with four or five stamens protruding. Similar species growing in Mediterranean area: Purple Viper's Bugloss (*E. plantagineum*) (20–60cm) usually branched with soft bristles, basal rosette plantain-like; fewer flowers (2–3cm long) with purple-red corolla (blue initially) with two stamens protruding. Pale Bugloss (*E. italicum*) (30–100cm tall) erect stems with spike-like inflorescence forming a pyramid. Flowers small (10–14mm), white or flesh-coloured

Blue Bugle *Ajuga genevensis*
Widespread on calcareous soils (Alps, Pyrenees, Massif Central). Low, creeping perennial with distinctly toothed leaves, no runners, stems hairy all round, flowers bright-blue. Common Bugle (*A. reptans*) common on damp woods, grasslands; runners rooting, stem hairy two sides, flowers powder-blue in leafy, often purplish spike.

Bastard Balm *Melittis melissophyllum*
Widespread but local in central and southern France, open woodland, scrub, shady hedgebanks. Plant (20–60cm) hairy perennial, strong-smelling. Leaves toothed, oblong/oval, heart-shaped at base. Flowers (25–40mm) usually white with pink markings on lip, occasionally all pink/purple.

Ivy *Hedera helix*
Common. Widespread. Woods, walls, hegderows, rocks. Woody climber, capable of covering ground or trees. Leaves glossy, three to five pointed lobes (non-flowering shoots), not lobed on flowering shoots. Flowers green-yellow anthers, carried in umbel; berries black. Flowers September to November.

Large Thyme *Thymus pulegioides*
Widespread in grassy and waste places. Low tufted perennial, stems hairy all round. Leaves hairless above, oval, stalked. Flowers small (6mm), pink, in whorled spike (July to September). Similar species: Thyme (*T. vulgaris*), southern France, aromatic dwarf shrub with velvety-white twigs. Leaves narrow, white below; flowers in rounded or elongated clusters, white or pinkish.

Meadow Clary *Salvia pratensis*
Widespread. Frequent on dry limestone grassland. Slightly aromatic medium perennial, leaves broadly lanceolate, unstalked, wrinkled, bluntly toothed.

Flowers in leafless spikes, whorled, bright violet-blue (May to August). Similar species: Whorled Clary (*S. verticillata*) southern Pyrenees, leaves stalked, purplish, flowers smaller, pinkish-purple with purple sepals; strongly aromatic. Jupiter's Distaff (*S. glutinosa*) mountain woods (eastern Pyrenees), yellow flowers with reddish-brown markings (30–40mm) in whorls of two to six.

Ivy-Leaved Toadflax *Cymbalaria muralis*
Common on walls and rocks. Trailing perennial with long-stalked ivy-shaped leaves. Flowers (8–10mm) lilac with yellow spot (April to November). Similar species: Pale Toadflax (*Linaria repens*) dry, bare places, short hairless perennial, flowers (7–14mm) in stalked spikes, pale-lilac, violet-veined orange spot on lower lip. Alpine Toadflax (*L. alpina*) mountain screes and river-beds, Alps and Pyrenees, sprawling stems, leaves whorled grey-green; flowers (13–22mm) violet with yellow patch on lower lip.

Large Self-Heal *Prunella grandiflora*
Widespread on limestone in woods and dry meadows, roadsides. Low creeping perennial. Flowers (20–25mm) violet-blue with a whitish tube and lower lip. Flower head rounded/flattened cluster, no leaves at base. Similar species: Self-Heal (*P. vulgaris*), flowers smaller, deep violet-blue (13–15mm) in dense oblong clusters with leaves at base.

Field Cow-Wheat *Melampyrum arvense*
Widespread in dry grassy and rocky places. Semi-parasitic plant (20–60cm), leaves lance-shaped, unstalked. Bracts green, whitish or reddish-pink, deeply toothed. Flowers (20–25mm), close-mouthed, purplish-pink marked with yellow in loose spikes (June to September). Similar species: Crested Cow-Wheat (*M. cristatum*) local, bracts purple, serrately toothed. Flowers (12–16mm) yellow and purple in short spikes.

Yellow Rattle *Rhinanthus minor*
Widespread in cornfields and grassy places, semi-parasitic. Short to medium, almost hairless annual; leaves oblong to lance-shaped, dark-green and toothed. Finely-toothed, hairless, triangular bracts. Yellow flowers with two lips, violet tip, in leafy spike (May to September). Similar species: Narrow-Leaved Rattle (*R. angustifolius*) mountain meadows (Alps and Pyrenees), stems black-streaked, leaves toothed, linear to lance-shaped, pale-green. Flowers pale yellow (16–20mm).

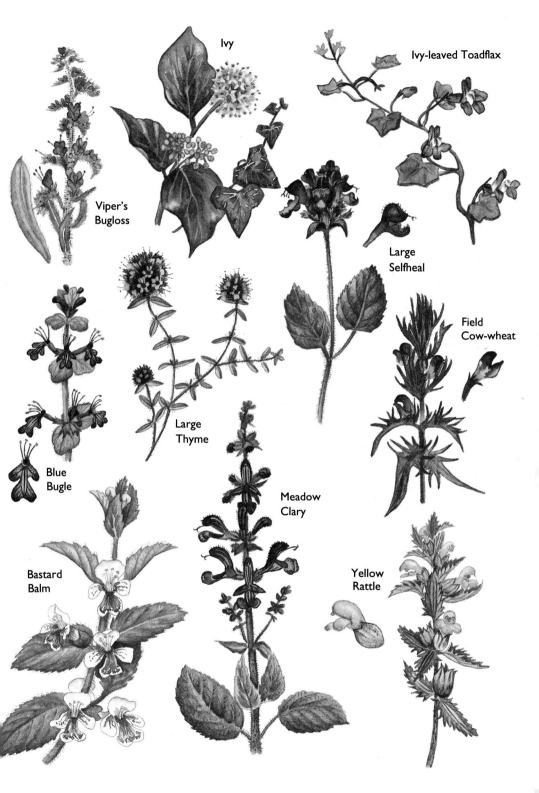

Ivy

Ivy-leaved Toadflax

Viper's
Bugloss

Large
Selfheal

Field
Cow-wheat

Large
Thyme

Blue
Bugle

Meadow
Clary

Bastard
Balm

Yellow
Rattle

Globularia *Globularia vulgaris*
Widespread on dry hills and sunny rocks in south. Short/medium evergreen with erect stems. Leaves elliptic to lance-shaped with flattened edges, three-toothed at tip. Flower-heads (25mm), blue, borne on 20cm long stems. Similar species: Shrubby Globularia (*G. alypum*) Mediterranean, bristle-leaved, much-branched evergreen shrub with brittle stems. Flower-heads (15–20mm) sweet-scented. Violent purgative; flowers (winter and spring).

Spreading Bellflower *Campanula patula*
Widespread. Frequent in woods, scrub and grassy places. Slender, erect-stemmed medium biennial or perennial. Leaves oblong; upper narrower and unstalked. Flowers violet-blue, (15–25mm) wide bells, in spreading cluster on stalks (June to July).

Nettle-Leaved Bellflower *Campanula trachelium*
Widespread in woods and hedgerows. Perennial medium to tall, hairy with angled, unbranched stems. Leaves irregularly toothed, nettle-like. Flowers violet-blue, 30–40mm long (July to September). Similar species: Clustered Bellflower (*C. glomerata*) common on limestone meadows, woodland edges, flowers deep-violet (15–25mm long) in tight clustered heads (June to October).

Goldenrod *Solidago virgaurea*
Widespread. Common in scrub, woods, heath, grassy and rocky places. Plant 20–100cm tall; leaves bluntly oval or lance-shaped, toothed, stalked. Flower-heads bright-yellow, 15–20mm in diameter, in branched racemes (July to October). Similar species: Goldilocks (*Aster linosyris*) local on limestone, usually coastal. Leaves linear, numerous; flowers in flat-topped cluster (September to November).

Corn Marigold *Chrysanthemum segetum*
Locally common weed of cultivation. Short to medium perennial. Leaves fleshy, toothed or lobed, oblong, upper clasping stem. Flowers solitary, bright-yellow, 35–55mm in diameter (June to October). Similar species: Crown Daisy (*C. coronarium*) Mediterranean region, often abundant beside roads, waste ground. Plant hairless (up to 80cm). Leafy stems: leaves feathery, finely divided. Flower heads up to 60mm; bright-yellow. var. *discolor* has bi-coloured ray florets: white at tips, yellow at base (March to September).

Ox-Eye Daisy *Leucanthemum vulgare*
Common in grassy and waste places. Medium perennial, slightly hairy. Leaves dark-green, variable, toothed or lobed; lower ones rounded upper ones longer clasping stem. Flower-heads single (25–50mm) white rays, disc florets yellow (May to September). Similar species: Feverfew (*Tanacetum parthenium*) smaller flowers (10–25mm) in umbel-like clusters, aromatic.

Globe Thistle *Echinops ritro*
Widespread on dry grassland, stony pastures. Plant medium to tall perennial, white-felted stems, usually branched. Leaves with narrow, spiny lobes; undersides felted. Flower-heads rich-blue, 35–45cm in diameter (June to September). Similar species: *E. sphaerocephalus*; plant stickily hairy and white woolly; flowers pale-blue, spiny.

Cabbage Thistle *Cirsium oleraceum*
Widespread in damp places. More or less hairless medium perennial. Leaves variable: lance-shaped, pinnately lobed to toothed. Rayless, egg-shaped flower-heads, straw-yellow, clustered, almost hidden by topmost leaves. Similar species: Yellow Melancholy Thistle (*C. erisithales*), hilly areas usually on limestone, lemon-yellow flower-heads, solitary or two- to five-clustered, nodding, not hidden by upper leaves.

Cornflower *Centaurea cyanus*
Locally abundant weed of cultivation: cornfields especially in limestone areas of Massif Central. Medium annual, with grey down, leaves unlobed or with pinnate lobes. Flower-heads bright-blue (15–30mm across).

Dandelion *Taraxacum officinale*
Common in grassy and waste places. Low to short perennial. Flower-heads (35–50mm) yellow. Bracts sepal-like. Dandelions divided into eight groups each with numerous micro-species. Can flower all year but mainly April to June.

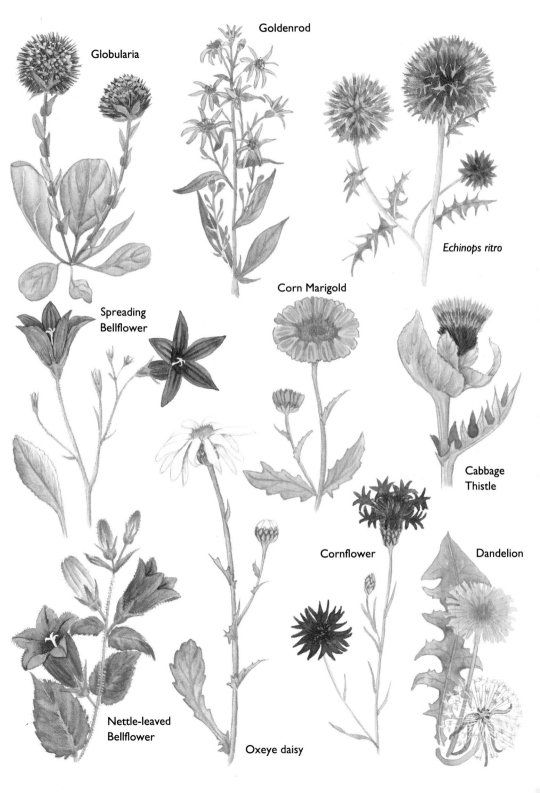

Globularia

Goldenrod

Echinops ritro

Spreading Bellflower

Corn Marigold

Cabbage Thistle

Cornflower

Dandelion

Nettle-leaved Bellflower

Oxeye daisy

Arrowhead *Sagittaria sagittifolia*
Flèche d'eau
Widespread in still and flowing water. Distinctive, large arrow-shaped leaves (in fast-flowing water the floating leaves can become oval with ribbon-like submerged leaves). Flowers (20mm), three-petalled, white with purple central spot (July to August).

Water Plantain *Alisma plantago-aquatica*
Widespread by fresh water. Leaves broad lanceolate, heart-shaped or rounded at base. Whorls of pale three-petalled lilac flowers (8–10mm). Fruit: nutlets with long 'beak'. Similar species: Narrow-Leaved Water Plantain (*A. lanceolatum*) has narrow leaves tapering into stalk. Fruit: with short 'beak'. Ribbon-Leaved Water Plantain (*A. gramineum*) has ribbon-like leaves, often submerged. Fruit: with coiled 'beak' (June to September).

White Asphodel *Asphodelus albus*
Widespread in south. Leaves all basal, strap-like, grooved. Flowers large (40–50mm), starry white or pink flushed in dense spikes (May–July).

Tassel Hyacinth *Muscari comosum*
Leaves long, strap-like. Flowers bell-shaped, of two types: lower, brownish-green; upper, violet-blue, smaller, more upright. Fields and rocky places (April–July).

Common Solomon's Seal *Polygonatum multiflorum*
Local, woods, hedgerows, scrub. Stems rounded (up to 60cm); leaves alternate, elliptical. Flowers at leaf-base, hanging in clusters of one to three, 'waisted', bell-shaped, greenish-white and unscented. Berry black. Similar species: Angular Solomon's Seal (*P. odoratum*) uncommon, on limestone, stems angled (15–20cm); flowers fragrant, not waisted, hanging singly or in pairs. Berry blue-black. Whorled Solomon's Seal (*P. verticillatum*), leaves narrow-lanceolate, whorls of four to five up stem, flowers bell-shaped; white, tipped green, unscented, arranged one to three at each whorl. Local, woods, woodland edges in mountain regions.

Yellow Iris *Iris pseudacorus*
Common by fresh water. Tall with branched stems, leaves with raised mid-rib. Flowers yellow, 80–100mm across (June to August).

Red Helleborine *Cephalanthera rubra*
Céphalanthère rouge
Local but frequent in limestone regions in Beech woods or scrub, roadsides. Short to medium perennial, stem and leaves with purplish tinge. Leaves nar-

row; stem wavy. Flowers deep rose-pink, not opening widely; lip whitish (June to July). White Helleborine (*C. damasonium*), leaves broad lanceolate, bluish-green, flowers yellowish-white barely opening. Yellow area at lip-base hidden. 'Beech woods, scrub (May to July). Sword-Leaved Helleborine (*C. longifolia*) leaves, long, narrow, parallel-sided, flowers white, opening more widely to reveal orange spot at lip-base. Open woodland, scrub (May to June).

Early Purple Orchid *Orchis mascula*
Orchis mâle
Plants (20–50cm) open woodlands, scrub, grassland, cliff-tops. Leaves, narrow, oblong usually blotched purple-black. Flowers magenta-purple; one sepal and two petals form loose hood, other sepals erect. Lip shallowly three-lobed, lighter towards centre, spotted; spur long, thickened at tip (May to July). Plants in high-mountain areas have sepal and petals in 'hood' extended, whiskery (ssp 'signifera'). Lady Orchid (*O. purpurea*) robust, leaves shiny, unspotted: sepals and petals form dark hood, lip pale-pink 'manikin'; broadly-lobed 'skirt', narrow arms. Woods, scrub on limestone. Military Orchid (*O. militaris*) leaves broad, oblong, unspotted. 'Manikin' with narrower legs, dark magenta near tips, 'tail' between. Frequent on limestone (May to June).

Woodcock Orchid *Ophrys scolopax*
Ophrys bécasse
Locally frequent in Massif Central and farther south on stony limestone slopes, meadows, under coastal pines. Plants 20–45cm, sepals vary from deep-pink through whitish to greenish, petals half the length of sepals. Lip dark-brown (8–12mm), three-lobed, side lobes hairy (small, blunt horns), markings variable: bluish- or brownish-purple edged white. Apex forward pointing. Late March in south; late May in Massif Central.

Bee Orchid *Ophrys apifera*
Ophrys abeille
Local but frequent on limestone soils: grassland, open scrub, dunes. Plant from 20–60cm with sepals from deep-pink to whitish-pink; petals, one-third sepal-length, greenish. Lip dark-brown, apex curved under to give 'blunt' appearance. Pattern shield-shape, reddish-brown or violet-brown edged in cream. Few cream spots elsewhere. Side-lobes hairy. Several varieties are known: var. *chlorantha*, lip yellow, perianth segments greenish-white. var. *bicolor*, lip light towards base, brown towards apex, pattern absent (May to July).

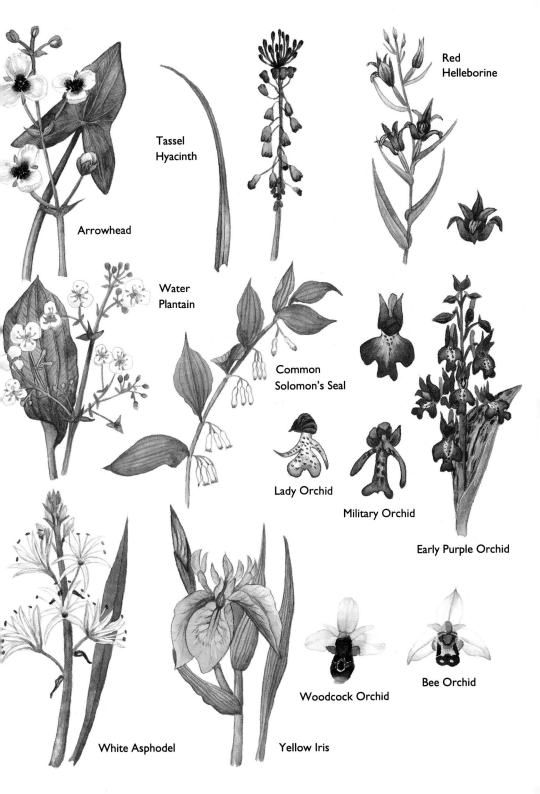

Tassel
Hyacinth

Red
Helleborine

Arrowhead

Water
Plantain

Common
Solomon's Seal

Lady Orchid

Military Orchid

Early Purple Orchid

White Asphodel

Yellow Iris

Woodcock Orchid

Bee Orchid

USEFUL ADDRESSES

Parc National des Cévennes
Chateau de Florac
48400 Florac
(Tel: 66-45-01-75)

Parc National de Port-Cros
50 Avenue Gambetta
83400 Hyères
(Tel: 94-65-32-98)

Parc National des Pyrénées Occidentales
59 Route de Pau
65000 Tarbes

Parc National des Ecrins
7 Rue du Colonel Roux
05004 Gap Cedex
(Tel: 92-51-40-71)

Parc National du Mercantour
23 Rue d'Italie
06000 Nice
(Tel: 93-87-86-10)

Parc National de la Vanoise
BP 105
73000 Chambery
(Tel: 79-62-30-54)

REGIONAL NATURAL PARKS

The central office for all the Regional
Natural Parks is in Paris. They can provide
addresses of individual park offices, and
have some further information:

Fédération des Parcs Naturels de France
4 Rue de Stockholm
75008 Paris

CONSERVATION ORGANIZATIONS

Société Nationale de Protection de la
  Nature (SNPN)
57 Rue Cuvier
BP 405
75231 Paris Cedex 05
(Equivalent to the Royal Society for Nature
Conservation in Britain, covering all
France)

La Société d'Etude et de Protection de la
  Nature en Bretagne (SEPNB)
BP 32
186 Rue Anatole France
29276 Brest Cedex
(Tel: 98-49-07-18)
(Covers nature conservation in Brittany
only)

Ligue Française pour la Protection des
  Oiseaux (LPO)
La Corderie Royale
BP 263, 17305 Rochefort Cedex
(Tel: 46-99-59-97)
(Equivalent to the Royal Society for the
Protection of Birds in Britain)

Fonds d'Intervention pour les Rapaces
  (FIR)
BP 27, 92250
La Garenne Colombes
(Tel: 47-71-02-87)
(Specifically concerned with the protection
of birds of prey)

OTHER ADDRESSES

Office National des Forts (ONF)
2 Avenue de Saint-Mandé
75012 Paris
(Tel: 40-19-58-00)
(Equivalent to the British Forestry

Commission; runs huge areas of forests, some with nature reserves)

French Government Tourist Office
178 Piccadilly
London W1V 0A1
(Tel: 071-491-7622)

Club Alpin Français
7 Rue la Boétie
Paris 75008
(Runs many of the mountain refuges)

Cox and Kings Travel Ltd
St James Court
Buckingham Gate
London SW1E 6AF
(Tel:071-834-7472)
(Run special-interest tours, including natural history, botany and photography to numerous destinations, including France)

BIBLIOGRAPHY

ENGLISH

Arnold, E. and Burton, J., *A Field Guide to the Reptiles and Amphibians of Britain and Europe* (Collins, 1980).

Campbell, A.C., *The Hamlyn Guide to the Seashores and Shallow Seas of Britain and Europe* (Hamlyn, 1976).

Chinery, M., *Collins Guide to the Insects of Britain and Western Europe* (Collins, 1986).

Corbet, G. and Ovenden, D., *The Mammals of Britain and Europe* (Collins, 1980).

Davies, P. & J. and Huxley, A., *Wild Orchids of Britain and Europe* (Chatto & Windus, 1983).

Davis, M., *The Green Guide to France* (Green Print, 1990).

Gibbons, R., *Country Life Guide to Dragonflies and Damselflies of Britain and Northern Europe* (Hamlyn, 1986).

Gibbons, R. and Davies, P., *The Pyrenees* (Batsford, 1991).

Gooders, J., *Field Guide to the Birds of Britain and Europe* (Kingfisher, 1990).

Gooders, J., *Where to Watch Birds in Britain and Europe* (Christopher Helm, 1988).

Grey-Wilson, C. and Blamey, M., *The Alpine Flowers of Britain and Europe* (Collins, 1979).

Higgins, L. and Riley, N., *A Field Guide to the Butterflies of Britain and Europe* (Collins, 1970).

Polunin, O. and Smythies, B., *Flowers of South-West Europe* (Oxford University Press, 1988).

Raine, P., *Mediterranean Wildlife: The Rough Guide* (Harrap-Columbus, 1990).

Schoenfelder, I. & P., *Wildflowers of the Mediterranean* (Collins, 1990).

Whalley, P., *The Mitchell Beazley Pocket Guide to Butterflies* (Mitchell Beazley, 1987).

FRENCH

Dubois, P., *Ou Voir les Oiseaux en France* (Nathan, with the LPO, 1989).

Reille, A. and Bonnin Luquot, C., *Guide des Réserves Naturelles de France* (Delachaux & Niestlé, 1987).

Vadrot, C-M., *France Verte: Guide des 1,000 Plus Beaux Sites Naturels* (Editions du May, 1987).

Guides Naturalistes des Côtes de France is a useful series published by Delachaux and Niestlé. Some are very general, and the best is that on Corsica.

INDEX

Page numbers in *italic* refer to illustrations; those in **bold** refer to field guide entries.

PHOTOGRAPHIC ACKNOWLEDGEMENTS

All photographs courtesy of Natural Image. Photographers and page references as follows:

Bob Gibbons 2–3, 4–5, 6, 8, 11, 12, 13, 14, 15, 17, 18, 20, 21, 23, 25, 26, 27, 28, 29, 30 (left and right), 31, 32, 35, 36, 37, 39 (upper and lower), 40, 43, 44, 45, 47 (upper and lower), 49, 50 (upper and lower), 51, 53, 54, 55, 57, 58 (upper and lower), 59, 60, 61, 64, 68, 70, 71, 73 (lower), 76, 77 (upper and lower), 79, 80 (left and right), 82, 83, 84, 87, 90 (left), 92, 95, 96, 99, 101, 102 (upper and lower), 105, 115, 120, 124, 125, 129, 132, 133, 135, 136, 138 (left and right), 139, 141 (left and right), 142 (upper and lower), 143, 144, 146, 148–149, 150 (left and right), 152, 153, 155 (left and right), 160, 161, 163, 164, 167 (upper and lower), 168, 172, 173 (upper and lower), 174, 175 (upper and lower), 177, 178, 179, 180, 181, 183 (upper), 185, 186, 187, 188 (upper), 189, 191; **Paul Davies** 41, 66, 72, 85, 90 (right), 93, 98, 106, 109, 110, 111, 112, 113, 118, 119, 121, 123, 157, 166, 192; **Robert Dickson** 56, 188 (lower); **Alec Harmer** 33; **Mike Lane** 69, 73 (upper), 103, 126; **A. Walmsley** 116; **Peter Wilson** 65, 131, 183 (lower), 184; **Michael Woods** 94.